Implementing Design for Six Sigma

Also available from ASQ Quality Press:

Leadership For Results: Removing Barriers to Success for People, Projects, and Processes
Tom Barker

The Executive Guide to Improvement and Change
G. Dennis Beecroft, Grace L. Duffy, John W. Moran

Design for Six Sigma as Strategic Experimentation: Planning, Designing, and Building World-Class Products and Services
H. E. Cook

Computer-Based Robust Engineering: Essentials for DFSS
Genichi Taguchi, Rajesh Jugulum, and Shin Taguchi

Defining and Analyzing a Business Process: A Six Sigma Pocket Guide
Jeffrey N. Lowenthal

Transactional Six Sigma for Green Belts: Maximizing Service and Manufacturing Processes
Samuel E. Windsor

Design of Experiments with MINITAB
Paul Mathews

Failure Mode and Effect Analysis: FMEA From Theory to Execution, Second Edition
D. H. Stamatis

The Certified Six Sigma Black Belt Handbook
Donald W. Benbow and T. M. Kubiak

The Certified Manager of Quality/Organizational Excellence Handbook: Third Edition
Russell T. Westcott, editor

Business Performance through Lean Six Sigma: Linking the Knowledge Worker, the Twelve Pillars, and Baldrige
James T. Schutta

Process Quality Control: Troubleshooting and Interpretation of Data, Fourth Edition
Ellis R. Ott, Edward G. Schilling, and Dean V. Neubauer

To request a complimentary catalog of ASQ Quality Press publications, call 800-248-1946, or visit our Web site at http://qualitypress.asq.org.

Implementing Design for Six Sigma

A Leader's Guide—Getting the Most from Your Product Development Process

Georgette Belair
John O'Neill

ASQ Quality Press
Milwaukee, Wisconsin

American Society for Quality, Quality Press, Milwaukee 53203
© 2007 American Society for Quality
All rights reserved. Published 2006
Printed in the United States of America

12 11 10 09 08 07 06   5 4 3 2 1

Library of Congress Cataloging-in-Publication Data

Belair, Georgette, 1969–
Implementing design for Six sigma : a leader's guide : getting the most from your product development process / Georgette Belair, John O'Neill. —1st ed.
   p. cm.
Includes bibliographical references and index.
ISBN 0-87389-695-5 (alk. paper)
1. Six sigma (Quality control standard)   2. Total quality management.
I. O'Neill, John, 1956–   II. Title.

TS156.B438 2006
658.5'7—dc22   2006016963

ISBN-10: 0-87389-695-5
ISBN-13: 978-0-87389-695-5

No part of this book may be reproduced in any form or by any means, electronic, mechanical, photocopying, recording, or otherwise, without the prior written permission of the publisher.

Publisher: William A. Tony
Acquisitions Editor: Annemieke Hytinen
Project Editor: Paul O'Mara
Production Administrator: Randall Benson

ASQ Mission: The American Society for Quality advances individual, organizational, and community excellence worldwide through learning, quality improvement, and knowledge exchange.

Attention Bookstores, Wholesalers, Schools, and Corporations: ASQ Quality Press books, videotapes, audiotapes, and software are available at quantity discounts with bulk purchases for business, educational, or instructional use. For information, please contact ASQ Quality Press at 800-248-1946, or write to ASQ Quality Press, P.O. Box 3005, Milwaukee, WI 53201-3005.

To place orders or to request a free copy of the ASQ Quality Press Publications Catalog, including ASQ membership information, call 800-248-1946. Visit our Web site at www.asq.org or http://qualitypress.asq.org.

∞ Printed on acid-free paper

Quality Press
600 N. Plankinton Avenue
Milwaukee, Wisconsin 53203
Call toll free 800-248-1946
Fax 414-272-1734
www.asq.org
http://qualitypress.asq.org
http://standardsgroup.asq.org
E-mail: authors@asq.org

This book is dedicated to the many people who have touched our lives and to the organizations that have allowed us to work with them, have celebrated with us when we've "hit home runs," and have been patient with us when the inevitable mistakes have occurred.

Contents

Preface . . . . *xi*
Acknowledgments . . . . *xiv*

Chapter 1   Introduction 1
   Is Your Product Development Process Helping You
      Win the Game Today? 1
   Do You Even Have a Product Development Process? 2
   So How Does DFSS Work Its Magic? 8
   What We'll Promise You 10
   Do You Have the Gottawanna? 13

Chapter 2   What Is Design for Six Sigma? 15
   Introduction 15
   What Is Six Sigma? 15
   The Idea of Improving Design Processes 25
   What Is DFSS: Narrow Sense? 26
   What Is DFSS: Broad Sense? 31
   Key Points 33

**Chapter 3   What DFSS Can Do for You
           and Your Company** 35
   Introduction 35
   Financial Benefits of DFSS (for Senior Leaders) 36
   Reducing Internal Friction through DFSS
      (for Middle Managers) 39
   DFSS Personal Benefits for Product Developers:
      What's in It for Me? (WIIFM?) 41
   One Company's Product Development Improvement
      Journey 42
   Key Points 47

Chapter 4 DFSS: The Method and Roadmap 49

Introduction 49
DMADVI: A Quick History and 50,000-Foot View 50
Define Phase: Overview and Tools 54
Measure Phase: Overview and Tools 57
Analyze Phase: Overview and Tools 61
Design Phase: Overview and Tools 66
Verify and Validate: Overview and Tools 70
Implement: Overview Tools 73
Key Points 75

Chapter 5 Gap Analysis and Readiness for the DFSS Journey 77

Introduction 77
Why Do You Want to Do DFSS? 78
Gap Analysis 82
Quality-Side Gaps 82
Gap Analysis: Current New Product
  Development Processes 83
Gap Analysis: Current New Product Development
  Organizational Structure 90
Team-by-Team Gap Analysis 92
Prioritize the Development Process Improvements 93
"A-Side" Gaps 93
Leadership Commitment 96
Tolerance and Motivation for Change 101
Planning for Change 103
Key Points: DFSS Gap Analysis 105

Chapter 6 Planning, Leading, and Implementing DFSS 107

Introduction 107
Planning the Deployment 107
Step 1. Define DFSS Goals and Charter Your
  DFSS Team 108
Step 2. Understand Gaps and Prioritize Changes;
  Align the Organization 111
Step 3. Plan the Changes 113
Step 4. Pilot DFSS Changes, Measure Results, Roll
  Out Full-Scale Changes 128
Step 5. Monitor and Improve the DFSS Process 129
Step 6. Integrate and Sustain the Gains 130
Dos and Don'ts to Successful DFSS Implementation 130

Dos to Successful DFSS Implementation 131
Don'ts to Avoid in Implementing DFSS 135
Key Points: Using This Book to Help You Along
   in Your Implementation 140

Chapter 7   Measuring Success 143

Introduction 143
What and When to Measure 143
DFSS Leading, or Early Deployment, Metrics 144
DFSS Mid-Deployment, or In-Process, Metrics 146
DFSS Lagging, or Independence, Metrics 149
Planning to Measure Your DFSS Success 151
DFSS Deployment Metrics Examples 151
Who to Measure 152
How to Measure 153
Key Points: Guide to Measuring Success 154

Chapter 8   How to Know When the
                  Organization "Has It" 155

Identifying the Success of Training 156
Benchmarking Success Against Other
   Organizations 158
Verifying Independence Day 158
Communicating Independence Day 161
Key Points: How to Measure and Communicate
   Your Success 162

Chapter 9   Keeping Up the DFSS Drive 163

Introduction 163
Sustaining DFSS: Enablers and Enforcers 164
Enablers 164
Enforcers 168
Ownership for the New Process 172
Key Points 172

Chapter 10 Where Do You Go from Here? 173

Introduction 173
Advanced versus New Product Development 173
Axiomatic Design 176
Customer Listening 177
Design Infrastructure Improvements 180
Holistic Development 182
Leaning the New Product Development Process 182

Organizational Change Management 183
Schedule Performance Improvement 184
Supplier Development 185
Systematic Innovation Technique 185
Taguchi's Robust Design 186
Theory of Inventive Problem Solving (TRIZ) 188
Key Points 188

Chapter 11 DFSS Case Study 189

Introduction 189
Define Phase: The Opportunity 189
Measure Phase: Defining Customer Requirements
  and CTQs 191
Analyze Phase: Identifying Concepts and Assessing
  Feasibility 195
Design Phase: Detailed Product and Production
  Process Design 200
Verify/Validate Phase: Verify Against Requirements;
  Validate Against Customer Needs 217
Implement Phase: Production and Quality/Business
  Results 217

Glossary *221*

References *231*

Index *233*

Preface

The comedian Bill Cosby often recalls his time playing college football. In one of his stories, the scene is the Temple University locker room. The coach is pumping the team up for a game against their feared opponent, Hofstra. When the team has reached a fever pitch, the coach yells, *OK, let's get out there and fight, fight, fight*! The team tries to rush onto the field, but the door is locked!

As leader in your company's product development organization, do you find yourself in a similar situation? Has your company tried to pump you up to go *do Design for Six Sigma*? When you've tried to run out on the Design for Six Sigma (DFSS) field, do you also find that the door is locked?

Between the two of us authors, we've spent over 20 years either developing new products or helping others get better at product development. We were introduced to DFSS quite a few years ago, and it took us a while to *get* what DFSS is all about. One of our Master Black Belt friends freely admits that it took her three experiences to finally understand the DFSS process. She took General Electric's DFSS course, she ran a DFSS project, and then she taught the GE course—after that, she finally *got it*. So it's tough enough to figure out how to *do* DFSS.

Have you also been challenged to move your organization from its current design and development process to one that can reliably produce Six Sigma designs? Implementing DFSS is a cross-functional effort that can be an even tougher door to break down. This door may be locked, and marketing, R&D, and operations may have all their weight pressed against the other side. We've written this book mainly to help you break down that door. There are some very good how-to books on the mechanics of DFSS, such as Yang and El-Haik's *Design for Six Sigma: A Roadmap for Product Development*.

Our main goal, though, is to provide you with a *game plan* to help you move the ball down the field—from your current product development world to one where DFSS has been embraced and is a working part of your processes and culture. Whether the products you develop are made of metal and plastic, or of credit plans and mutual funds, this book will help you improve your development process, so that you may deliver better products and services to your customers. Whether you develop tangible products like cars or cough syrup, or you deliver service products like mortgages and retirement plans, DFSS can help you develop robust products that your customers will want and will want to pay for.

At a high level, there's no mystery to the approach we'll offer you. We want to help you understand how your current development process is performing, diagnose the current strengths and weaknesses of your new product development approach, and plan and implement changes that will improve your organization's ability to deliver Six Sigma designs. If your company has already adopted Six Sigma, you'll recognize that our approach is to apply the Define, Measure, Analyze, Improve, Control (DMAIC) improvement method to your new product development process.

HOW WE'LL GET THERE

In Chapter 1, we'll start in the locker room as your *coach*. Some of the questions we'll pose may seem harsh, but we've got to help you decide why you want to *do DFSS*.

Chapter 2 will provide the theory and rationale behind striving for Six Sigma designs. Just in case your company hasn't embraced Six Sigma as an improvement approach, we'll provide you with the necessary Six Sigma background. We'll start to build the case for DFSS in Chapter 3, to help you think about how to *sell* DFSS in your organization and build some momentum and desire to want to break down those doors.

Consider Chapter 4 your benchmarking visit. Here, we'll give you a picture of *what good looks like*—the phases, steps, tools, and deliverables of a mature DFSS process.

With the theory and groundwork laid, it's time for you to get to work. Chapter 5 will guide you through a gap and readiness analysis—what are the differences between your current development process and *what good looks like*. It's one thing to be aware of the gaps; it's quite another to be ready and motivated to take the necessary improvement actions. We'll focus on the change management aspect of DFSS here.

We're going to get tactical in Chapter 6. We'll take you through a step-by-step approach to planning and implementing the design process changes. We'll address process changes, training and skill building, infrastructure changes, and overall change management of your DFSS initiative.

So how do you know your changes have made a difference? Measuring results is addressed in Chapter 7. What kind of metrics should you have on your scoreboard, and how do you know you're winning the game? We'll continue this theme in Chapter 8—discussing how you will know your organization is ready to transition from DFSS implementation to sustaining mode.

It's understandable to want to rest after a long game, but there's a danger in slipping back to old habits if we rest too long. Chapter 9 will address how to regain your organization's energy and keep the DFSS drive alive.

We've alluded to your work of implementing DFSS as a game. We'll close by suggesting some future *plays* in Chapter 10—directions you may take to continue to improve your development process.

Finally, even though it's not the main focus of this book, in researching this book we heard over and over that a DFSS case study would be very useful. Have fun reading our historical DFSS example in Chapter 11!

We can't promise you that DFSS will cause your stock's price to double in the next year. We can only promise that, if you dig deeply into your new product development process and follow the guidelines in this book, you can implement major improvements to this important process. We've played on the DFSS field ourselves and have been fortunate to be asked to help others do the same. We've seen the results DFSS can bring. We're hoping you'll join us. OK, let's get out there and fight, fight, fight!

A FEW NOTES

- We've included a number of references to other DFSS books and information. Some of this information is referenced via Web site URLs. As time goes by, we can't guarantee that the website will exist when you go to look for it. If you can't find it where we did, Google it!

- Although it is a common business term today, we recognize that Six Sigma is a registered service mark and trademark of Motorola, Inc. Similarly, Minitab is a software package owned by Minitab, Inc., and Crystal Ball is a software package owned by Decisioneering, Inc.

Acknowledgments

From Georgette: To my brothers and sisters, mom and dad, and my dear friends Karl, Megan, Marlene, and Jona. You have encouraged me to ask questions, to seek new paths, and to keep an open mind as I navigate through this world. To the great mentors I have had the pleasure of working with: David Perry, Mark Pomeroy, Kathy Vigue, Lucia Buehler, and Ed Kopkowski. Thank you for sharing your passion for excellence!

From John: To Larry Pabst and Mario Fedele—my *engineering fathers*, to Dr. Kazuyuki Suzuki—my *reliability big brother*, to Bill Hensler for that fateful DFSS call, to Eric Mattenson and the late Bill Lindenfelder for the chance to help shape GE's DFSS program, to Liz Iversen for the chance to help shape J&J's Design Excellence initiative, and, of course, to my wife, Nancy, and children, Mary and Michael, for allowing Daddy the time to devote to this book!

1
Introduction

IS YOUR PRODUCT DEVELOPMENT PROCESS HELPING YOU WIN THE GAME TODAY?

Think about the products your company has recently launched. Have these products achieved what you hoped for—rapid customer uptake, high sales volume and revenue/profit, high Sigma levels for critical-to-quality requirements, and low complaint rates and return/warranty costs? How are your costs compared to your competitors'?

Is R&D still trying to stabilize products with its manufacturing partners? Are you overwhelmed with the number of parts you have to manage to produce your products? If you have a Six Sigma initiative, how many of your Black and Green Belts are working on reducing product defects whose causes lie in design decisions? Are your product development efforts mostly producing line extensions of existing products?

Now think about the products that your company does consider successful. How much bigger could the product have been? How much higher could sales/revenue/profit be? How about planning the next generations of your products? As these products mature in the market, is your company actively developing/acquiring the technologies you'll need to meet the market demands of tomorrow?

Now think about what is going on inside your product development process. Do R&D teams have clear goals for what they are trying to develop? Do they have a clear understanding of what the customer wants in the product? Does product development take too long because your engineers are still mired in a build, test, fix, "design" mode? Do the two monsters of scope and feature creep roam your hallways? Does manufacturing complain about designs that can't be built? There is a corollary to this question: Does R&D

understand the capabilities of manufacturing processes and how this variation will impact what the customer sees?

Do you still *throw things over the wall* (marketing requirements to R&D, R&D specifications to manufacturing, parts requirements to suppliers)? How many of your development projects are *science projects*, where the team is trying to invent a technology and where schedule and budget are way over projections?

If these questions seem a bit brutal and personal, don't feel too bad. You and your company are not alone. While companies have spent millions of dollars on systems to better manage their manufacturing and supply chain operations, only a few have really focused on improving their *Archimedes' lever*—the design and development process.

One of us recently tried to purchase a radio-alarm clock—a simple, mature product—and returned two brands back to the store. Ah, you say, manufacturing must have screwed up! No, both were design issues.

We had a hard time finding our favorite rock station because the first clock's tuning dial would allow only coarse adjustments (we're just glad we didn't buy that clock as a gift for an elderly person with arthritis). We took that clock back to the store and purchased another brand. Ah, now the sweet sounds of heavy metal in the morning! The second brand, however, had an annoying habit of running fast, about an hour a month. We could have developed a *work-around* and reset the clock once a week, but that would reward the company for its incompetence. Back this one went, too.

Clearly there were design issues with both of these products. But why should this occur? In the 21st century, why would any company release a product that will inevitably annoy and disappoint customers? How can we even imagine it happening on mature technology like dial radios and alarm clocks? What are we missing?

DO YOU EVEN HAVE A PRODUCT DEVELOPMENT PROCESS?

Recently, we were talking with a young mechanical engineer just hired by a company who has been on a several-year DFSS journey. We asked why he had decided to change companies. He was quick to respond, "At my old company, we had a chaotic approach to product development. We didn't do market research, there was no discipline to product development, and there was a lot of conflict between the development staff and production." He went on to say that he made his job move because he was eager to learn "what a good development process can look like and how you get from bad to good!" In a few words, he had captured one of our basic learnings and a key hypothesis of this book: (1) design is a process and (2) the design process can be improved.

When we see problems in a manufacturing process, it's usually pretty easy to track those back to the *6Ms:* the method, the man, the material, the machine, the measurement system, and Mother Nature. Although sometimes they are not quite as obvious, problems in product development will usually fall into these categories.

Method Issues

Too many companies have no *real* product development process. We worked in the power plant engineering department of a large electric utility a few years ago. The department managed by engineering work orders (EWOs). Once you were assigned the EWO, every Monday morning you were asked to report on your work status. That was as good as it got for a design process. Unfortunately, the customers of the department—the power plants—weren't very happy with the quality, consistency, cost, and schedule performance of the engineering process.

At a consumer products company, pictures of their five-step product development process were posted in all of the hallways. When asked about the process, the scientists and engineers either didn't know about it or would freely state that nobody followed that process. After we trained several teams at the company's South American R&D center in the Design for Six Sigma method, one of the team leaders came up at the end of the session. She thanked us for the training and said, "Before you came, our development process was just a series of gates. You've shown us how to successfully get from one gate to another!"

Tool Issues (The Fishbone's Machine Category)

Companies employ poor or underperforming design tools. A lot of great tools can really help improve the development process. We've seen companies go through the waves of quality function deployment, Taguchi, concurrent engineering, stage gating, reliability, and so on. It often seems, though, that the main effect of introducing these tools is to add buzz words and acronyms to the development lexicon. As one of our friends noted, "At the fountain of knowledge, most people simply gargle and spit!"

Let's consider quality function deployment (QFD) as an example. Originally developed in Japan in the 1970s, QFD was introduced to U.S. companies by thought leaders such as Bob King and Don Clausing. Japanese companies had shown them how QFD could lead to faster, better product launches. So here's a tool that actually works, one that has been demonstrated to provide a measurable benefit to product development.

In typical applications, though, the gargle and spit approach often occurs. Here's a sequence of events we've seen all too many times. QFD is sold as a new idea to a company. A QFD consultant is hired and trains the R&D staff. The contract might include mentoring one or two teams in how to develop QFD's house of quality. Once the first couple of houses are built, the company will proclaim, "Yes, we know how to do this." The consultant is patted on the back, collects the fee, and goes off to the next client.

If you were to visit this company a year later, though, we'll bet one of two scenarios will have occurred. In the first, the company is back doing product development the old way. Some associates will remember (perhaps not so fondly) building the *house of pain,* and their typical comments will be "took too long, didn't see the benefit, our old way was good enough." If you wandered through the R&D offices, you'd see the QFD training books on the shelves, maybe a few computers with QFD software still installed and, perhaps, that lone QFD champion's voice still crying in the wilderness, but not much else.

In the second scenario, QFD is still employed, but it has become one of the checklist items in the development process. We walked into a development team room a while back and were pleasantly surprised to see a quite detailed house of quality on the wall. The big "oops" came when we asked an engineer what they did with the house. "We showed it at our last stage gate and management was happy. Now we are developing the product that we think the customers want!" As another of our friends says, "Well, that looks like some pretty expensive wallpaper to me!"

Now we happen to think that QFD is a great development tool. But if we are going to use the tool, let's make up our minds to drink deeply and not just gargle and spit.

One of the other failure modes we've seen is a focus mainly on the mechanics of the tool. In the QFD example just described, notice that we mentioned only R&D being trained in the tool. We often forget that it takes a *team* working together to deliver the best product for the customer. For QFD, the house of quality is the tangible deliverable. The truly important outcome of QFD, though, is the *alignment* that the team achieves around the requirements for the new product. If the meetings to "build" the house of quality do not include all key team members and do not incorporate building consensus around the requirements, the tool has failed to accomplish its purpose. The QFD house should, as a minimum, include participation from market research, R&D, and operations. We can't overstress the importance of these "soft" issues associated with many DFSS tools and methods.

People Issues

We'll try to keep this one short, especially because we'll talk much more about it later in this book. You probably know most of these issues in your company, anyway.

Silo mentality. Marketing, R&D, and operations are the usual trinity we have to address. Misalignment of goals, mistrust, and a throw-it-over-the-wall culture are just some of the issues we deal with. One R&D director tells the story of how she was asked to look into a development project that just wasn't going anywhere. She talked to R&D first and asked what the project was about. The answer: "Oh, we are developing a new adhesive technology." Next, she visited marketing. The answer: "This project is about a new platform of 'X' that we want to launch." Finally, she talked with operations. The answer: "Well, we are looking to really increase production efficiencies with this project." Three groups, three different goals for the same project!

Reward and recognition. In one company, marketing takes the lead on product development projects. Unfortunately, individuals are rotated into these positions for periods of only 18 to 24 months and they are rewarded mainly if they launch a product. The development cycle is constrained to the time they spend in that role. In 18 months, this company's development process is capable of delivering a line extension, but not much else. The company wonders why most of its development projects are low risk, low reward!

Leadership. We are not going to rant and rave here that your leaders need to be like Jack Welch, Larry Bossidy, or Attila the Hun, but this is an obvious, important development process factor (we've devoted the entirety of Chapter 6 to this factor).

Two common leadership themes seem to appear over and over, though. The first concerns prioritization. Too many development projects are thrown at finite development resources. Talking with a package designer the other day, we asked her how many projects she's working on. The answer was 15! Do the math—even working a typical 60-hour week, that's about 4 hours per project per week. This company needs to learn about the Theory of Constraints and apply that learning to its development process's bottlenecks and throughput!

Second, we've found that the risk tolerance of many companies is usually pretty low. One of our friends did a risk/reward chart for his firm's development projects (Figure 1.1). Virtually all of the projects were in the lower left quadrant, not good news, because the company had some pretty aggressive growth targets.

In just 15 minutes a day, your development process can look like GE's, Johnson & Johnson's, or . . . (fill in the blank!)

This is the part of the introduction where we unveil the answer to all your product development woes. Well, not quite. Here's the best news we can give you.

Over about the last 10 years, companies around the world from GE to Johnson & Johnson have been improving their development processes using a framework known as DFSS.

Light bulbs, x-ray tubes, automobiles, appliances, medical devices, shampoo, soft drinks, and even frozen dinners are being designed faster, with a focus on what the customers truly want and with a view to preventing defects from occurring as far upstream in the development process as possible (no more throwing it over the wall). DFSS methods and tools have also been successfully applied to designing and redesigning business processes and services.

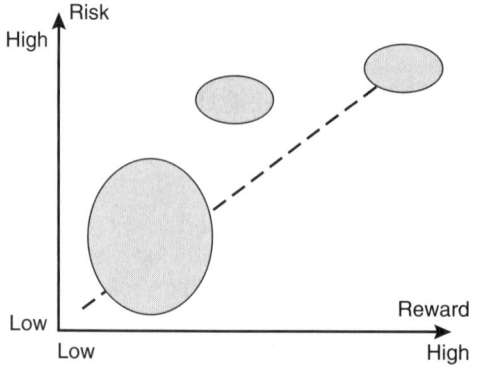

Figure 1.1 Risk/reward profile.

Before we get carried away, though, we'll make two disclaimers. First, we recognize that product development is a key contributor to organizational success. However, we know of companies that are successful in spite of their poor product development processes and vice versa. DFSS by itself will not guarantee a rapid rise in your stock price. If some of your other processes and structures are in poor shape, work on improving those, too.

Our second disclaimer is that time moves on. We'll share DFSS success stories from a number of companies. However, remember that Rome had both a rise and a fall. While we'll discuss sustaining the DFSS drive, we haven't been able to figure out how to make DFSS a permanent part of an organization's systems, structures, and culture.

Given these disclaimers, though, we've found that for the companies who have taken DFSS seriously, their results are positive and encouraging. For example, one company has seen its initial scrap/rework rates dropping from historical averages of 10 to 15% to 2 to 3% for products developed using a DFSS process. Another has seen its customers' satisfaction with new products increase dramatically. Following is a specific example from General Electric.

> **The Product:** LightSpeed Computed Tomography (CT) Scanner (launched 1998)
>
> **The DFSS Process:** GE incorporated input from more than 100 customers around the world to make sure the technology was meaningful, not just new.
>
> The LightSpeed Scanner's advancements were the direct result of GE's Design for Six Sigma quality efforts, an approach that enabled GE scientists and engineers to develop more benefits and introduce the scanner at least one year earlier than what otherwise would have been possible. Specifically, this approach allows GE to develop nearly flawless products through a disciplined process control approach that is delivering tremendous results.
>
> Six Sigma allowed GE to manage this complex technology— including R&D breakthroughs in materials science, computers, software, and electronics—to achieve a system with unprecedented speed and image clarity (according to PressLink Online AP Photo Express Network, PRNZ).

(Continued)

(Continued)

> **The Customer Response:** "The speed is breathtaking," said Dr. Carl Ravin, professor and chairman of the Department of Radiology at Duke Medical Center. "A body scan that used to take three minutes now can be completed in approximately 20 seconds."
>
> **A GE Manager Response:** "In the past, many projects were approved and implemented based on gut feeling and intuition. Designing a process to deliver 6σ capabilities requires quantitative data. Using gut feeling in a Design for Six Sigma methodology will not permit passing a tollgate."

SO HOW DOES DFSS WORK ITS MAGIC?

There's both a narrow and a broad answer to this question. Let's start with the narrow answer. The essence of DFSS is to develop a design where important product requirements are being delivered at Six Sigma levels of performance. Here, you will start by identifying the product's critical-to-quality (CTQ) requirements. These CTQs are based on what is most important about the product from the customers' perspective. Then, as you develop the product and production process, you'll deploy and allocate these requirements (this is called *flowdown*) to lower level (for example, subsystem, assembly, parts, process) requirements. You'll then predict how the variation in parts and process and noise variables will affect the variation the customer sees at the CTQ level. You'll use design scorecards to report the predicted design performance. You'll cascade requirements and establish transfer functions relating the design Xs to the CTQs. You'll perform Monte Carlo simulations to determine how variation in the Xs contributes to variation in the CTQs (recording the results on your scorecard). Just incorporating these DFSS elements in your design process can help. At the very least, you'll have checked your design against the variation enemy and made design improvements where insufficient margin to CTQ specification limits exist. Your product can then enter manufacturing with some degree of assurance that defect probabilities will be low.

Over the last few years, a broader view of DFSS has evolved. A number of companies view DFSS as encompassing the entire product development process and are using DFSS to improve their overall design process. Here, DFSS's scope has been expanded to address all product development functions from market research (voice of customer, QFD) to concept selection (TRIZ, Pugh methods) to detailed design (design cascade, design prediction, reliability, design for manufacturing/assembly) and production system design (process control, statistical process control [SPC], error-proofing, and lean). Some companies have also included advanced technology development and product portfolio management under the DFSS banner. In this broad view, DFSS aims to help you:

- Identify, prioritize, and resource the right product development projects.
- Manage advanced technology development outside of/in parallel with product development.
- Understand critical-to-quality customer requirements (the Ys).
- Develop superior design concepts to meet the CTQs.
- Predict design quality and eliminate defects upstream.
- Manage risks through failure mode and effects analysis.
- Identify and optimize critical process variables through simulations and design of experiments.
- Benchmark to demonstrate design superiority.

While these are noble and lofty goals, as a product development manager you face two questions—first, what to do, and second, how to do it. It's nice to talk about getting your VOC and using QFD to define your CTQs, which are then cascaded to CTPs through DOE and FMEAs, and then optimized and controlled through SPC and Poka-Yoke error-proofing (oops, sorry, we slipped into Buzzword City). That's your future world.

Today, though, you are faced with the current state of your product development process and staff. Your development staff today may do little in the way of customer research, likely defines product features as requirements, performs the failure modes and effects analysis (if at all) just before the next design review to make sure the box is checked, and thinks Poka-Yoke is something you do with chicken eggs.

Everybody knows they need to manage their diet and exercise, but there is no easy way to get there; no magic pill. The tough thing is changing habits. This same challenge applies to improving your product development process. Successful change will encompass personal, team, and organizational habits.

WHAT WE'LL PROMISE YOU

In developing this book, we actually followed the DFSS and Six Sigma process—including gathering the voice of our customers. Here's what our research told us you wanted:

DFSS Business Case

Building the Business Case for DFSS. What will the business achieve with DFSS? What are the benefits/costs? (chapters 3 and 5)

Success Examples from Others (Outside/Inside)—Value. What have others achieved? What can we expect to see (early wins, longer-term wins)? How can we share within our organization? (chapters 3, 6, 7, and 8)

Leadership

Leadership Linkage. How can senior leadership be sold on DFSS? What behaviors are expected of leaders? What can they expect of their organization? (chapters 5 and 6)

Commitment. How can we get the organization committed to adopting DFSS? (Chapter 5)

DFSS—What, How, and When

Emphasis on Process, Methods, and Application. Focus on the DFSS process (not details around specific tools—those details can be obtained elsewhere). (Chapter 4)

Specific Tools—Where, When, and When Not. Show where tools are useful/not useful; relevant examples of tools application within the DFSS process. (chapters 4 and 11)

Minimum Requirements and Expectations. What are the minimum expectations for development teams? (chapters 6 and 8)

Application/Impact of DFSS Method/Tools on Day-to-Day Design. How can we ensure that the adopters see

DFSS as benefiting the design process, not as extra work? How can we ensure that application occurs after the training? How do we keep the organization focused on DFSS? (Chapter 6)

Application in My World. How are development efforts currently performed? Where are the inefficiencies? How can DFSS make product development (in my world) better, faster, and cheaper? How can current design best practices be integrated with DFSS? (Chapter 5)

Chartering. How do we ensure that the right development projects are selected? How can we keep the DFSS momentum going beyond the charter? (chapters 4, 7–10)

Planning. How do we develop a vision of a DFSS organization? How can we introduce DFSS? What are effective models for deploying DFSS in different design organizations? What specific behaviors should leaders exhibit during implementation? What should the deployment plan look like? (chapters 5 and 6)

Deployment Strategy. What deployment strategies are effective for different types of design organizations? Give me tips for successful rollout strategies. What are best practices for training for teams? Who are the key DFSS stakeholders, and how do we engage them? (chapters 5 and 6)

Outlining Deployment Strategies and Drivers. What are the key deployment drivers? What messages should management hear? (chapters 6 and 8)

Cost of Implementation. What will it cost to implement DFSS? (Chapter 6)

Change Management. How will we lead the organization through the change (transformational leadership)? How will we avoid preaching DFSS as gospel and engage staff in a scientific, logical manner? How can senior leadership learn to think DFSS and talk DFSS with teams, creating expectations for application of key DFSS methods/tools? (chapters 5 and 6)

Doing. What does *good* look like for DFSS? How can we make the leadership issue tangible for leaders—specific behaviors to look for, specific questions to ask? What resources will be required? How can we make it part of doing business, not something special or extra? (chapters 4, 5, 6, and 11)

Design Process Integration. How can we integrate DFSS into the current design and development process (or vice versa)? (Chapter 6)

Integration with Existing Design Process. Think about implementing DFSS as a Six Sigma project. How do we ensure that DFSS doesn't slow down design/development? (chapters 5–8)

Infrastructure. What infrastructure will be needed to support DFSS (training is obvious; others include databases, references, websites, software, and rewards and recognition)? (Chapter 6)

Roles and Responsibilities. What are the specific roles and responsibilities? What are the expectations for each role deploying and doing DFSS? (Chapter 6)

Role of Training. How does learning work in a specific organization? Should we use internal or external trainers? How do we link training to action? How should training be applied—key projects versus the masses? (Chapter 6)

Consulting and Support. What is the role of the consultant? How should he or she work with the deployment team? Are dedicated resources (for example, DFSS Master Black Belts) required? How can they be best employed? (Chapter 6)

Subject Matter Experts (SME). What SMEs are needed? How can they help the deployment process? What coaching models work and don't work? (Chapter 6)

Mentorship. What mentorship models work? (Chapter 6)

Check and Act. What assessment models work? How can success be measured? (chapters 5, 6, 7 and 8)

Metrics. What are examples of good metrics for the design process? How should metrics evolve? How should behaviors be reinforced? (Chapter 7)

Sharing and Learning. What sharing models work? How can teams share learnings? How can they avoid the same struggles? (chapters 5 and 6)

Path to DFSS and Assessment Tool. How can DFSS maturity be assessed? (chapters 5, 6, and 7)

Pitfalls. What are the pitfalls of implementing DFSS? How can these be avoided? (Chapter 6)

DO YOU HAVE THE GOTTAWANNA?

Many of the organizations we have worked with have a common cultural barrier to DFSS—they are already successful. Nothing stifles success like success. But fortunately for many of these organizations, they also shared one other major cultural element: Their leaders were not satisfied with "same as" success. They wanted to give their customers products that actually met and exceeded the customers' needs. They wanted to stop wasting resources "cleaning up the mess" of a barely producible product. They wanted to be leaner, faster, and more profitable every year. We will show you how DFSS has helped these organizations and how it will help you, too, if you have the *gottawanna*.

If you are ready, let's get on the field and start our way to DFSS victory!

2
What Is Design for Six Sigma?

INTRODUCTION

Before we can help you implement Design for Six Sigma, let's spend a few pages describing what DFSS is. In case you aren't familiar with Six Sigma, we'll start with some basic concepts.

Our first exposure to Design for Six Sigma was as an improvement to an existing design process. Over the last few years, though, DFSS's scope has expanded to include virtually the entire product development life cycle. We'll bracket this by first describing DFSS in its narrow sense and then expanding to the bigger picture of today's DFSS.

WHAT IS SIX SIGMA?

If you are already familiar with Six Sigma concepts, you can skip this part and head on down to "What Is DFSS—Narrow Sense?" section. On the other hand, this won't take you too long to read and may provide insight into some of the DFSS method and implementation discussions later.

Six Sigma has come to mean a lot of things. As an *improvement system,* Six Sigma has been around since the late 1980s. Motorola was the first company to develop and apply Six Sigma as a disciplined, breakthrough improvement method. General Electric then adopted Six Sigma and popularized the method through both its Six Sigma results and the public spotlight that Jack Welch put on its Six Sigma application. Most large companies have at least tried Six Sigma, with varying degrees of adoption and success. Although the idea of Six Sigma is less than 20 years old, the tools and methods associated with Six Sigma are not new. Many of these, especially the statistical and process analysis methods, were around for quite a few years before the phrase *Six Sigma* popped up.

Six Sigma *performance* corresponds to a certain defect rate—about 3.4 defects per million opportunities. Where did this come from? Well, the basic idea behind Six Sigma is simple. If your process can produce parts or products whose characteristics have very little variation in relation to the customers' specification limits, then you will produce very few defects. The key word is *variation*. Most of us are comfortable with using the *mean* as a measure of average performance. Fewer are comfortable with measuring variation in terms of a *standard deviation,* or *s*.

Simply speaking, the *Sigma level* of a process measures how far the mean of your process is from the specification limits *measured in standard deviation units*. Figure 2.1 shows you the formula for the mean and standard deviation and also shows a process whose mean is four standard deviations from the specification limit (that is, a *Four Sigma level* process).

For example, say your customers expect you to produce a part that has a requirement that is of particular importance to them. We'll call that requirement "critical to quality" or CTQ. The customers want you to hit a target of 100 and stay below 105 for the part's CTQ. You make 50 or so parts and calculate your process's mean to be 100. Good news! Your process is centered on the target. However, if you calculate the standard deviation of the parts to be 5, you should be worried about the variation in your process. A little statistical theory, invoking the normal distribution, will predict that your process will produce 16 defective parts out of 100 opportunities. Figure 2.2 shows you the picture of this situation.

Because this process's mean is one standard deviation away from the specification limit of 105, we'd conclude that this process

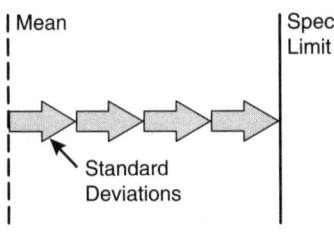

Figure 2.1 Mean, standard deviation formula, Sigma-level picture.

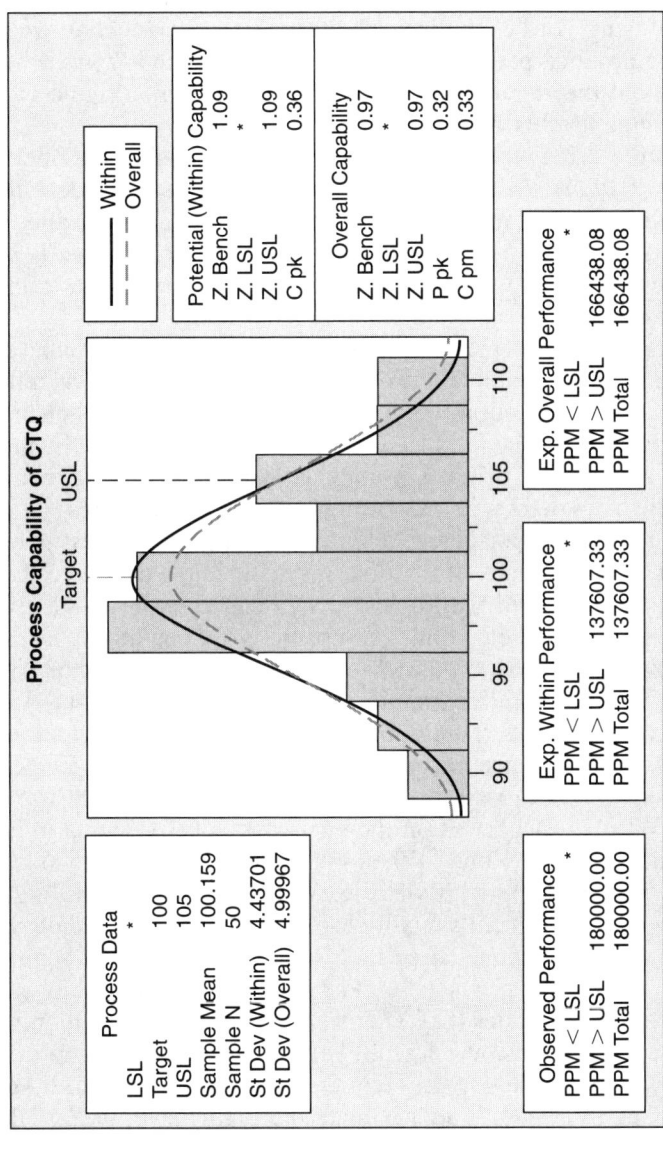

Figure 2.2 Process capability with mean = 100, sigma = 5, target = 100, USL = 105.

is performing at One Sigma. Be careful; the language can be confusing. When you hear the term *One Sigma process,* that's not the value of the standard deviation, but rather how many standard deviations the process' mean is away from the spec limit(s). To keep from confusing you, we will use the term *Sigma level* when we're describing product, part, or process, performance, and *Sigma* when talking about the standard deviation. In our example, Sigma is 5, but the Sigma level is 1.

In Figure 2.2, notice the Z term in the upper right box labeled *Potential (Within) Capability.* Z is the symbol used to describe Sigma level. You will hear these two terms used interchangeably in the Six Sigma world. You will hear "Z equals 6," or "Z value is 6," "Sigma level is 6," or "the process is running at a Six Sigma level." All of these mean the same thing.

Figure 2.3 shows a process that is operating at a Six Sigma level. As you can see, when there are six standard deviations between the mean and the specification limits, there is a very, very small chance that a given part will be produced outside of the spec limits. Even if this process shifts and drifts over time, it can be expected to produce no more than 3.4 defects in one million parts or opportunities.

So why is Six Sigma good? Why not Five Sigma? If Six is good, why isn't Seven Sigma better? First, here's a simple answer. When Motorola benchmarked world-class performance in the 1980s, the best-in-class Japanese electronics companies were operating at about a Six Sigma level. Why were *they* operating at Six Sigma? The deeper answer lies in the economics of production. The best-in-class Japanese companies were minimizing the loss associated with their products' variation; in other words, they were following Genichi Taguchi's quality approach.

Don Wheeler elaborates on the economics of Six Sigma in his paper "The Six Sigma Zone." When we wrote this book a downloadable copy was available at his website, www.spcpress.com. His argument is similar to Taguchi's quality loss concept and is based on the *excess cost of production.* These excess costs are incurred when the product or part is not produced on target. If you can achieve operational process capabilities (Cpk) in the 1.5 to 2 range, you will minimize these excess costs, which will likely either increase your profits or allow you to reduce your price in the face of competition. If you multiply Cpk by 3, you'll approximate the Sigma level or Z of the process. Hence, a Cpk of 2.0 is equivalent to a Six Sigma level process. Don't be fooled by fuzzy arguments for why you should pursue Six Sigma; there is sound *economics* behind this important business concept!

What Is Design for Six Sigma? 19

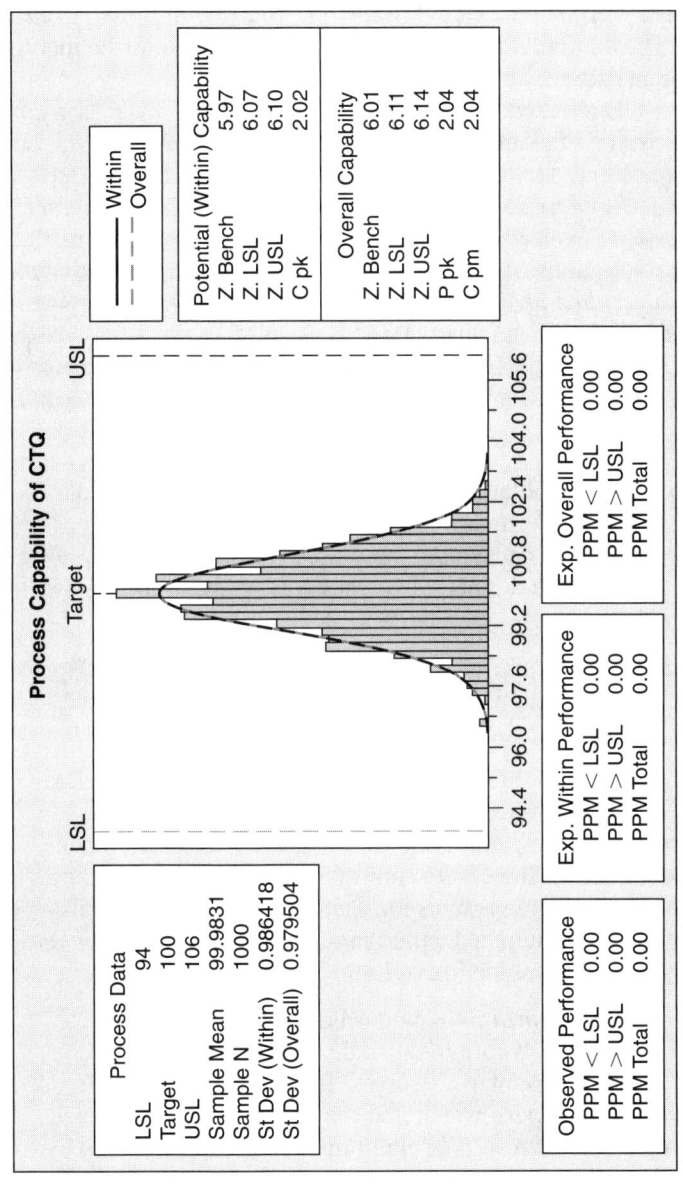

Figure 2.3 Six Sigma process.

So with Six Sigma being the goal, and since most companies find they operate at somewhere between Two and Four Sigma, how do you get there? To help them achieve Six Sigma, Motorola developed a four-step methodology: *Measure, Analyze, Improve, Control (MAIC)*. The continual application of MAIC helps Motorola identify and eliminate sources of variation in its processes.

When GE adopted Six Sigma, its management added a *Define* step, which identifies the current process and clarifies what the customer cares about: the process' CTQs. GE found that this prestep was helpful when applying MAIC to *transactional* rather than *manufacturing* processes. This leads us to today's DMAIC improvement method. You'll see variations of DMAIC. For example, one business is concerned with *replicating* improvements, so it employs DMAIC-R (R = Replicate). We've found that *DMAIEC*—splitting the Improve step into two parts: Identify Improvements and Execute Improvement—is useful in the kind of improvement projects we work with. We'll use DMAIEC here:

Define—The problem is defined and the business value of the problem quantified; resources are marshaled; the customers, their needs, and the critical-to-quality metric operationally are defined; and finally the current process is defined.

Measure—The current process performance is measured, the baseline Sigma level calculated, and the process sliced and diced to see whether some leverage area exists (Pareto analysis for defects, theory of constraints for bottlenecks, etc.).

Analyze—The process variables responsible for performance are identified (if the CTQ is our outcome or *y-variable,* then the Analyze step represents the search for the inputs or *x-variables*) through a detailed process analysis, a statistical analysis, or a combination of both.

Identify improvements—Countermeasures to improve and stabilize the Xs are identified, practical methods to implement the countermeasure(s) identified, cost-benefit tradeoff studies performed, and the process changes piloted (with data-based results backing up the countermeasures' effectiveness).

Execute improvement—The full-scale change is implemented with the necessary process changes being executed across the department or organization. Results of the full-scale change are measured to ensure its effectiveness.

Control—The Control step recognizes that effective changes need to be made a permanent part of the process. A process control system is developed and implemented, identifying who is accountable for process performance, what the standard process is, how it should be measured, and what actions are to be taken if the process is not performing as desired.

Figure 2.4 shows the steps and the key activities performed in each.

The Six Sigma toolkit today resembles a well-stocked hardware store. Here is a list of tools from a four-week course delivered by one of the authors:

- MS Office (including Project and Visio)
- Statistical software (Minitab, JMP)
- Black Belt roles and responsibilities
- Improving existing products and services—DMAIEC
- Project chartering
- Project reporting and reviews
- Voice of customer feedback
- Developing indicators
- Basic data collection
- Measurement system analysis
- Line graphs
- Run charts
- Sampling
- Histograms
- Process capability
- Process flowcharts
- Process analysis methods
- Bar charts
- Pareto analysis
- Pie charts
- Radar charts
- Cause and effect analysis
- Contingency analysis
- Scatter diagrams
- Correlation analysis
- Regression analysis—simple, linear
- Probability distributions
- Hypothesis testing
- Parameter estimation
- Confidence intervals

Sampling

Single-factor experiments

Analysis of variation (ANOVA)

Design of experiments

Reliability terms and definitions

Reliability management

Failure modes and effects analysis (FMEA)

Fault-tree analysis

Weibull analysis

Selecting and implementing process changes

Cost-benefit analysis

Evaluating the effects of changes/standardization and replication

Controlling processes

Process management charts

Control charts

Creativity methods

Performance and process benchmarking

Tolerance development and analysis

Reliability testing/accelerated testing

The people (usually future leaders) who receive this training and lead improvement projects are known as Black Belts. Black Belts are often assigned full-time to solve important business problems or attack business opportunities. Green Belts will work part-time on smaller business problems/opportunities. Master Black Belts actively support business improvements and mentor Black and Green Belts.

Other Six Sigma roles include Champions and Sponsors, who can provide resources and remove barriers for the improvement teams, and Finance (or Money Belts) to ensure the projects make business sense and to provide their blessing to recorded project benefits, especially in today's Sarbanes-Oxley world.

To help the organization implement Six Sigma, drive its application, and assess Six Sigma's effects, a Six Sigma Program Office may be established and there may be Six Sigma leads assigned within the business' various departments/divisions.

Executives are accountable for promoting the application of Six Sigma in their divisions, ensuring that the rewards and recognition systems are consistent with the behaviors Six Sigma demands, and, most important, ensuring that the business strategy is defined, measured, and accomplished by Six Sigma projects (where needed).

The previous text describes a basic Six Sigma initiative. There are as many flavors as there are companies that have adopted Six Sigma. For example, Six Sigma and lean improvement methods are

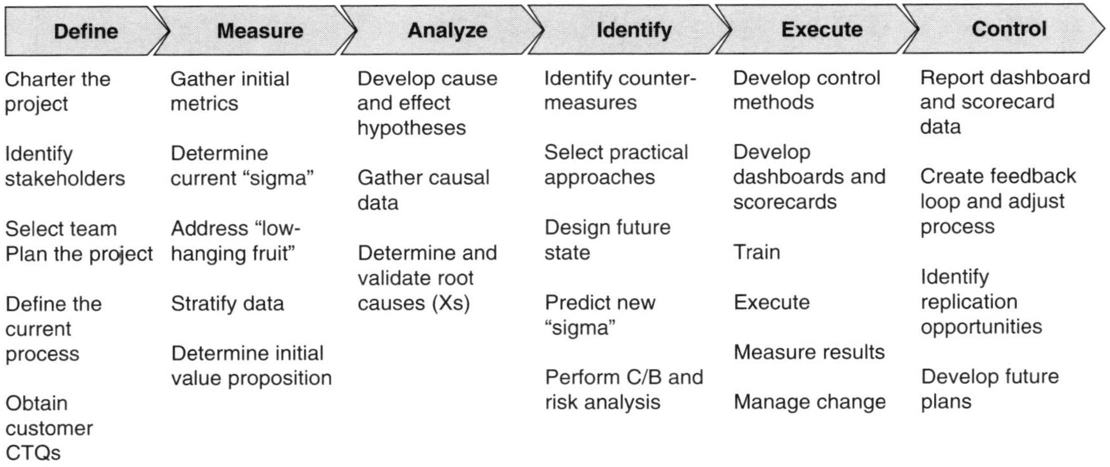

What Is Design for Six Sigma? 23

Define	Measure	Analyze	Identify	Execute	Control
Charter the project	Gather initial metrics	Develop cause and effect hypotheses	Identify counter-measures	Develop control methods	Report dashboard and scorecard data
Identify stakeholders	Determine current "sigma"	Gather causal data	Select practical approaches	Develop dashboards and scorecards	Create feedback loop and adjust process
Select team	Address "low-hanging fruit"	Determine and validate root causes (Xs)	Design future state	Train	Identify replication opportunities
Plan the project	Stratify data		Predict new "sigma"	Execute	Develop future plans
Define the current process	Determine initial value proposition		Perform C/B and risk analysis	Measure results	
Obtain customer CTQs				Manage change	

Figure 2.4 DMAIEC process improvement method.

often linked as companies strive to take waste out of their supply chains and become more responsive to the market. In the software world, we've seen Six Sigma used to support improvement of software development processes. At least one company has integrated Six Sigma with its goal of achieving Level 5 on the Software Engineering Institute's capability maturity model-integrated (CMMI).

While it sounds obvious, many companies miss the connection between Six Sigma and achievement of *strategic goals*. Strategy often comes down to either improving existing processes' performance or designing new products/services/processes. Six Sigma's methods are perfectly suited for this.

Although application of Six Sigma tools and methods will *lead* to reduced costs (less waste, rework, warranty), some companies have corrupted Six Sigma by treating it primarily as a cost-reduction program. If your Six Sigma program is focused only on cost reduction, you can expect that it will only last for about a year before it disappears!

A thriving basic Six Sigma culture will lay the foundation for your efforts to promote Design for Six Sigma. To the extent that one or more elements are missing or not working well in your company, your DFSS implementation will have to compensate. Three simple examples will suffice:

1. If manufacturing has embraced Six Sigma, you will be able to enlist the staff's support for your DFSS effort. They are probably tired of having to perform DMAIC projects because of the defects your current design process is producing.

2. If your people have already been trained in the Six Sigma toolkit, you'll find that quite a few of these are also part of the DFSS toolkit. This can reduce the learning curve and the amount of time you have to devote to training and skill-building. Consider, though, which functions have these skill sets. Often, manufacturing and operations have been trained in and are skilled in Six Sigma, but not the research and development staff.

3. If your company has tried Six Sigma and discarded it, then you are in for an even greater challenge trying to implement DFSS. You might be able to pull off a design process improvement initiative, but you may be better off not calling it DFSS.

THE IDEA OF IMPROVING DESIGN PROCESSES

OK, let's move on to Design for Six Sigma. It may be hard to believe, but occasionally we run across individuals who do not accept the idea of design as a process. Just in case you have doubts, we'll try to dispel those with the following example.

In 1988, one of us (John) was working at Florida Power & Light (FPL) in a statistical specialist role (today, we'd call him a Master Black Belt). At the time, FPL was learning and applying its quality improvement program to business problems/opportunities.

FPL's Japanese counselors had spent almost three years helping us learn how to improve our business processes through systematic process and root-cause analysis. It had been a long road. We weren't dumb, but it took us a year to just get good at doing Pareto and cause/effect analysis in our counselors' eyes. Just as we started to think we could DMAIEC our way to business excellence, one of the counselors remarked, "You must now learn to move from preventing the recurrence of problems to preventing problems through prediction!" You could see the FPL eyes rolling: "Oh, boy, here we go again."

The counselor had an important point, though. He was telling us to start looking at the processes we employed to *design* power plants and transmission and distribution systems. He was asking us to identify and eliminate defects during design *before* they were translated into steel, copper, and concrete.

For example, counselor Dr. Noriaki Kano reviewed our plans to add two gas turbines to one of our power plants. He asked Bill Hensler, the plant manager, for his *quality plan*. Of course, we didn't have a clue what he was talking about. It turned out Dr. Kano was simply looking for evidence that we knew what the Ys (outcomes) were for this project and that we had identified *and were managing* the critical inputs, or Xs, that would drive achievement of these outcomes. So, with their encouragement, we dug in and found that there were lots of opportunities in our design processes.

We supposedly cared a lot about our system's reliability. But do you think we demanded reliability from our equipment suppliers? Not really. How about doing a simple failure modes and effects analysis for a new transmission system design? No, too much trouble—we don't have time for that! How about keeping the drawings updated so the engineers could work with a good set of as-builts? Again, some folks didn't quite see the value in that. We were in a meeting once where the drawing manager actually stated, "Engineers don't need updated drawings!"

So as we started working on these opportunities, we had a couple of novel thoughts. First, design *is* a process. It has inputs, a *product* is produced (the design output), and some defined steps have to occur between the input and the output. Second, by treating design as a process, we could identify the Xs in the process that were producing design defects and work to eliminate those defects. We also found that the same systematic process/root-cause analysis approach we were applying to power plant failures could be used to analyze and improve our design processes. At one point in the late 1980s, we had over 60 teams working on design process improvements.

WHAT IS DFSS: NARROW SENSE?

So, now we'll address the Design for Six Sigma process. Suppose you are the head of a Stone Age research and development organization. You are working on a new idea—combining the wheel and axle to transport objects. Imagine that you're tired of dragging those big blocks needed to build Stonehenge. There is a large market for these, and you plan to build an assembly line to make the product. Fred will be in charge of boring the hole through the wheels and Barney will shape the axles' outside diameters. Wilma and Betty will assemble the two components (Figure 2.5).

Let's apply DFSS to this situation. There is only one requirement you are worried about—the gap between the axle and the wheel. There is an upper specification of 0.005 feet; if it's greater than this, the wheel will slip off the axle. There is also a lower specification of

Figure 2.5 Wheel/axle assembly.

0.00 feet; otherwise there will be an interference and Wilma and Betty won't be able to assemble the two parts. Figure 2.6 shows our specifications.

This critical requirement, a CTQ, is a Y (outcome) that you can't control directly. To control the CTQ, you need to identify the Xs (variables or factors) that drive the CTQ and how they combine to achieve the Y; we'll call this a *design cascade*. Here, the only two Xs are the inner diameter of the wheel (Fred's responsibility) and the outer diameter of the axle (Barney's responsibility). We'll examine a simple relationship between the Xs and the Y:

$$Y = f(x_1, x_2)$$
$$\text{Gap} = \text{Wheel diameter} - \text{Axle diameter}$$

The formula is known as a *transfer function,* because it helps us *transfer* both the mean and variation from the Xs to the Y.

Suppose the axle diameter has been set at 0.400 feet. If you wanted to achieve an average gap of 0.0025 feet, the wheel diameter must be set at 0.4025 feet. Entering these average values into the transfer functions confirms that the targeted gap will be achieved.

But let's not forget the specification limits. Because Fred and Barney will be making a lot of these shafts and axles, we can expect some variation to occur in the part dimensions. The question that we now face is how much variation is allowable in the parts—or, equivalently, what specification limits should we place on the part dimensions? We really can't answer the question until we've posed another interesting question: How often are we willing to fail at achieving the CTQ? Or, asking the question in just a slightly different way, What is our target Sigma level for this CTQ? If we set the target Sigma level at 6, we already know that fewer than 3.4 out of a million axle assemblies will be defective. If that seems to be too

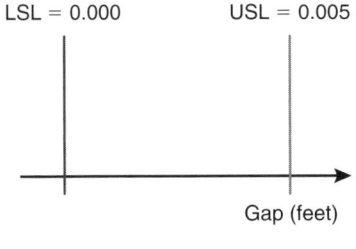

Figure 2.6 Axle/wheel specifications.

Table 2.1 Sigma level and corresponding defect rate.

Sigma level (Z)	Defects/million opportunities (DPMO)
2	308,537
3	66,807
4	6,210
5	233
6	3.4

good, you may decide to choose a lower target Sigma level, by looking at Table 2.1.

Remember that this economic decision is not just based on the cost of defects; there is an *excess cost of production* associated with any deviation from the target. Let's go with a targeted Sigma level of six and see where it takes us. To achieve this at the assembly level, the parts' and assembly process' allowable variation (spec limits) must be defined, consistent with the CTQ requirement. This raises yet another question: How can we transmit variation from a Y to its associated Xs?

For an assembly such as our axle and shaft, we can use a simple but important statistical property known as *additivity of variances*. If you know the standard deviations of the inputs to the assembly, and the *transfer function* between the Y and its Xs is linear, the sum of the squares of the Xs' standard deviations equals the square of the Y's standard deviation:

$$s_Y^2 = s_{X_1}^2 + s_{X_2}^2 + \ldots s_{X_n}^2$$

Where S_y = Standard deviation of the output, Y

S_{xi} = Standard deviation of the inputs, $x_1, x_2, \ldots x_n$

If you'll permit us a little magic at this point, we can also use this relationship to define the allowable tolerances of the Xs to achieve a required Y tolerance:

$$T_Y^2 = T_{X_1}^2 + T_{X_2}^2 + \ldots T_{X_n}^2$$

Where T_y = Total tolerance of the output, Y

T_{xi} = Tolerance allocated to each of the inputs, $x_1, x_2, \ldots x_n$

For the axle-shaft assembly, the tolerance width is 0.005 feet (USL = 0.005 feet, LSL = 0.000 feet). The transfer function from the gap to the axle and shaft diameters is linear, so we can use the additivity of variance property:

$$T_{Gap}^2 = 0.005^2 \, feet^2 = T_{Axle}^2 + T_{Shaft}^2$$

Suppose Fred and Barney use similar fabrication processes to make the axle and shaft. We decide to equally allocate (or budget) the allowable tolerance to them:

$$T_{Gap}^2 = 0.005^2 \, feet^2 = 2 \times T_{Component}^2$$

or

$$T_{Component}^2 = T_{Gap}^2 / 2$$

$$T_{Component} = \sqrt{T_{Gap}^2 / 2} = \sqrt{0.005^2 / 2} = 0.00354 \, feet$$

With a resulting tolerance half-width of:

$$0.00354 / 2 = 0.00177 \, feet$$

Of course, Fred and Barney have to hold these component tolerances at a Six Sigma level in order for the assembly to be produced at Six Sigma level. Note that we're assuming Wilma and Betty's assembly process doesn't introduce any variation, which is generally not the case in the real world.

Applying these specifications to our suppliers is all well and good, but how do we know they can meet the component requirements (for Fred's wheels: 0.4025 +/− 0.00177 feet at Six Sigma Level; for Barney's axles: 0.4000 +/− 0.00177 feet at Six Sigma Level)? Because this is a Stone Age example (pre-computers), we'd probably have them make 30–50 samples, measure the results, and perform a capability calculation. By the way, we had better check Fred and Barney's measurement systems—these will introduce additional variation into the mix.

In today's Silicon Age we will use a Monte Carlo simulation to predict the design's performance before we actually cut tools and build parts. The simulation will allow us to predict how well we expect to achieve the CTQ's performance as a function of the design and assembly Xs, identify the key contributors to CTQ variation, and then, if necessary, trade off variation across suppliers or change how variation transmits from the suppliers to the CTQ (for example, improve the robustness of our design). Figure 2.7 shows a typical variation simulation, using the Crystal Ball Monte Carlo package.

Once we're happy with the simulated design's results, we'll order tools and verify that the design meets its predicted performance.

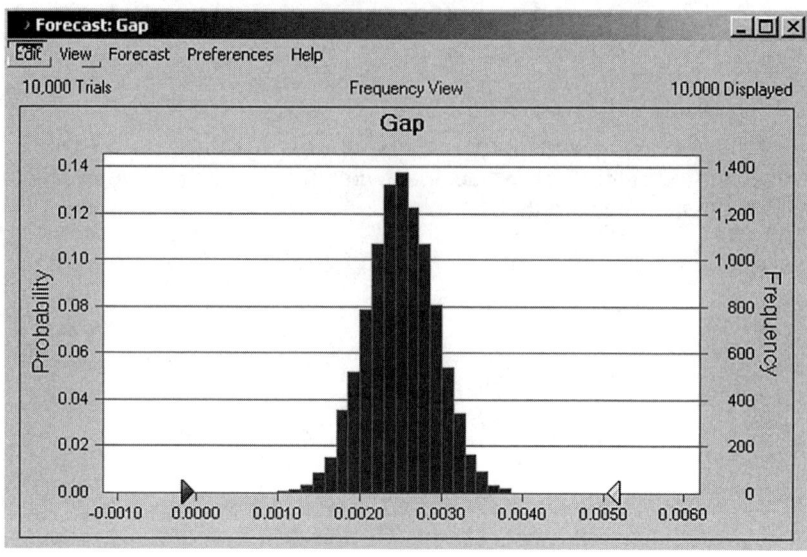

Figure 2.7 Monte Carlo simulation of gap CTQ.

Real parts will be assembled and the Sigma level of the CTQs actually measured.

So that's Design for Six Sigma (narrow sense) in a nutshell. Let's summarize some of the key ideas:

CTQ definition—DFSS depends on clearly defined product requirements that can be measured. The complete CTQ will generally include a product function, a metric, targets and limits as appropriate, and a Sigma level target.

Cascade—Once the CTQs (Ys) are defined, during design we will systematically identify the important Xs that drive achievement of the CTQ. Cascade includes both a qualitative understanding of the Ys and Xs and, through the transfer function, a quantitative understanding of the Y = f(X) relationship.

Tolerance allocation—For complex systems, as the design work progresses, the design team will define lower-level (that is, subsystem) requirements in terms of both a target and associated allowable variation (tolerance band plus targeted Sigma level).

Design prediction—To ensure the design meets its CTQ goals, the team will predict how the variation in parts and assembly processes will transmit to the variation that the customer sees at the CTQ level.

Trade-off and design robustness—If the predicted performance is less than adequate, the design is iterated, either through tolerance tradeoffs across suppliers or through the robustness of the design to sources of variation it will experience.

What benefits do you see from this approach? How much of this are you already doing? For example, many design teams we work with do stack-ups of dimensional tolerances. But they often stop the stack-up short of the CTQ level or perform it for other reasons—for example, analyzing assembly interferences. As you begin your DFSS journey, identify these supporting practices and use them to help get the DFSS message across to your developers.

WHAT IS DFSS: BROAD SENSE?

In the previous example, we started with a known product, with known CTQs and a given design. We also assumed that there was a market for the product, willing to pay enough for the product for us to cover our costs and make some amount of profit.

You can see where we're going with this. If we design a Six Sigma product but don't really know the right CTQs, we'll have a high-quality product that is just sitting on the shelf, because it doesn't fulfill customers' needs. If there is little market for our Six Sigma product, again, that's bad news. Our design concept may be flawed in that it is not robust to sources of variation. Here, no matter how tight we squeeze our suppliers' specifications, we will fail to achieve Six Sigma at the CTQ level (or we will do so at excessive cost). Our goal, in fact, should be to develop a design that is tolerant of variation at the parts/process level.

Given these challenges, a number of companies have taken a broader approach to Design for Six Sigma. They treat DFSS as an opportunity to improve the overall new product development (NPD) process. For example, one consumer products company was faced with the problem that its NPD process generated only line extensions of existing products and technology. Its early DFSS wins came from developing good product development *charters* that quantified the value of the design opportunity.

A medical products company had a *prototyping* culture. Its engineers were encouraged to quickly jump to design solutions, assuming that they understood the doctors' and hospitals' needs and wants. This company's early DFSS wins came from improving its voice of customer listening processes. Instead of presenting product prototypes and getting limited feedback on features from the doctors, the engineers learned how to better observe the doctors working in their surgical environment and truly *hear* the doctors' voices. This improved *listening,* in combination with a disciplined cascade approach, allowed them to develop products with the performance factors and functions the docs really cared about.

Table 2.2   NPD gaps and improvement ideas.

NPD function	Gap	Improvement ideas
Selecting NPD opportunities	Choosing NPD projects with small value	Improve portfolio management; focus on business case for projects and adopt multi-generational thinking to identify bigger wins
Defining and resourcing the project	Poorly defined project scopes, insufficient project resources	Improve project chartering, adopt disciplined, cross-functional review approach to defining and assigning project resources, and apply lean principles to the NPD process
Understanding customers' needs	Prototype-First approach, limited customer voice in product development	Improve customer listening processes, improve requirements definition (e.g., through Quality Function Deployment), improve cascading of requirements into the design; consider product validation activities throughout NPD process
Developing a feasible product	Focus on a single prototype, science projects in development, poor manufacturability of designs	Adopt Pugh Concept Convergence approach, incorporate TRIZ and/or axiomatic design principles in NPD process, require design prediction of performance (design scorecards) prior to release to detailed design, incorporate *Design for X* (X = manufacturing, assembly, reliability, etc.) practices and reviews, bring manufacturing staff (and others!) into design process as early as practicable

Continued

Table 2.2 NPD gaps and improvement ideas. _Continued_

NPD function	Gap	Improvement ideas
Developing a producible product (and production process)	Tight tolerances identified on drawings relative to suppliers' capabilities, difficult to assemble designs, designs sensitive to parts, assembly variation	Include robust design principles and practices (e.g., Taguchi approach), include lean principles in process design, predict performance of design (variation transmission from parts, process to CTQs)
Verifying and validating the NPD output	Surprises in verification, validation, early production with high yields, followed by yield degradation	Add verification and validation activities throughout design process. Incorporate robust design principles and practices and _test_ prior to manufacturing release
Post-launch production issues	Too long to stabilize design in production; production issues require reinventing the design	Design capability predictions prior to launch, design reviews to include manufacturing staff, improve capture and transfer of design knowledge to production staff (design intent)

In the broad sense of DFSS, you may identify gaps in almost any area of your NPD process and then work to close those gaps. Table 2.2 lists just a few ideas.

Obviously, you will have a hard time tackling all of these issues at one time. Don't treat DFSS as a "one-shot" deal. If you consider it a journey, you'll be more successful. We'll talk more about this in chapters 5 and 6.

KEY POINTS

You should walk away from reading this chapter with:

- A basic understanding of Six Sigma as a performance metric and as a business improvement approach

- An understanding of what it means to design a product for Six Sigma performance at the CTQ level and how to achieve this through design analysis and prediction

- A foreshadowing of how you will begin to implement DFSS—through a gap analysis of your current NPD process and systematic improvements to same

3

What DFSS Can Do for You and Your Company

INTRODUCTION

Now that you have a basic idea of the DFSS process, let's talk benefits. Dr. Joseph Juran is one of our heroes. Many years ago, we listened to him talk about a company's *language*. To engage engineers, he said, you must speak their technical language. When speaking to senior management, you engage them by speaking in their language—that of money. Middle managers must then be bilingual, because they need to communicate in both directions. Of course, there is that rare senior leader such as Mr. Soichiro Honda, who noted that he would rather hold a piston than a financial statement.

This chapter will follow Dr. Juran's advice. First we will discuss the financial benefits of DFSS. To obtain support and the resources needed to begin your DFSS journey, you'll have to build the business case and convince senior leaders that there are dollars to be gained. Next, we'll talk about the organizational benefits—reducing the friction that occurs in a typical product development organization (middle managers will live here). Finally, we will talk about the benefits your engineers will see when they begin practicing DFSS methods and tools. To wrap up, we'll share a *DFSS journey* example. This example will help you see both the benefits of systematically improving your development process and the work needed to get there—no pain, no gain! Looking back, we would have given an arm and a leg to have had something like DFSS when we were younger.

FINANCIAL BENEFITS OF DFSS
(FOR SENIOR LEADERS)

We'll start with the cost side of the equation, where the case is relatively easy. Most studies of new product development processes start out with figures on the percentage of new products that fail in the market. Typical reported numbers fall between 40 and 80%. The Product Development and Management Association defines *failure rate* as "the percentage of a firm's new products that make it to full market commercialization, but which fail to achieve the objectives set for them." The financial consequences of these failures can range from a few thousand dollars for the backyard inventor to the $5 billion catastrophe of the Iridium satellite system.

What is the cost of such a failure? Tangibly, the time spent by the development team, investment in plant and equipment, raw materials and purchased parts/assemblies, sales, advertising, and warranty costs all go into the expense side of the equation. Stand these figures up against the revenue gained from the product. Intangibly, what have product failures cost you in the eyes of your customers? How has your reputation suffered because of the failures? What other products might you have launched with the resources you had to waste making things right?

How many of your new products launched over the last few years fall into this category? Do the numbers—what does this tell you about your product development process? Next on the list of financial costs of poor design quality is the cost of recalls. Although we love our 1995 Mustang, there have been several recalls on the car since we bought it. How much does Ford spend on these recalls?

Recently, a large medical device company has been in the news because of alleged design defects in their products. For example, three of its products are the subject of a class I recall by the Food and Drug Administration. This means that there is a reasonable probability that if a particular device is malfunctioning, it will cause serious adverse health consequences or death. The cost of these design defects can be measured in terms of product replacement costs, potential legal liability, and the impact on the company's value on the stock market—not a pretty picture.

Finally, the basic Six Sigma message needs to be restated. Whether you want to invoke Taguchi or Wheeler, there is a *quality loss/excess cost of production* when a part or product is produced off target. Figure 3.1 shows this picture.

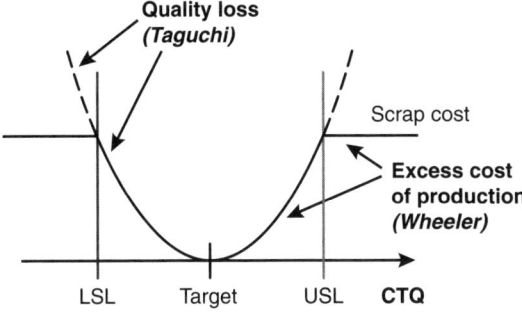

Figure 3.1 Quality loss/excess cost of production—off-target performance.

In keeping with the introduction's theme, we're not going to claim that DFSS will make all of your product launches wild successes. This sounds like an undersell, but the best we'll promise is a reduction in the failure probability (with a resulting decrease in failure costs).

You will decrease the probability that a low-value product will enter the pipeline. You will lower the probability of developing a product that does not meet its customers' needs. You will decrease the chances that your product will languish in development while a needed technology is being invented. You will decrease the likelihood that the product will have problems in production. You will decrease the probability of expensive warranty/recall costs. And, finally, you will decrease the quality loss/excess cost of production caused by the variation your customers see in your products.

Some examples follow.

Consumer Products Company

Although this company adopted and trained its staff on a full-scope DFSS development process, its biggest, earliest benefit came from the front end of the process. The organization had a habit of throwing resources at a lot of product development ideas without considering the market/business opportunity. When we did the initial team training, we didn't think that *project chartering* would be a big deal, but it turned out to be a huge benefit.

Of five pilot DFSS teams, two were killed at the charter. Leadership viewed this positively because those development resources were deployed to other, more valuable projects. The organization soon began requiring each development team to pull a charter together. Seeing what was happening, the R&D director organized charter reviews; he and his direct reports would take a day out of their busy schedules and review seven or eight teams, with the first couple of teams usually getting the most attention.

In addition, the teams were encouraged to think in *multigenerational* terms. The focus was on how to take an idea that was considered small and grow the idea through additional products that used the technology or through extensions of the first-generation product.

Medical Device Developer

A medical device company had grown quickly by being a *fast-follower* in the market. To continue its growth, it had to develop innovative products that would leapfrog the competition. We'll highlight two of many changes this company made to its development process:

Voice of customer/product requirements—In its fast-follower mode, the company focused on a prototyping approach to new products. "Let's get something in the hands of the surgeons and see how they like what we've done to it!" To transition to a market leader, the company recognized that a better, richer voice of customer (VOC) gathering process was needed. Marketing took the lead on benchmarking VOC best practices and developed an approach that would help the product developers really understand the surgeons' needs. Although sometimes frustrating at first (what new process isn't?), the approach did begin to improve the identification of product requirements. The teams began to understand what product functions, instead of features, the surgeons were looking for and how well those functions needed to perform. These solution-open requirements gave the developers the opportunity to explore different design concepts instead of locking into a solution too quickly.

Cascade and prediction—To ensure that the products met the requirements and were producible, the requirements/CTQs were cascaded to parts and process requirements, clearly linking the Ys with the Xs. Predictions of the designs' capability allowed developers and sponsors to clearly see (and mitigate before production) the designs' risks.

Results—One of the product leaders came to kick off a DFSS training session. Her comments to the class included, "We're starting to knock some balls out of the park with our product launches. One surgeon picked up a new product and, without any instruction, began to use it intuitively. Our stabilization times used to average 12–15 months; now we're down to one month!"

Another product team saved hundreds of project hours because they were able to predict their product performance instead of spending the time and money building prototypes to test product performance. The project leader conservatively estimated that they launched the product two months earlier than they would have without DFSS.

Finally, a third product team was established to work with an outside company on an acquisition of new technology. The technology seemed quite promising, but the purchasing organization (our client) was disciplined enough to put a strong contract in place that allowed the team to investigate (a) the true needs of the customer and (b) the ability to mass-produce this product before it was required to pay the bulk of the contract. The team used a disciplined VOC gathering process and analyzed manufacturability of the design. They found that the prototype in their hands wasn't of great use/value to the customers, and it couldn't be mass-produced either. They released the contract in record time, allowing the seller to work on other ideas and allowing the buyer's engineers to work on a more valuable product.

These are generally the visible costs. If they aren't enough to motivate your leaders to improve the development process, consider some of the internal costs.

REDUCING INTERNAL FRICTION THROUGH DFSS (FOR MIDDLE MANAGERS)

We spoke with some folks recently about their nutrition products development process. While the company is currently successful because of a blockbuster product it developed, its pipeline isn't as full or productive as it would like. It has been launching products, but there have been significant production problems. Instead of development resources being occupied with new product development, executives are flying around the country to their plants and supplier facilities trying to fix production problems. They are honest enough to admit that they don't spend enough time on getting the design *right*—so that it can be produced reliably. The R&D folks are in a squeeze. They are being pressured to get product to market faster, but they are also having to deal with today's crisis. The time they spend trying to stabilize the product prevents them from putting development resources where they belong: in up-front *preventive, predictive design activities*. They just don't have the resources to do both.

DFSS will minimize these problems through its emphasis on *cascade/flowdown*—linking the product requirements qualitatively and quantitatively to parts and process Xs. By predicting the influence of X variation on the product requirements/CTQs, you will build assurance that the product can be produced within the required tolerances. If there is a problem in production, the documented cascade will help production engineers quickly pinpoint either which X is contributing to the Y problem, or what impact a change in an X will have on the product's Ys.

Another source of friction is the rework that occurs in development. You are probably familiar with the throw-it-over-the-wall syndrome—market research obtains requirements from the customer, throws them over the wall to development, which in turn develops a product and throws that over the wall to operations and sales.

If this isn't bad enough, consider how many times things change during development. Marketing or sales rushes into the development team meeting with a new feature that *absolutely* must be incorporated into the design. Development comes up with specs that suppliers can't meet, and the design has to be reworked. How many times have tools been ordered and reordered because the parts don't work together?

One of our clients tells the story of a production machine that was built overseas and shipped to their facility but had to be scrapped (cost: $20 million) because it didn't mate with the rest of the processes. Had they sent over the mating equipment (at a shipping cost of about $30,000), the problem would have been avoided. Just read *Dilbert* each day and you'll see Scott Adams poke fun at cases like these. How much does this cost?

Although not unique to DFSS, the method incorporates both business reviews and design reviews. At appropriate design points, we'll conduct a disciplined business review of the current state of the design by all stakeholders: market research, R&D, operations. This helps ensure that everybody agrees with design decisions and the current risks. Design reviews (usually before an associated gate) help ensure that the technical aspects of the design have been examined by peers and/or outside experts. See Chapter 4 for the purpose of each review. More importantly, DFSS is clear about the deliverables associated with each phase and how these deliverables are *frozen* (OK, at least somewhere close to being frozen) for the specific product under development. This helps the organization minimize changes that affect both the quality of the design and its development/launch schedule.

DFSS PERSONAL BENEFITS FOR PRODUCT DEVELOPERS: WHAT'S IN IT FOR ME? (WIIFM?)

We've lived and worked in engineering and development organizations. We've sat with our friends at lunch and complained about what was wrong. We've sat across the table from our customers and listened to their complaints about our products. That's not fun! As a product developer or engineer, you want to be successful. You want to have your name associated with successful products that make customers happy and make a lot of money for your company. You hate it when the development process prevents you from doing a good job.

So how will DFSS help you, the product developer? One of our friends is a pharmaceutical developer in Belgium who has embraced DFSS. He likes to ask a simple question: "What would you pay for . . .?" As a product developer/engineer, what would you pay for?

- A clearly scoped development project
- Understanding what the customer really wants, rather than the opinion of marketing, management, sales, or (fill in your favorite player here)
- Product requirements that are rational, that you personally helped develop, and that you can clearly measure
- The ability to develop a product concept that focused on meeting customer needs
- Not having to invent a new technology in the middle of a development project
- Not having whiplash from all the changing requirements or a product with ever-changing features
- The ability to predict how well your product will perform in the face of process and supplier variation
- A rational identification and mitigation discussion around the risks associated with your product

The knowledge and assurance that your product will be producible

Having to give up all those airline miles and hotel nights because you don't have to solve postlaunch problems with the design

No more late in the day (or at night) phone calls from manufacturing with the dreaded question "Can you tell us why . . ."

Actually being able to say, "That part of the design is frozen"

Feeling less and less like you're trapped in a *Dilbert* cartoon

One young engineer came up to us after a DFSS class. She said, "We've had a stage gate process for about a year, but you've shown us how to be successful in getting from one gate to another!"

ONE COMPANY'S PRODUCT DEVELOPMENT IMPROVEMENT JOURNEY

Because of confidentiality issues, this example of a company's journey toward improved product development has been disguised. You'll see that this company has gotten better, that the journey may not be pretty, but that its managers are convinced they are on the right path. What follows was adapted from a speech by the head of R&D to his product development teams.

The Company

About 20 years ago, YouAreHere, Inc., was founded with a clear purpose: to provide the military, business, and consumers with access to global positioning technologies and applications. Today, we are recognized as a leader in these solutions, and YouAreHere positioning systems can be found throughout the world in ships, aircraft, military vehicles, trucks, autos, yachts, and personal, hand-held applications.

As a GPS technology leader, our in-house product development expertise is responsible for overall product design and we control all key processes including development, manufacturing, sales, and service. To date, we have avoided the virtual model adopted by some of our competitors where they develop conceptual designs and then outsource detailed design and manufacturing. Our motto comes from Einstein's saying, "Everything should be as simple as possible, but no simpler."

Product Development History

Fifteen years ago, the GPS industry was still new. A few large companies dominated the military industry, but as the GPS signals were made available to civilian applications, many small companies were formed, developing products and bringing them to market. Quality standards were practically nonexistent. The technology available was new and marginally reliable. Customer expectations and service were generally low.

Our Product-Development "Infancy"

The first products we developed were trivial by today's standards and developed with no recognizable process or methodology. Simply by applying good engineering to innovation, we produced a new product every year or so. By 1995 we still only had about 10 products in our portfolio but were in the early stages of planning to invest heavily in a new, custom-built factory. The factory was planned to cost our entire year's sales.

By then, we had grown our development team to about six engineers. The "team" wasn't organized. There was an intrinsic feeling of what needed to be done but absolutely no processes or organization or management to make it happen. We worked on an interesting collection of projects with no concept whatever of project management or planning.

In fact, it was never entirely clear who reported to whom. However, new products did appear, and we moved into our new factory with, for the first time in our history, a significant corporate debt.

In 1998 we were still trying to find our feet in our new factory, still spending heavily, still had no detectable new product development process. However, due to the rapid development in electronics and the growing application and awareness of GPS technology, the market was growing rapidly and we were forced to make changes.

It's Hard to Grow Up

In the late 1990s, YouAreHere was in real trouble. We had a new plant to pay for and expensive automation systems that didn't work.

The causes included a familiar litany: no particular structure anywhere in the company, no real management. Product failures, poor delivery and service performance were rampant everywhere. We needed to take action quickly. The first semblance of a management team was put together with each member being assigned very clear responsibilities.

To say we put in place a new product development process would be a very gross exaggeration. We had to develop and get to market enough new products fast enough to survive. As in most potentially catastrophic situations, it was essential to make decisions quickly. This wasn't the time for hiring consultants or team-based decisions (we didn't even know what a team was). People were just told what to do.

One management principle is that the fastest way to do anything is to put together a small autonomous group of the right people, with a strong leader and a clear objective. Our product development process was driven entirely by one or two people, directly supervising a handful of engineers. This was essentially our entire new product development process, and it was simple but not sustainable.

We launched products in rapid succession, creating a full range of consumer, automotive, and marine GPS applications. The products were far from perfect and were driven into an uncontrolled manufacturing process. However, they were well received and kept us in business. So it was obviously possible to develop new products much faster than we had done previously, but how should it be done?

To survive and grow, we had to use all the knowledge in the company to develop new products better, more reliably, and faster than our increasingly competent competition. New product development needed to become a "total company" process.

Are We Adults Yet?

The biggest change to our new product development process was actually driven by our manufacturing leaders. In 2000, they convinced senior management to embrace Six Sigma as a "total company" improvement method. We restructured the entire company around a team-based implementation of Six Sigma.

Our implementation of Six Sigma required analysis of everything that we did to get a product to a customer; broke this down into manageable, clear process steps; and gave responsibility for each process to small teams (Six Sigma Improvement Teams, SSITs). Every SSIT owned a process, or several processes, over which they had complete control. They were given responsibility to supply the next downstream team with continuously improving quality. Linking all of these processes together gave us a chain connecting our whole business from suppliers to customers, encompassing everything we did.

Although this showed us the connection from market input through design to purchasing and manufacturing to sales and our customers, it did not show us how to make the process of new product development and introduction actually work.

With the Six Sigma process structure in place, we tried to find the best method to utilize it to develop and introduce new products. One of our Master Black Belts came from a large company and had experience with Design for Six Sigma. Through her guidance, we chose a six-phase model of product introduction, based on the DFSS Define–Measure–Analyze–Design–Verify/Validate–Implement (DMADVI) model along with a "kit" of design tools such as QFD, design of experiments, statistical tolerance design, and so forth. We worked out how to overlay and mesh this with our SSIT structure and expected an immediate transformation in our new product introduction process.

Oops, A Few Steps Backward!

Surprisingly, it didn't work. In fact, virtually nothing worked for some time. Our productivity didn't improve, our quality may even have gotten worse, and our new product introduction rate was flat. We flipped between standing back and trusting our SSITs to do the job, and jumping in and telling people what to do. Since the total company was based on the SSIT structure and new product introduction was a total company activity, if the SSITs didn't work, neither would new product introduction.

However, we needed to continue to deliver new products to stay in business. We tried to understand and use the new business processes, but when a product had to be delivered on time, it was easier to use the established methods. The gaps between where we were and where we wanted to be were very stressful, but the new products continued to appear.

So what was wrong? We probably expected too much too quickly. DFSS is a skill, a process in itself to be improved with practice over time. The demands placed on our team leaders are very high, the right people are essential, and it takes time to recognize this and find the right people. Our DFSS application was initially focused on just use of the tools and missed some essential steps, mainly around the management of new product development projects. For example, we were still working in silos, where marketing would gather the customer needs, the engineers would then use

QFD to develop requirements and the product design, and then turn it over to manufacturing with little up-front input from our operations partners.

We thought that just applying the tools and continually improving the functional processes would make our development process better. Finally we realized that we had to also adopt a cross-functional view of product development, with leadership through our management team. Although we were using DMADVI, we needed to learn to focus on the DFSS *process*. Among other things, this meant that we needed to ensure that DMADVI's "gates" were taken seriously (for example, through a disciplined review of the development deliverables and "sign-off" by all stakeholders). We also needed to break down the functional barriers—for example, our QFD sessions are now conducted with the whole team in place— marketing, R&D, and manufacturing. Even though we are in a fast-paced industry, we needed to stop the "requirements churn" that frustrated our engineers.

OK, We're Out of the Nest

So where are we now? I would like to say that we have a highly effective, smooth running, reliable, predictable new product introduction process that consistently delivers the right product at the right price at the right time.

However, DFSS is not about just being better than your competition. It's about getting better faster than your competition. Nothing stands still. Although the standards we work to now and the quality of our products make our efforts of 20 years ago look amateurish, the whole world has moved just as fast, or faster, than we have. Instead of our competition being a handful of small specialized, quirky companies, we are now head to head with global, vastly competent, multinational firms.

We have deliberately moved forward in technology, closer to the leading edge. This, ironically, reduces product life times and gives us the privilege of discovering the bugs in our suppliers' new components technologies!

Our expectations of new product introduction are higher. Each new product is critical to our business plans. Delays cost profit and growth. A quality problem at launch can virtually kill a product. However, like our products, the "devil is in the details." We need to continue to refine our processes; improve team effectiveness; eliminate unnecessary, non-value-added design and development work; and focus our design efforts on our strategic goals.

Next Steps

Where do we go next? With our fundamental DFSS development processes (almost) working and improving, hopefully quickly enough, we now need to be sure that we point this sharp, powerful, DFSS tool in the right direction. Our new product "hit rate" has always been high. We introduce very few products that flop. However, the stakes are now higher and our wide range of capability means we could do almost anything we choose to do. It's more important than ever that we choose to do the right things.

Since the company was started, there has always been an almost instinctive feeling of where we are going and how to get there. With a small company this is easy. A few times it has been spelled out, sometimes before we go somewhere, sometimes just after we have arrived!

We are now trying to improve our sense of direction and get everyone in our 500-plus-strong company to go in the same direction. Much of our energy now goes into defining our strategies and, in particular, our product development strategies.

We're moving from chaotic new product development to a strategically driven new product introduction process. Everything we do, every product we develop should take us a step forward toward our strategic vision, and then before we reach it, we should move the goal forward. It (hopefully) never stops!

KEY POINTS

You should walk away from reading this chapter with:

- The ability to define the *financial* benefits of DFSS—lower product failure rate, fewer product recalls, lower warranty costs, lower costs associated with excess variation (Wheeler's and Taguchi's points)

- The ability to define the *friction-reducing* benefits of DFSS—fewer R&D resources wasted fixing production problems, less rework during development, fewer disagreements between key product development functions

- The ability to define "What's in it for me?" benefits of DFSS—higher job satisfaction, or as Deming said, "Joy in Work" for your organization

- An ability to talk to different stakeholders about these benefits

4

DFSS: The Method and Roadmap

INTRODUCTION

Here, we'll show you what *good* can look like in a DFSS-based new product development process. This process will help you understand the broad application of DFSS as we described in Chapter 2.

At the 50,000-foot level, a quick web search will reveal several, seemingly different methods: DMADV, DMADVI, DMADI, I^{2}DOV, and so forth. At this level, there's not much difference. As you drift down to about 10,000 feet, you'll start to see some minor differentiation.

The real differences appear as you get closer to the ground. If you design complex equipment, DFSS will have a systems-engineering flavor. If you design products whose malfunction can cause harm or injury, DFSS will have a strong risk management flavor. For some companies (pharmaceutical pill production, for example), the basic production equipment may not change a lot from product to product. For them, the process design challenge is more about getting the recipe right. For equipment and devices, though, the production process may be unique for each product or one line may produce a variety of products. Here, DFSS will incorporate lean principles and practices.

For this chapter's journey, we've decided to use DMADVI as our DFSS framework. We'll describe how DFSS works for a developer of moderately complex products—somewhere between the Stone Age R&D shop of Chapter 2 and the next generation of the starship *Enterprise*. This will allow us to illustrate the main themes and methods without getting the description too simplistic or too complicated.

A note on the tools/methods described here: A great many tools/methods have been developed to support product development efforts. We have not tried to include them all but rather have attempted to identify at least one way of accomplishing the intended function. If you have a favorite (or even better) tool/method, please feel free to employ it in your development process' toolkit.

DMADVI: A QUICK HISTORY AND 50,000-FOOT VIEW

DMADVI stands for *Define–Measure–Analyze–Design–Verify (and Validate)–Implement*. In the late 1990s, GE tried to stretch DMAIC method into a design process that could be applied to business processes, the result being DMADV. Early applications of DMADV were focused on redesigning existing processes, particularly in GE's financial services companies. Teams were expected to first *Define* the business problem or opportunity, *Measure* the current process' performance, and then *Analyze* the root causes of the performance gap. So far, the method is not much different from DMAIC. The switch occurred in the Design phase, where the teams would design the new business process and test it in the Verify phase.

While this approach can work well for redesigning a process, GE's Eric Mattenson recognized that the company's growth goals required development of new services. He wanted a method that could be used to design a completely new business process—from a clean sheet of paper. In the late 1990s, we helped Eric turn DMADV into a new process design method by changing the intent of the MADV phases. *Measure* became a requirements definition phase employing quality function deployment to define the new process' requirements. *Analyze* became the concept definition and feasibility phase. The *Design* phase was beefed up to include more prediction and risk management tools such as design scorecards, variation prediction through simulation, and failure modes and effects analysis. Because we changed the intent of the Measure and Analyze phases, we should have changed their names. However, "DMADV" had already gained some brand recognition inside GE and so we left the phase names alone and focused instead on the phase details.

So how did DMADV cross over to become a product design method? Around the turn of the century, Johnson & Johnson decided to include design excellence as one of the pillars of its Process Excellence initiative. Elizabeth Iversen (a GE alumnus) brought together an internal team of product design experts to define the methodology and toolkit. They picked DMADV as their new product development framework and then worked to turn DMADV into a real, robust product development method. We were fortunate to be on the consulting team that supported this J&J effort. J&J has since applied DMADV (or a tailored version of DMADV) to medical device design, consumer product design, and pharmaceutical design as well as applying it to design/redesign of business processes, its original incarnation.

One thing that has always bothered us about DMADV is that it seems to trail off just when the fun starts—implementation. The design is ready for launch at the end of Verify/Validate, but it's still not out there. Therefore, we'll add an *Implementation* phase, and our method becomes DMADVI. Figure 4.1 provides a DMADVI block diagram.

At the 50,000-foot level, then, DMADVI's phases have the following objectives:

Define phase—The business decides to apply resources to a product design effort. To ensure that the opportunity makes sense from a market and business perspective, the team first focuses on developing their project charter. Define is obviously critical; if the wrong projects enter the pipeline, the organization will be wasting development resources. Part of the chartering effort will be to identify gaps in existing knowledge about the opportunity; the idea may enter DMADV with varying degrees of maturity. Define is also the getting-started phase, and the team develops their initial project plans and project management processes. A charter review by project sponsors ensures that the team is working on the right product for the right market with the right goals.

Measure phase—Measure is all about the customer and current competition. The team gathers the customer's voice, understands the competitive environment, and then translates this information into a set of prioritized, measurable product-level requirements. The most important of these are the critical-to-quality requirements, or CTQs. A business review at the end of the Measure phase aligns the team and its sponsors on the requirements that the development team will try to achieve.

Analyze phase—Design concepts are identified and analyzed for their feasibility. Here, feasibility includes capability to meet the set of product requirements/CTQs, identification of potential product risks (with mitigation plans), and an early look at how producible the design will be (design for manufacturing and assembly), how reliable the product will be (design for reliability/maintainability), and so forth. We will seek the customer's feedback to either

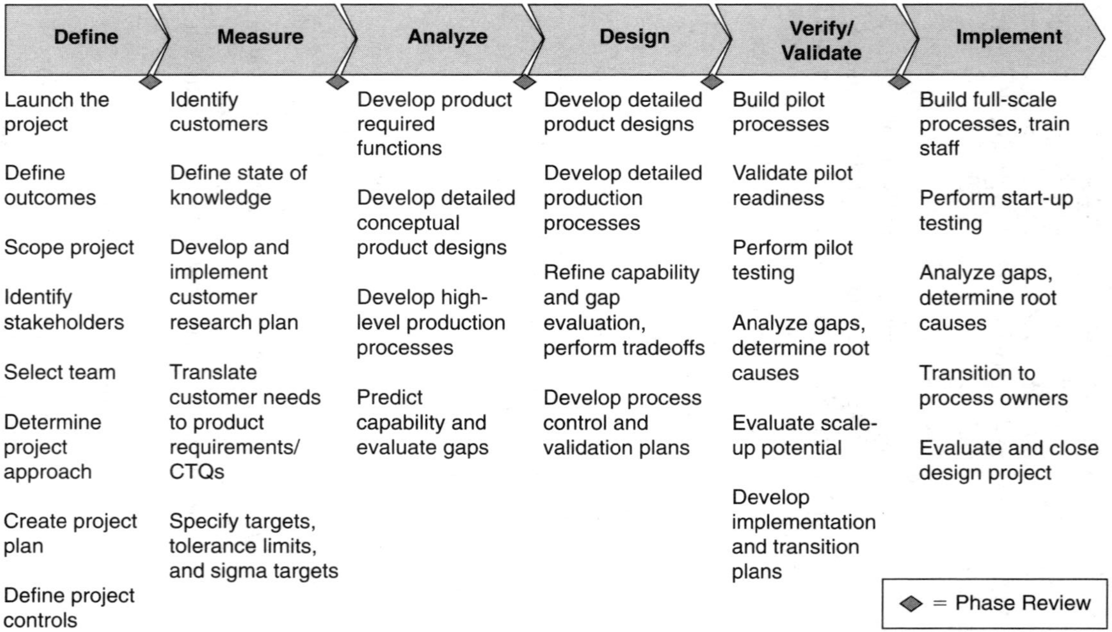

52 Chapter Four

Define	Measure	Analyze	Design	Verify/Validate	Implement
Launch the project	Identify customers	Develop product required functions	Develop detailed product designs	Build pilot processes	Build full-scale processes, train staff
Define outcomes	Define state of knowledge	Develop detailed conceptual product designs	Develop detailed production processes	Validate pilot readiness	Perform start-up testing
Scope project	Develop and implement customer research plan	Develop high-level production processes	Refine capability and gap evaluation, perform tradeoffs	Perform pilot testing	Analyze gaps, determine root causes
Identify stakeholders	Translate customer needs to product requirements/CTQs	Predict capability and evaluate gaps	Develop process control and validation plans	Analyze gaps, determine root causes	Transition to process owners
Select team	Specify targets, tolerance limits, and sigma targets			Evaluate scale-up potential	Evaluate and close design project
Determine project approach				Develop implementation and transition plans	
Create project plan					
Define project controls					

◆ = Phase Review

Figure 4.1 DMADVI product development phases.

physical or virtual prototype(s) here. A business review, likely preceded by a technical design review, approves the design concept for further development where large capital expenditures can occur.

Design phase—Once the concept's feasibility has been demonstrated, detailed design occurs. The product is optimized both to achieve targeted performance and to minimize variation around the targets. Sigma Level predictions will be developed for the CTQs and, perhaps, for other important/high-risk requirements. The production process is also designed and optimized to achieve its quality, capacity, cost, and safety requirements. Production tools will be designed and ordered, and the assembly process layout will be developed with lean principles guiding the layout of both the process and its associated supply chain. The company will begin to make the capital investments needed to produce the product. A final technical review of the design ensures that the design meets its requirements and that necessary trade-offs are recognized, and then the product design is frozen. A business review at the end of Design ensures the business that all important product risks have been identified and mitigated.

Verify and Validate phase—In this book, *verification* is defined as the ability of the product/process to meet its requirements; *validation* is defined as the ability of the product to meet the needs of the customers. Given these definitions, testing of the product will occur against its requirements, the process is verified to be able to consistently produce the product within specifications, and customers' reaction will be obtained to validate that the product meets their needs. The design predictions begun in the Analyze and Design phases will be verified using the assembly process and supplier parts. A business review during this phase provides the team with the approval to launch the product.

Implement phase—There can be significant overlap between Verify/Validate and Implement phases. Somewhere along the way, a production process is built. Process qualification activities (installation qualification for new equipment, operational qualification to demonstrate equipment capability and process qualification to verify overall process capability) will generally occur in the Verify/ Validate phase. Activation of the supply chain, ramping up to production volumes, and shipment/distribution of the product are all Implement activities. Early problems with the production process must also be addressed (if we've done a good job in DMADVI, there are not too many problems).

So when does DMADVI end? Some companies will hold a post-launch review of the product (six months post launch, for instance); we'll use a milestone such as this to define the end of a DMADVI project. Note that you may also consider a performance-based end, perhaps when certain business and process goals (for example, quality and quantity goals) are being met.

At a high level then, DMADVI just looks like a normal design and development process. We're going to drill down a bit further into the phases now to show you where the Six Sigma-ness of DMADVI kicks in.

As you review these phases, keep in mind that we're describing DMADVI in a linear fashion so that it's easy to understand. Practically, teams will implement DMADVI in a nonlinear fashion. For example, when we spoke recently with a product development leader about his team's activities, he had work going on in the Measure, Analyze, *and* Design phases. Likewise, when we discuss phase reviews, we're not suggesting that all work for that phase must be complete before the review is held and approval to move ahead obtained. The key questions at each phase review are "Do we have enough information to decide to move ahead with this project?" and "Are the key players (marketing, R&D, operations) in agreement about the decision?"

As you start to think about implementing DFSS in your organization, one of the early choices you'll make is whether to adopt DMADVI as your design framework or to map DMADVI into your current design process. Also, as we've noted several times, you should think about the current gaps in your design and development processes. You may decide to start your DFSS journey by improving just a few steps or elements of your current process.

DEFINE PHASE: OVERVIEW AND TOOLS

Purpose

In the Define phase of DMADVI, the product development project is chartered, planned, and resourced. The market concept for the product is clarified, in terms of unmet customer needs and/or a value proposition. The development team (at least a core team of marketing, R&D, and operations) will be in place. They have determined project scope, initial business, customer, and technical goals; have some understanding of the market/competitive environment and project risks; and have an initial plan to do the development work. The team also understands how their project fits within the overall product portfolio plan for the company.

The Define phase is where the company transitions from the "fuzzy front end" to actually committing development resources. There may be a significant body of "knowns" that the team can use in developing their charter—inputs from customer/market research, technology and competitive assessments, business strategy, and previous product generations. As part of chartering, though, the team will likely work to address "unknowns"—questions they want answered to provide assurance that the new product has a reasonable probability of being desired by the customer and that it will make money for the business.

Key Inputs

- Business and strategic plans
- Market research
- Customer needs (high level)
- Competitive information
- Current-generation products
- "Mature" technology

Steps

Note: The activities are listed in a very general sequence of events. A number of these activities can occur in parallel.

Launch the project—Decide that this product should be designed/redesigned (based on market research, company strategy, customer input, and value proposition). Assign overall responsibility for the project.

Scope project—Determine the boundaries of the project. Determine the project deliverables, what is in and out of scope for the project. Product designs may be divided into a series of releases or generations. Note that the product should employ known technologies with technology development occurring outside the DMADVI process. This is important to avoid schedule-busting science projects.

Define outcomes and goals—Determine how the success of the project will be measured (hint: consider customer, business, and technical goals). What unmet customer needs will be addressed? Will the design/redesign reduce cost or increase revenue or market share? Are there technical goals, such as compatibility with previous generations or other products in the portfolio?

Identify stakeholders—Who will be affected by the new design and can influence the success of the design project?

Select team—Determine full- and part-time members of the team. Which disciplines or departments should be involved? Early on, a skeleton team may take the design through feasibility (end of Analyze), with a larger team working through the rest of DMADVI.

Determine project approach—DMADVI provides a generic framework; determine how DMADVI will be tailored to the specific project. For example, a line extension will likely require less voice of customer input than a new product.

Create project plan—Develop a work breakdown structure, network diagram (for example, a PERT chart), and/or a Gantt chart. Estimate time, cost, and resource requirements for the project. Assess the risk of achieving the plan (methods include critical path method, Monte Carlo simulation of the plan, critical chain method; the latter is based on Goldratt's theory of constraints).

Define project controls—Develop communication plans, change control (for the design), change management (for stakeholders, staff), review plans (design and business), and review risk and opportunity management processes. Table 4.1 shows the primary tools used in the Define phase.

Key Outputs

- Approved project charter (scope/deliverables, goals, metrics, targets, business case, milestones)
- Skeleton team
- Project approach and plans (draft)

- Design process controls
- Risk/opportunity management processes
- Stakeholder analysis
- Multigenerational plans

Phase Review

The first project review occurs when the team completes the Define phase. Sponsors review and approve the team's charter, multigeneration plan, and draft project approach and plan. Sponsors review the team's current risk and opportunity assessment of the project and concur with the team's mitigation actions. Some companies include a "charter check-in" in the middle of Define to make sure that the project fits strategically, will be supported, and will get funded; this can help kill projects early.

MEASURE PHASE: OVERVIEW AND TOOLS

Purpose

In the Measure phase, the team will obtain the voices of the various customers of the product. These will include customers external to the business who will buy and use the product, trade partners (for example, retail outlets such as Wal-Mart or Target), internal customers and the stakeholders who will be affected by or who may influence the success of the project (management, regulatory bodies, among others). The goal of this phase is to develop a set of requirements (some of which will be critical to quality) that the design team can use as inputs to their design. A clear linkage between the voices and requirements must be established in this phase.

Key Inputs/Use

- Approved project charter (scope/deliverables, goals, metrics, targets, business case, milestones)
- Stakeholder analysis
- Multigenerational plans
- Preliminary voice of customer
- Existing customer information
- Market research studies

Table 4.1 Define phase tools.

Tool	Use
Market research studies	Understand unmet needs of the customer, identify opportunities for new products.
Process capability studies	Understand current production process capabilities, technology gaps.
Technology survey/assessment	Understand technologies that may be applied to achieve unmet customer needs or improve capability to meet existing needs.
Competitive analyses	Understand current competitive products, predict future direction of competitive offerings.
Benchmark studies	Understand current and future competitive offerings, but scope is broader than own industry.
Analysis of government/regulatory requirements	Understand regulatory direction and threats to current products and opportunities for new products (for example, environmental protection changes).
Value proposition	Understand all internal and external stakeholders and what benefits the new product will offer each.
Chartering	Understand and achieve agreement on scope, goals, business case, timeline, and resources needed for the development project.
SIPOC mapping	Understand usefulness of scoping a project using SIPOC (Supplier–Input–Process–Output–Customer) maps.
Multigenerational product planning	Develop and scope a vision for series of product releases, aimed at sustaining market leadership position and identifying needed technologies (for research by advanced technology process).
Project risk and opportunity management	Identify, quantify, prioritize, and mitigate business risks; understand technical, organizational, external, and other risks and opportunities faced by the project. SWOT (strengths, weaknesses, opportunities, and threats) analysis is useful here. Project risks may be mapped on a severity/likelihood map. Stakeholder analysis is useful throughout the project.
Project management and planning	Develop and resource the overall plan for the product development project. Develop project control processes (configuration management, scope change management, communication plans, etc.).
Team management	Develop and implement processes to ensure effective, efficient teamwork (idea generation, decision making, conflict management, meeting, etc.).

Steps

Note: The activities are listed in a very general sequence of events. A number of these activities can occur in parallel.

Identify customers—Determine external, internal customers; review stakeholder list generated in Define phase.

Define current state of knowledge about your customers' needs—Review existing customer information, including complaints, compliments, and market research studies.

Determine what more you need to know about the customer—Review your project charter and existing knowledge of customer needs, looking for the gaps in knowledge your team needs to fill.

Develop and implement customer research plan—Determine what information must be collected, determine appropriate voice of customer methods (interviews, focus groups, surveys) to fill the gaps in your knowledge of the customer.

Translate customer needs to product requirements/ CTQs—The voice of the customer is generally obtained in their language. A filtering and translation process takes the customers' voices as input and develops a set of requirements stated in the technical language of the product. We call these *product requirements*. Quantitative research is used to help the team prioritize the customers' needs.

Quality function deployment (QFD) can be employed to organize and structure the VOC gathering/translation process. The translated requirements (and other business requirements, regulatory, code requirements) are measurable, testable, and feature-free requirements. The most important of these product requirements are identified as the CTQ requirements (planned for heavier focus because they are differentiators or difficult to design against). Deciding which requirements are critical helps the team focus on what will differentiate their product in the market. A typical product may have 30–100 requirements, but only 3–5 of these will be CTQs.

Specify targets, tolerance limits, and Sigma targets—Numerical goals are set for the product requirements. Allowable variation and defect rates (that is, Sigma targets) are established to help the design team objectively judge their design. As a minimum, the CTQs will receive extra design attention; these are recorded on a design scorecard. Table 4.2 shows the primary tools used in the Measure phase.

Table 4.2 Measure phase tools.

Tool	Use
Voice of customer/market research tools (in-depth interviews, focus groups, surveys)	Gather detailed qualitative needs from customers (interview, focus group), prioritize needs or translated product requirements through quantitative research (surveys).
Image diagrams	Method of obtaining a picture of what life is like for the customer using the product.
Requirements diagrams	Organization method to identify and group product requirements into themes.
Affinity sort	Organize large number of ideas (here, customer needs) to identify themes.
Structure tree	Develop a hierarchy of ideas (here, high-level to detailed customer needs), often used as input to QFD's house of quality.
Quality function deployment (QFD)	Matrix-based translation tool. In the Measure phase, QFD is applied to translate prioritized customer needs into a set of product-level requirements (with associated priorities, metrics, targets, and limits).
Conjoint analysis	Market research technique used to identify the utility customers have for product features or requirements.
Kano analysis	Market research technique to identify "must-be," "one-dimensional," and "delighter" needs or product requirements.
Radar chart (also known as spider diagram)	Graphical technique to display many attributes' performance on one chart. A common Measure phase use is to show importance and satisfaction gaps of needs/requirements.
Product requirements management	Systematic identification, deployment, and verification process to ensure requirements are met by the design; trade-offs are consciously made.

Key Outputs

- Voice of customer/stakeholder (all research performed as part of Measure phase: customer segmentation analyses/decisions, complaint/complement analysis, interview/focus group transcripts, competitive analyses, importance/satisfaction survey results, etc.)
- Product requirements, including function, metric, targets/limits, and variation or Sigma Level targets (the most important of these identified as the CTQs)
- Basis for defining product requirements: quality function deployment, needs/requirements matrix, others

- Design scorecard at the CTQ level
- Updated Define phase deliverables (charter, multigenerational plan, risk/opportunity management, stakeholder management, etc.)

Phase Review

The second business review occurs when the team completes the Measure phase. Sponsors review and approve the team's product-level requirements/CTQs (and their basis in the VOC/competitive information is gathered). Updates/revisions to the charter, multigenerational plan, and the project plan are also reviewed and approved. Sponsors review the team's current risk/opportunity assessment of the project and concur with the team's mitigation actions.

ANALYZE PHASE: OVERVIEW AND TOOLS

Purpose

In the Analyze phase, the design team will identify and evaluate possible design concepts to meet the requirements defined in Measure. The decisions made in this phase will determine a large percentage of the ultimate quality and cost of the product. Moving too quickly through this important phase can limit the potential market for and ultimate success of the product. Here, the team will develop concepts that may fulfill the product requirements, analyze these concepts, and select the optimum design concept. Finally they will begin to verify that the design concept will meet its customers' requirements, through feasibility analyses and early capability predictions.

Key Inputs

- Project charter
- Project plan
- Multigenerational product plan
- Risk/opportunity management plan
- Product requirements/CTQs
- Design scorecard—CTQ level

Steps

Note: The activities are listed in a very general sequence of events—a number of these activities can occur in parallel.

Develop product functions—Functional analysis takes a complex product and breaks it down into the functions that must occur for the requirements (CTQs, for instance) to be met. This analysis sets the stage for identification of product concepts.

Develop conceptual product designs—Benchmarking, structured invention (for example, TRIZ), and other creative methods are employed to identify concepts for the product functions (in parallel with intellectual property searches to ensure that the technology is available for use). The various functional concepts are virtually assembled into an overall product concept. Alternative concepts are evaluated and a best-fit concept is selected. The Pugh matrix approach is a useful means of identifying, iterating, and converging on the best concept.

Design *cascade* begins here. Cascade (or flow-down) is the systematic linking of the highest-level Ys (product requirements) to lower-level Ys (for instance, subsystem, assembly, component, process requirements) and eventually to the process parameters (fabrication and assembly Xs) that will determine the product's quality. Qualitative cascade ensures the design effort is focused on meeting its overall requirements and can be accomplished by continued application of the QFD method, structure trees, or other hierarchical analysis. Quantitative cascade allocates the allowable variation at the CTQ level to each of the lower-level requirements that affect the CTQ (error budgeting). The team uses their engineering knowledge, simulation, or experimentation to develop transfer functions that help them understand how their CTQs will behave as a function of the design (and eventually process) Xs; that is, the $Y = f(X)$ relationships.

Identify high-level production processes—Production process technologies are investigated for the selected concept. Feasibility studies will ensure that the product can be produced with available, mature production technologies (again, avoiding science projects in the middle of development).

Evaluate feasibility, predict capability, and evaluate gaps—Depending on the product requirements, analyses, predictions, and prototype tests are made to assess the ability of the concept to meet requirements and to ensure the design concept is as "robust" as possible. This is *flow-up*, moving from the Xs to the product CTQs or Ys. Taguchi's parameter design principles recommend that the design concept be subject to different noises—with design parameters then set to minimize the sensitivity of the design to noise. Design simulations (such as finite element analyses) can be used to predict the performance of the design and assess feasibility. Design for X principles will be proactively applied to the design (here, X = manufacturability, assembly, environment, human factors, reliability, maintainability, inspectability/testability, and others, as appropriate). The output of the prediction/feasibility efforts is recorded in the requirements workbook and on the design scorecard for the CTQs. Product risks are identified, prioritized, mitigated, and documented via failure modes and effects analysis. Table 4.3 shows the primary tools used in the Analyze phase.

Table 4.3 Analyze phase tools.

Tool	Use
Quality function deployment	Analyze phase application of QFD is to deploy product requirements to subsystem and/or subassembly requirements.
Functional analysis breakdown (tree diagram)	System engineering technique to identify and decompose functions required to be performed by the product. Physical/software/human architectures are defined to meet these functions.
Creativity techniques	Brainstorming, attribute listing, mind mapping, and other techniques used to identify design concepts (individually or in a group setting).
Benchmarking	Systematic method of identifying technologies that can be applied to the design concept (either product or process).
Intellectual property analysis	Systematic identification of technologies aimed at avoiding use of technologies owned by others (early in concepting) and then protecting company-developed technologies (through patents, trademarks, copyrights, trade secrets, etc.).

Continued

Table 4.3 Analyze phase tools. *Continued*

Tool	Use
Pugh concept convergence	Matrix-based approach to identify, evaluate, and converge on a superior design concept that meets the product requirements (can be used at any design level, including production process concepts).
Cascade/flowdown	Process of deploying and allocating higher-level to lower-level requirements. Analyze phase cascades product-level requirements to subsystem requirements (minimum).
Transfer functions	Quantitative relationships from CTQs (and other important requirements) to lower-level requirements and, eventually, to process variables.
Simulations (e.g., finite element analysis)	Computer representations of the product developed for the purpose of more rapidly, cheaply (and, in many cases with greater insight) predicting product performance than physical prototypes.
Design of experiments (DOE)	Statistical technique to evaluate which design factors affect the CTQs/requirements, optimize the design, and ensure its robustness (i.e., Taguchi techniques). Analyze phase purpose is to identify most important design factors as part of feasibility assessment.
Industrial design/human factors	Discipline whose purpose is to ensure that the human interface with the product is well designed.
Design control/ configuration control	Design process to ensure that requirements, features, and design parameters are identified and controlled.
Design for X	Proactive design techniques to consider "X-factors" such as design-to-cost, manufacturability, assembly, environment, maintainability, inspectability, and testability.
Reliability methods	Proactive design techniques to ensure that CTQ performance is achieved over the intended product life. Examples include reliability target setting and allocation, reliability prediction, failure modes and effects analysis (FMEA), fault tree analysis (FTA), reliability testing. If the product is maintainable, this includes setting and allocating maintainability targets, as well as maintenance strategy development.
Consumer feedback	Market research methods to obtain feedback on design concept(s).
Design reviews	Meetings between the team and peers/experts to review the design and associated analyses. Analyze phase purpose is to challenge the design concept and identify weak points before moving to the production-version design.

Key Outputs

- Functional analyses, correlated to goals/needs
- Selected conceptual design(s) (including *virtual* or prototype models)
- High-level design drawings (layouts, flowcharts, schematics)
- Subsystem (and lower-level) requirements (from cascade—traceable in both directions—up to CTQs, down to subsystem or lower level)
- Process technology selected
- Supporting feasibility analyses/test results:
    - Calculations (including transfer functions)
    - Predictive analyses (FMEA, EMEA, FTA, FEA, stress)
    - Experimental results
    - Test plans/results
    - Design for "X" analyses (manufacturability, assembly, maintainability, environment, human factors, others)
    - Regulatory and environmental impact analyses
    - Cost estimates to produce product
    - Customer/consumer feedback on concept
- Maintenance strategy
- Design scorecard (typically comparing average performance to targets)
- Updated deliverables from Define and Measure phases

Phase Review

The third business review occurs when the team completes the Analyze phase. Sponsors review and approve the team's design concept (and its ability to meet the product requirements, as determined by the feasibility studies). A technical design review of the concept by peers and/or experts can provide valuable input to the business decision makers. Updates and revisions to the charter, multigenerational plan, and project plan are also reviewed and approved. Sponsors review the team's current risk assessment of the project and concur with the team's mitigation actions.

DESIGN PHASE: OVERVIEW AND TOOLS

Purpose

Here the production version of the product, as well as that of the production process, is developed and finalized. Design analyses/prediction activities are refined and completed; the product has been determined to meet its requirements; trade-offs are made where necessary. In preparation for verification and validation of the design, process controls and validation plans are developed.

Key Inputs

- Outputs of Define, Measure, and Analyze phases
- Feasible concept(s)
- Preliminary production process design

Steps

Note: The activities are listed in a very general sequence of events—a number of these activities can occur in parallel.

Develop detailed product designs—The work done in the Analyze phase is continued at the detailed level. Materials are selected; assembly and parts designs are completed. Cascade continues to part requirements. Drawings are developed with critical parameters/ dimensions noted. By this phase's completion, the design will be developed to the point where it can be produced using production-version equipment and processes.

Develop detailed production process design—Likewise, the production process design is developed. Technologies are selected for part fabrication and assembly processes defined. Suppliers are selected for outsourced parts/ assemblies. Tooling design and analysis (such as mold fill analysis) occurs. Measurement systems are selected and/ or designed. Cascade is completed with identification of the critical process parameters (Xs) that affect the design's quality.

Refine capability and gap evaluation, perform tradeoffs—In the Analyze phase, capability analyses were begun to assess the ability of the design to meet its requirements. Generally, these analyses will ensure that the design meets its targets. Here in Design, the team will also determine how variation in the product and part Xs will flow up to the CTQs or other Ys. Many development teams are familiar with performing tolerance stack-ups to ensure that design requirements are met. The concept of predicting variation in the CTQs should not be a novel idea, although actually doing so is generally new to many teams. The design scorecard should be completed here, with accurately predicted variation (rather than simple tolerance highs and lows).

The team should be able to walk into a design or business review and state how well the design is predicted to perform in terms of both average and Sigma levels (as well as for the product's life–reliability predictions). Cost estimates, design for X analyses, and product and process FMEAs are completed. For maintainable equipment, preventive maintenance plans are developed, including spare-parts lists.

Develop process control and verification/validation plans—Testing and product verification/validation activities are planned. In preparation for these efforts, the necessary process controls—procedures, protocols, bills of material, device master record, critical parameter identification, measurement, and sampling and reaction plans—are developed. Table 4.4 shows the primary tools used in the Design phase.

Table 4.4 Design phase tools.

Tool	Use
Quality function deployment	Design phase application of QFD is to deploy product requirements to parts and process requirements.
Functional analysis breakdown (tree diagram)	System engineering technique to identify and decompose functions required to be performed by the product and production process. Physical/software/human architectures are defined to meet these functions.
Creativity techniques	Brainstorming, attribute listing, mind mapping, and other techniques are used to identify parts and process concepts (individually or in a group setting).

Continued

Table 4.4 Design phase tools.

Tool	Use
Benchmarking	Systematic method of identifying technologies that can be applied to the parts and process design.
Intellectual property analysis	Systematic identification of technologies aimed at avoiding use of technologies owned by others (early in concepting) and then protecting company-developed technologies (through patents, trademarks, copyrights, trade secrets, etc.).
Pugh concept convergence	Matrix-based approach to identify, evaluate, and converge on a superior design concept that meets the product requirements (can be used at any design level, including production process concepts).
Cascade/flowdown	Process of deploying and allocating higher-level to lower-level requirements. Design phase cascades product-level requirements to parts and process requirements.
Transfer functions	Quantitative relationships from CTQs (and other important requirements) to lower-level requirements and, eventually, to process variables.
Simulations (e.g., finite element analysis)	Computer representations of the product developed for the purpose of more rapidly, cheaply (and, in many cases with greater insight) predicting product performance than physical prototypes.
Design of experiments (DOE)	Statistical technique to evaluate which design factors affect the CTQs/requirements, optimize the design and ensure its robustness (i.e., Taguchi techniques). Design phase purpose is to optimize the product design (and also production process design).
Industrial design/human factors	Discipline whose purpose is to ensure that the human interface with the product is well designed. Design phase focus will be on usability testing of product.
Design control/configuration control	Design process to ensure that requirements, features, and design parameters are identified and controlled.
Design for X	Proactive design techniques to consider "X-factors" such as design-to-cost, manufacturability, assembly, environment, maintainability, inspectability, testability, and others.
Reliability methods	Proactive design techniques to ensure that CTQ performance is achieved over the intended product life. Examples include reliability target setting and allocation, reliability prediction, failure modes and effects analysis, fault tree analysis, and reliability testing. If product is maintainable, this includes maintenance plans (reliability-centered maintenance, predictability-centered maintenance) and predictions, spare parts decisions, and others.

Continued

Table 4.4 Design phase tools. *Continued*

Tool	Use
Consumer feedback	Market research methods to obtain feedback on product design.
Lean production principles	Principles applied to production process design to ensure waste, work-in-progress are minimized, that the product is produced "just-in-time" to meet customer demand.
Control planning	Method to control the quality of the product by ensuring that the production process Ys and Xs are identified, control and critical control points are identified and measured, and reaction plans are developed with accountability for action when necessary.
Design reviews	Meetings between the team and peers/experts to review the design and associated analyses. Design phase purpose is to challenge the final product design and associated production process design to identify weak points before moving to verification/validation activities.

Key Outputs

- Functional analyses
- Production-version product design (including parts and assemblies)
- Subassembly, parts, and process requirements (from cascade)
- Design drawings (layouts, flowcharts, schematics)
- Bills of material
- Product specifications
- Production process design (including equipment, tooling, layout, and measurement systems)
- Control plans, procedures, protocols
- Supporting design analyses/test results:
  —Calculations (including transfer functions)
  —Predictive analyses (FMEA, EMEA, FTA, FEA, stress analyses)
  —Experimental results

- —Test plans/results
- —Design for X analyses (manufacturability, assembly, maintainability, environment, human factors, others)
- —Regulatory and environmental impact analyses
- —Cost estimates to produce product
- —Customer/consumer feedback on production version product
- —Production process analyses (capacity, lean, mold fill, environmental impact, others)

- Maintenance plans, spare-parts plans
- Design scorecard (by end of Design, CTQ variation predictions are developed and compared to specifications, predicting design capability)
- Product/process verification and validation plans

Phase Review

The fourth business review occurs when the team completes the Design phase. When the product design is deemed complete, a design review occurs. Following this review, the design is frozen so that process design work can occur with minimal changes/schedule impacts. Sponsors review and approve the team's product and process design. Updates/revisions to the charter, the multigenerational plan, and the project plan are also reviewed and approved. Sponsors review the team's current risk assessment of the project and concur with the team's mitigation actions.

VERIFY AND VALIDATE: OVERVIEW AND TOOLS

Purpose

Verification confirms the product and process meets their requirements; validation confirms the product meets the needs of the customers for the intended use environment. Pilot testing can be a key part of the product's validation. Based on the results of these activities, the decision to scale up to full production is made; implementation and transition plans to support the scale-up are developed.

Key Inputs

- Design outputs from previous phases
- Process control plans
- Product/process verification and validation plans

Steps

Note: The activities are listed in a very general sequence of events—a number of these activities can occur in parallel.

Build production processes—Production facilities, equipment, information systems, and so forth are procured and constructed in preparation for qualification tests. For some businesses, these may be on a pilot scale, with full-scale processes built after successful pilot results.

Verify process readiness—Start-up testing of the production processes is completed. The processes are tested to determine whether they are capable of producing the product. Typically, this involves installation qualification, in which the production equipment is installed and demonstrated to work, followed by operational qualification; here, the equipment is tested to ensure it meets its requirements (as cascaded from customer, business, and other stakeholder requirements).

Perform pilot testing—Typically, this involves performance qualification, in which the process is verified to be able to produce product within all of its requirements. The design scorecard is updated; verification results (Sigma levels) are compared against design predictions. Production version product is produced. The product is offered to customers; validation that the product meets the needs of the users in the intended use environment is performed.

Analyze gaps, determine root causes—Problems experienced by the customer are identified, root causes are determined, and the product/process is revised to eliminate the gaps.

Evaluate scale-up potential—A business decision is made to scale up the product to full scale.

Develop implementation and transition plans—Plans to fully implement the product are developed. Table 4.5 shows the primary tools used in the Verify/Validate phase.

Table 4.5 Verify/validate phase tools.

Tool	Use
Pilot/qualification testing	Various tests are designed to ensure that the production process will produce the product within specifications. Examples include installation qualifications (ensuring the production equipment operates) and operational qualifications.
Design reviews	Meetings between the team and peers/experts to review the design and associated analyses. Verify and Validate phase purpose is to review the results of design verification/validation and process verification activities to ensure the product is approved for launch.
Root cause analysis tools	Methods such as Define–Measure–Analyze–Identify–Execute–Control (DMAIEC), tools such as cause/effect diagrams, fault tree analysis, and five-whys are used to analyze process problems and their root causes so that corrective action can be taken.
Project management	Planning and managing methods to ensure that the production start-up and product launch are performed as quickly and efficiently as possible.

Key Outputs

- Verified production processes
- Verified and validated product
- Process control plans (updated)
- Configuration control plans (products, processes, suppliers)
- Implementation/transition plans

Phase Review

The fifth business review occurs when the team completes the Verification and Validation activities. Sponsors and business leaders approve product launch. Updates/revisions to the charter, multigenerational plan, and project plan are also reviewed and approved. Sponsors review the team's current risk assessment of the project and concur with the team's mitigation actions.

IMPLEMENT: OVERVIEW TOOLS

Purpose

Here the product is launched. The design is transitioned to the operating forces (that is, for products), and the device master record is completed and transferred to production. Further commercialization of the product may occur, and the design of the next product generation begun. The close of this design project is at hand. Lessons learned, as well as the history of the design, are documented. As appropriate, the design team is rewarded and recognized.

Key Inputs

- Verified production processes
- Verified and validated product
- Implementation/transition plans

Steps

Note: The activities are listed in a very general sequence of events—a number of these activities can occur in parallel.

Build full-scale processes, train staff—For many products, existing facilities are adapted to support the new production processes. In some cases, new production facilities/processes will be required.

Perform start-up testing—Necessary testing of the new production processes is performed. Production is ramped up to full scale.

Analyze gaps, determine root causes—Problems noted with early production units/processes are identified, root causes are determined, and appropriate countermeasures are implemented.

Transition to process owners—As the new product enters production, the design team performs a turnover to operating forces. Bills of material, device master records, process procedures, and control plans are transitioned. Design history files are updated.

Evaluate and close design project—Before the design team disbands and begins to work on the next products, lessons

Table 4.6 Implement phase tools.

Tool	Use
Project management	Planning and managing methods to ensure the production start-up and product launch are performed as quickly and efficiently as possible.
Process control methods	Method to control the quality of the product by ensuring that the production process Ys and Xs are identified, control and critical control points are identified and measured, and reaction plans are developed with accountability for action when necessary.
Root cause analysis methods	Methods such as DMAIEC are used to analyze process problems and their root causes so that corrective action can be taken.
Configuration/change management	Methods ensure that the as-designed product configuration is maintained and that those changes to materials, processes, or supplier-provided parts are evaluated for their effect on the product and its requirements. For example, the device master record contains all the routine instructions required to manufacture the product. The design history file contains or references the records that demonstrate that the design was developed in accordance with the approved design plan and the requirements of this part.

learned are generated, good practices are recognized, and improvement opportunities are identified. All of these should be fed back to the owners of the design process to improve the overall design processes. Table 4.6 shows the primary tools used in the Implement phase.

Key Outputs

- Production processes operating at desired quality and capacity levels
- Commercialized product
- Device master record
- Design history files
- Lessons learned/best practices
- Updated multigenerational plans

Phase Review

The last business review occurs when the organization defines the design effort to be complete (for instance, six months postlaunch or upon achievement of specified performance goals). This last review is intended to capture lessons learned (identifying both problems that occurred and the best or improved practices), determine next steps for the product line, and reward and recognize the team for their efforts.

KEY POINTS

You should walk away from reading this chapter with:

- Understanding that DMADVI is an *end-to-end* design process and that DFSS is adaptable to many product development challenges in many industries. In addition, although our focus has been on physical products, DFSS has been applied to business process/service designs.

- Understanding that the core of DMADVI includes gathering voice of customer information to identify product requirements/CTQs, developing design concepts to meet the requirements/CTQs, cascading requirements from product to process and predicting/verifying that the design meets these requirements—both targets and specification limits.

- A choice for you to consider: Bring the DMADVI framework into your organization as the DFSS method or use your existing framework and incorporate DMADVI's tools and methods.

5

Gap Analysis and Readiness for the DFSS Journey

INTRODUCTION

After the first four chapters, we're sure you agree that DFSS makes sense and that DFSS could help improve your organization's new product development. That's the easy part. On the other hand, the hard part is figuring out how to make it work for *your* organization. Everybody wants to win the game, but doing it is hard!

We've been easy on you so far in this book. You've had the chance to understand a bit about DFSS. We hope you understand why companies have found it valuable to integrate DFSS in their product development processes.

In the next four chapters, we're going to turn the spotlight on your organization's new product development function. We have seen companies try to implement DFSS, only to have it become another "program of the month." We don't want that to happen to you.

We've mentioned Six Sigma's improvement method, DMAIEC, throughout this book. To help ensure that you get it right, we're going to use DMAIEC thinking to help you plan and execute your DFSS implementation. This chapter will address most of the Define, Measure, and Analyze step activities; the next chapters will take you through Identify, Execute, and Control.

You'll find that *change management* is critical in driving and sustaining a DFSS culture. With resources stretched in all areas of organizations, leaders are finding it critical to make effective, sustainable changes with the least amount of resistance. DFSS is more than a set of processes and tools. It truly represents a cultural shift in the way you do business. We will share ways with you to assess your organization and determine whether it is truly ready for a change like DFSS.

In this chapter, you are going to figure out whether DFSS is for you by answering three basic questions:

- Why do you think DFSS is needed in your organization; that is, why do you want to do this?

- Do you understand the gaps between your current product development process (if you can even call it that) and *what good looks like?*

- Is your organization ready for the changes that DFSS demands? How much of a change can your organization take now?

WHY DO YOU WANT TO DO DFSS?

By 1985, Florida Power & Light (FPL) had been playing with its quality improvement program for about four years. While we had seen a good bit of local improvement, our execs weren't happy—the program wasn't making as big an impact on the company as they'd expected. A group of 12 respected middle managers (informally known as the *quality apostles*) were charged to benchmark quality programs around the world. They learned about Crosby, Deming, and Feigenbaum. They went to Detroit, to Europe, and finally to Japan. Here, they happened to find the Kansai Electric Power Company (KEPCO).

KEPCO had just won the 1984 Deming Prize, and its overall performance was excellent. Because it was similar to FPL in size and characteristics, KEPCO was judged to be a good model from which FPL might learn. The apostles met with KEPCO representatives, discussed their approach, and asked how they did it—who helped them, and so forth.

In due time, we were introduced to Dr. Tetsuichi Asaka, the lead Union of Japanese Scientists and Engineers (JUSE) counselor for KEPCO. Our senior leadership arranged a meeting in Japan with Dr. Asaka and several other counselors. We thought at first that these counselors were like typical Western consultants: throw money at them and they'd do whatever we wanted.

That was a big mistake, and it was our first of many in dealing with these strict teachers. The first question Dr. Asaka asked our leadership was "Why do you want to do this?" We gave him such reasons as we wanted to get better and we think this will be good for our reputation. He wasn't happy with our answers. We were sent home (without a commitment!) to figure out *why*? Six months later, we went back with an answer that satisfied the counselors. It was only then that Dr. Asaka agreed to work with us.

What made the difference? Well, from several fuzzy, feel-good reasons, we had been able to articulate a clear business reason to change our management systems. These reasons included: (a) concern that the *economic* disaster that General Public Utilities experienced after Three Mile Island could happen to us (FPL owned two nuclear plants at that time), (b) concern over our customers' *satisfaction* with our electric service and its price (this, after the two oil shocks of the 1970s; the rest of our generating capacity was oil fired), and (c) concern that the *regulatory environment* could shift, deregulating the electric utility industry, because we had just seen the telephone industry deregulated and Bell Telephone broken into pieces. So we're going to apply the same hard question to you that Dr. Asaka posed over 20 years ago: Why do you want to adopt the discipline of DFSS?

Chapter 2 gave you some reasons why others have done so. So here's your first homework—building the business case for DFSS. Answer the following questions. Go out and get the data. Table 5.1 shows a sample of possible pieces of the business case for DFSS.

Table 5.1 Examples of DFSS business case elements.

Audience	Candidate reasons	My company's situation
Senior leadership (language = *money*)	New product failure rate: The percentage of your new products that make it to full market commercialization but that fail to achieve the objectives set for them Cost elements: • Development resources • Plant and equipment investment • Raw materials and purchased parts/assemblies • Sales and advertising	

Continued

Table 5.1 Examples of DFSS business case elements.

Audience	Candidate reasons	My company's situation

Senior leadership (language = *money*)	• Warranty costs
	• Intangible:
	  —Reputation
	  —Difficulty placing new products with distributors
	• Product recalls:
	  —Cost of recalling product,
	  —Product replacement
	  —Legal liability
	  —Stock price decline (loss of capitalization)
	• Excess cost of production (because of off-target performance):
	  —Scrap and rework
	  —Cost inside the spec limits
	• Wasted development resources:
	  —Rework in product development
	  —Stabilization of new product
	  —Projects proceeding past their "kill-by" date
	• Lost revenue opportunities:
	  —Successful product with no follow-on
	  —Product launched too late (competitive product appeared first)
	  —Product overwhelmed by superior competitive product
	  —Inadequate development pipeline	

Continued

Table 5.1 Examples of DFSS business case elements.   *Continued*

Audience	Candidate reasons	My company's situation
Middle management (bilingual)	All of the above money reasons All of the below technical reasons	
Development staff (language = technical)	• Frustration with: —Poorly scoped development project —Lack of understanding what the customer really wants —Irrational product requirements —Inability to develop a product concept that focused on meeting customer needs —Having to invent a new technology in the middle of a development project —Being whipsawed with changing requirements or a product with ever-changing features —Inability to predict how well the product will perform in the face of process and supplier variation —Irrational risk management approach —Lack of knowledge and assurance that the product will be producible —Nights away from home solving production problems —Continually changing product requirements/ product features list	

What did this research tell you? Can you put a case together for improving your product development process? Does this case convince you? How about others in your organization (try it out with a few friends first)? Will this case be good enough to sell your senior leadership? If the answer to these questions is yes, move on to the gap analysis. If not, stop reading this book and move to the next book on your list!

GAP ANALYSIS

The *why* questions tell you that something's wrong and/or that there's an opportunity to improve your current development process. The next key question is: What are the gaps between your current process and what "good" looks like?

General Electric's change management approach starts with a simple but powerful equation:

$$Q \times A = E$$

Here, Q stands for the quality of a change or decision, A for the acceptance of the decision, and E for the effectiveness of the change or how well it will "stick" in the organization. We refer to "Q-side" issues as the *hard stuff* and "A-side" issues as the *soft stuff*. Your gap analysis must include both sides.

QUALITY-SIDE GAPS

We'll start your gap analysis on the Q-side of the equation. You want the highest-quality new product development system you can create, so we'll ask you to start by identifying gaps in your current development system. (We'll define *gap* as simply a difference between what *is* and what *should be*.) What are the biggest issues with your organization's current product development system? Why are they issues?

There are two main factors you'll consider here: design and development processes and organizational structures. We'll focus first on identifying development processes that need an overhaul and then organizational structures that are impeding you from developing a world-class Six Sigma product development process.

Prepare to take a deep dive into your development processes. Don't just get a copy of your product development procedure; look at the methods each product development team actually uses. Look closely at each step of the product development process, identifying the gaps between current practice and best practice (review Chapter 4 for what "good" looks like). This is important. Be sure to identify true *current practice,* not what is documented as your process. We've found too often that the documented new product development process and the one being followed can be very different. We mentioned earlier how one company had pictures of their process posted in all the hallways, but the reality was that *nobody* followed that process. Your success in sustaining DFSS is to make sure in the end that the process you put in place and document is a process your teams *can* and *will* follow. It really helps to be a good detective here. Adopt the Missourians' show-me attitude and look for data-based evidence, even if that evidence isn't numerical.

For example, one team we worked with built a cardboard-and-string mobile that listed the critical customer requirements at the top and strung the cascading critical requirements level by level. The mobile hung over their team table, so every team member saw it every day, reminding them that every level of detail linked back to the customer. This team *got it.*

Other teams could show management their "progress" with fancy PowerPoint presentations, but these were often cobbled together the night before the briefing. These teams were just putting up a *storefront.*

GAP ANALYSIS: CURRENT NEW PRODUCT DEVELOPMENT PROCESSES

Before we do a deep dive into your development process, here are a few basic questions. Do you have a defined product development process? Do your product development teams do things differently, without defined steps, gates, or milestones? Is that OK or even *condoned* and *encouraged*?

Think about the main functions associated with each step of DMADVI:

- *Define*—Organizing the development project
- *Measure*—Obtaining VOC and developing product requirements
- *Analyze*—Developing the feasible concept
- *Design*—Developing the production product and production processes

- *Verify and Validate*—Verifying and validating product and process performance
- *Implement*—Launching and stabilizing the product

Even if you're not using a DMADVI-like process, how are the teams performing these basic functions today? Can you build a map of the process (a flowchart, a schematic, whatever your favorite process picture is)?

If you've got major gaps here, your DFSS strategy and implementation plan (see Chapter 6) will start lower on the maturity scale. Your first steps may be to install a basic development process with decision gates. Go ahead and use DMADVI then as your basic development process.

Gaps I've Found:

Now let's look at your product development process step by step to find your detailed gaps. Although we'll walk you through all the design functions covered by DMADVI, you should focus on the most important gaps. We'll mix metaphors here and suggest that you use the Pareto principle and not try to eat the elephant in one sitting.

How Robust Is Your Define, or Chartering, Phase?

Based on the DFSS roadmap in Chapter 4, how far off are your teams' processes from the "what good looks like" for the Define phase? Do your teams use a chartering process to get the development project going? Are they reviewed and approved by management? Do all key stakeholders (at least marketing, R&D, and operations) sign off on the charters?

Are some teams chartered to develop a product with a wink and a nod from a manager, while others in your organization clearly define each goal, deliverable, and a project timetable? Although this question relates more to your overall development portfolio, how big are the development projects (balancing the project's risk with its reward)? Are the development projects linked to your business strategy? Is that evident in the charters?

Go out and sample a few of your teams' charters. What do the charters look like? Do the charters include the detailed product features the teams are tasked with designing (red flag here)? Or are the charters focused on the unmet customer needs, allowing the design teams the space they need for true ideation (green flag here)? Are the charters up to date, or can you see a bit of mold around the edges? For example, how does the scope defined in the charter match up with what the team is working on? Take a charter and, without letting them see it, ask team members a few questions. Make them obvious, such as what are the goals, scope, and deliverables of the project?

Gaps I've Found:

How Robust Is Your Voice of the Customer Collection?

To assess your gaps here, start with the product of the VOC process—the team's product criteria or design specifications. First, do your teams refer to a list of criteria during product design? Are these criteria simply a list of features that are to go into the product, or are they real requirements? Here's the linkage—the customer has *needs,* the product has *requirements,* and the resulting design has *features.* If your customer would like to dig a hole quickly, the *requirement* for the product could be "customer can remove X amount of soil from the ground per minute." This statement of a requirement allows your development team the opportunity to consider different solutions. If they listed the requirement as "surface area of the shovel blade," they've (a) just defined a feature and (b) have locked themselves into a solution.

Is this list of customer requirements referred to throughout the design and validation/verification cycles? Does anyone check to see whether the requirements were met by the design? Are there data to back up these claims? How much confidence do you have in these data? What is the business decision-making process if there are gaps here? Do the teams go back and redesign the product or do they shrug their shoulders and say, "Oh, what the heck, we'll launch it anyway?"

Now, work backward to the source of the product's requirements. What process was used to develop the requirements? Do the requirements come from customer visits, interviews, and confirmation surveys that are traceable to the appropriate customer segments? How well have your past launches met your customer expectations? How do you measure that satisfaction? It is very important to take a deep dive into your product development teams and take an honest look into their approaches to VOC.

Third, look for how teams are prioritizing these requirements. Is there evidence that the Pareto principle has been applied; that is, has the team selected those few critical drivers/customer differentiators? Or are all requirements "created equal"? We have seen teams list all of their requirements equally and then go through endless redesigns until they "meet" them all. Teams waste months, if not years, designing the product to hit every requirement perfectly. With DFSS, a team can learn to differentiate between requirements, from the many that have to perform adequately to satisfy the customer to the critical few that need to outperform everyone in the market. The time saved by applying this differentiation can be the difference between being first to market with the next iPod and fighting to convert customers to a me-too product.

Finally, look at the customer requirements' stability from the start to the finish of projects. Do you see the criteria change as new players come on to the team? As we stressed in Chapter 4, a robust VOC collection method will stand the test of time through product development, and it will stand the test of team-member shifts as well.

Gaps I've Found:

How Robust Is Your Concept Development (Analyze) Process?

Do you see evidence that the teams are evaluating their concepts objectively, according to how well each concept will deliver on the CTQs? Do you see evidence that more than one concept is being evaluated? Can you see that the concepts have been refined and combined, torn apart and put back together again, until the team can show that they have the best combination of features rolled up into one superior concept? Or are teams jumping to one solution too quickly? Ask them to prove that they've evaluated other possibilities.

What feasibility studies are performed to assess the concepts? Do your teams use a build-test-fix approach or a design-analyze-confirm approach? Do you see the teams wasting time with unnecessary prototypes that don't answer key questions? Are your teams using modern feasibility techniques such as simulation methods like finite element analysis or the SPICE circuit simulator? How do your teams seek and incorporate customer input to the design concept?

How many of your teams are stuck in *science projects,* trying to invent the technology needed for the product?

Are your teams thinking ahead to the production processes and other Design for X considerations (manufacturability, assembly, environment, reliability, human factors, testability, inspectability, maintainability, and other -ilities)?

How are your teams identifying risks associated with the concept? Who does the failure modes and effects analysis (FEMA)? When? Are the risks prioritized? Is there an opportunity for the results of the FMEA to be fed back into the design? Ask the teams for evidence where one or more high-risk failure modes (identified from the FMEA) were then mitigated through a design change.

Is the end of the concepting phase defined clearly for each team, marked by the milestone of a single concept selected, risk analysis performed around that concept, and mitigation of those risks?

Gaps I've Found:

How Robust Is Your Design Cascade Process?

Take a look at your design teams' outputs. Walk through their team rooms or meeting areas. Do you see solid evidence that the team members keep their eyes on the customer? Or do you see evidence that each member is approaching his or her subsystem with a narrow focus, suboptimizing the parts instead of optimizing the system?

You may gather evidence about this gap further downstream in the design process; how many times have problems come up when subsystems are brought together during systems integration?

Do you see engineering analysis that starts with manufacturing and assembly variation and predicts the resulting system capability? This is the second-largest gap we see in organizations. In many organizations, the engineers develop flawless performance calculations of the most complex systems and subsystems, but they are calculated only to the nominal. Many teams then turned to the quickest method for building safety into it, the 2X safety factor. Review your teams' approach to safety factors. If you see safety-factor-of-two calculations, then that team may not really understand their manufacturing capabilities.

We found another curious practice. One team of electrical designers told us they used worst-case analysis to ensure that their circuits performed within specs. First, a worst-case analysis of more than a few components is very conservative. Second, the designers told us that it wasn't component variation that caused problems, but variation in assembly processes such as soldering! So they were doing a "useless" prediction that ignored the important sources of product variation!

A team that understands the manufacturing capabilities will be able to use the predicted variation in their calculations instead of simple safety factors or worst-case analyses that may or may not truly be "safe" or "worst."

Also look at prototypes built during DMADVI's Design phase. Why were the prototypes built? How many versions of prototypes were built? Ask the team what questions they were answering when they built each set of prototypes. If the answer is always "to see if it works the way we want," throw up a red flag. The DFSS approach will help teams learn to evaluate and predict "how well it will work" by variation analysis and deep-dive into the cascade. Are teams building each version they design in order to check the functionality? If so, the chances are pretty high that the team doesn't truly understand

---

Gaps I've Found:

the design cascade from system down to component and feature. They are "building and testing," a costly and time-consuming practice that DFSS will help minimize. On the other hand, a team that builds a prototype to verify an analytical model will get the knowledge they need up front, requiring fewer prototypes through their project.

How Robust Is Your Verification and Validation Process?

We defined *verification* as the ability of the product to meet its requirements. What process do the teams use to verify their designs? Can they show you evidence of verification activities for product-level requirements? If design predictions were performed, how does the data from the verification activities compare; are there large gaps?

How has the production process been verified to perform its fabrication and assembly functions? Are sample products produced with just nominal settings, or does verification also include testing at the process extremes?

How is the final product, produced under production conditions, validated with the customer? Can the teams show you evidence that the product meets the customers' needs?

In today's resource-strapped world, it is understandable to want to reassign the development team to a new project the minute the first commercial product hits the shipping docks. But the best thing you can do for your organization is to allow the team to evaluate their results and identify what they could have done better. The whole team needs to be held accountable to deliver the quality product and manufacturing process that they promised. If you see teams being disbanded before the launch and subsequent product validation, consider that gap a significant obstacle to improving your product development process. The feedback cycle should identify both problems that occurred during this particular development effort as well as any good practices that could be replicated in future efforts.

Gaps I've Found:

GAP ANALYSIS: CURRENT NEW PRODUCT DEVELOPMENT ORGANIZATIONAL STRUCTURE

As you've performed the process gap analysis, you've probably identified a number of organizational practices that will also require change. You should look for structures, policies, and practices that have outworn their usefulness. Here are a few structural issues you should consider in your gap analysis:

- *Development team organization*—Do you use dedicated development teams or are development resources shared across teams? (Note that we're not suggesting either of these approaches is wrong, but rather that you consider team organization as a potential gap.)

- *Development resource utilization*—How are your development resources being used? How long do they stay in their roles (too short or too long)? DFSS emphasizes a design-analyze-confirm approach. Do your development resources have time and skills to perform this work? Have a few developers log how they spend their time for a few days (first, explain why you are doing this). How much of this time is non-value-added—that is, time they spend in meetings, chasing information, making PowerPoint presentations, and so forth? Because you will be asking them to do additional work (at least, up front), what can you tell them they can stop doing?

- *Reward and recognition systems*—This can be one of the most important factors either helping or hindering your new product development improvement initiative. What practices, behaviors, and so forth are rewarded? For example, are bonuses based on achieving time-to-market goals or time-to-profitability goals? Do the reward and recognition systems suboptimize your development process? Take a close look at what motivates each player, especially marketing, R&D, and operations. When GE wants to change something in its organization, it seems very good at aligning its systems to reward the right behaviors.

Which of the current structures, policies, and practices will hinder or prevent you from driving DFSS through your organization?

For example, in one organization, marketing staff members are rotated on an 18-month cycle. To make his or her mark, the marketer needs to quickly come up with a product idea and drive that idea through the development process to launch. This behavior leads to product development projects that are started with little voice of customer input and that are mainly variations of existing product lines. The company suffers from a plethora of line extensions being launched with few truly innovative (and hence higher revenue/profitable) products. Until this rotation policy is changed, the company will have little success in improving its new product development process.

What structures need to be in place to allow robust product development, strategic decision making, and business-driven portfolio management? For instance, one company put into place a phase-gate system for business checks and balances two years before deploying DFSS. This proved to be a valuable first step in the success of DFSS. The phase-gate process provided that organization with a strong, cross-functional project management approach that held teams accountable throughout the development cycle.

Because this was a large development organization, it took two years to get used to the phase-gate process. Some organizations may be able to implement a phase-gate process at the same time as the DFSS process, but every company's tolerance for change is different. Evaluate the tolerance for change within your organization before you decide whether to deploy the phase-gate process and DFSS simultaneously.

How robust is your decision-making process? Do products get launched because the organization is too weak to kill a bad idea? Do teams feel penalized if they find that a product is not worth pursuing? Do you practice killing the messenger? Do products get launched because teams and sponsors have pet projects and don't want to stop driving the product even though the data point toward killing the project? The DFSS process works if only teams and sponsors let data and strategy drive decisions. If your organization has weaknesses in the decision-making process within product development, stop where you are and work toward fixing this problem before you spend any time on DFSS implementation.

What about the portfolio management process? How do projects enter the pipeline? Is there a robust strategic alignment around new product ideas or unmet needs that allows leaders to use data to determine which projects feed the product pipeline? Do the teams use multigenerational product planning to manage their pipeline? Without a robust portfolio management process, DFSS may greatly improve your design robustness, but your company will feel a loss of morale as you fail to see the market growth you expect from DFSS. DFSS will improve your product development process only from charter to launch. Getting the right product ideas or unmet needs fed into the pipeline is as important as DFSS itself.

Gaps I've Found:

TEAM-BY-TEAM GAP ANALYSIS

So far, we've focused on the common cause sources of variation in your new product development process. These sources will generally affect all of your teams. We've also found that there can be a lot of variation across each development team. We've found that one of the most effective DFSS implementation approaches is to *make it personal.* If one team has done an outstanding job of collecting voice of customer information but is struggling with concepting or cascade/prediction work, you should recognize and celebrate the former and then focus your help on the latter.

To help you examine your individual teams' performance and processes objectively, develop and apply an evaluation tool like the one shown in Table 5.2 for your organization. This tool will help you do an individual team gap analysis by assessing the maturity of each team relative to what "good looks like."

In our example tool, we've included three levels of maturity: *unacceptable performance, watch for trends,* and *best practice.* You may decide to be more or less granular, but we would suggest you don't go above five levels of differentiation.

Be careful here and assess your culture's tolerance for *labeling.* Some cultures may be fine with a 1-through-3 rating, or 0 to 100%. Some may be tolerant of red–yellow–green coding. Don't underestimate the importance of your organization's cultural norms before using this assessment. The goal of this assessment is to gain the alignment of the teams, agreeing that there is improvement to be made. Your goal is to simply hold up a mirror for these teams to look objectively at themselves. Let the data do the talking.

Share the results with each team immediately. This sharing is the real heart of the A-side of the equation. Once teams see how they look in the mirror realistically, they usually want to change that reality. If you are objective in your evaluation of each team, you may find teams actually coming to you to request that you evaluate them next.

PRIORITIZE THE DEVELOPMENT PROCESS IMPROVEMENTS

Some organizations may have the willpower and resources to fix many of the DFSS gaps at once. In our experience, however, most companies do not have the resources or the patience for an extreme makeover. Instead, we've found that focusing on the most pressing process failures and structural gaps is the most effective way to proceed. This will allow the DFSS deployment team to fix the biggest gaps first and show the organization early and significant improvements. From a $Q \times A = E$ approach, you'll gain traction with the organization as you fix the biggest "pains" experienced by your new product development teams.

In Chapter 6, we'll ask you to create a DFSS implementation charter and deployment plan. By now, you've gathered just about all the information you need to do this, including those gaps you are going to fill in the organization first. This will help you maintain the quality of your change. You can now focus on the critical elements to fix: those elements that the organization can't help but agree are broken. With the individual team gap analysis tool, you also have a mirror that you can hold up to any team or department to help them see what they look like.

"A-SIDE" GAPS

Having defined and prioritized the "Q-side" gaps, you, the development leader also need to consider "A-side" issues as you plan implementation of DFSS-driven improvements. Don't do a "metric system." Most people recognize that the metric system has a lot of benefits over the English system used in the United States. However, general acceptance of the metric system stalled in the United States a

Table 5.2 Example of DFSS preevaluation criteria.

	Define	Measure	Analyze		Design		Verify/validate and implement	
Best practice	Preliminary Charter	CTQs Defined	Concept selection Re: CTQs, cascade	Cascade to transfer Functions	Scorecard	Scorecard	Actual capability	
	Charter aligns unmet customer needs, strategic plan, and market size.	CTQs are aligned with unmet customer needs and are new, unique, or difficult to fulfill. CTQs are measurable with targets and ranges.	Multiple concepts are evaluated. Diligence is shown around risk analysis, concept feasibility, and prediction around the ability to perform to the CTQs. Trade-offs can be articulated to show the optimal concept was selected.	Transfer functions have been developed that link all the CTQs to the critical parameters (i.e., subassembly, components). Every CTQ is cascaded through mathematical analysis.	Predicted capability	Transfer functions and variation analysis are performed to predict the capabilities of the CTQs. Components can be clearly linked as critical drivers based on the variation analysis and transfer functions.	CTQs are tested to verify the actual performance capability. Critical components tested to verify the actual capability of each critical feature. Any gap is identified and accounted for, and design is reoptimized if necessary, with clear understanding of what the drivers were to optimize the design.	

Continued

Table 5.2 Example of DFSS preevaluation criteria. *Continued*

		Define	Measure	Analyze		Design	Verify/validate and implement
Watch for trends	Preliminary		CTQs	Concept selection	Cascade to transfer Functions	Scorecard	Scorecard
	Charter		Defined	Re: CTQs, cascade		Predicted capability	Actual capability
		Mature technology to be used is defined. The value proposition points to market research and/or a multi-generational product plan.	All of the CTQs are solution-free.	Only two or three concepts were evaluated, with little or no difference between the concepts.	Cascade is shown, but links are weak and anecdotal.	CTQ scorecard is complete with predictions.	Scorecard is complete with capability analysis, measurement system analysis for each CTQ, and each critical component. Verification plan shows capable measurement system.
Unacceptable		Team is chartered to solution, with no real design/ innovation room allowed.	No CTQs are identified. All requirements are treated equally.	Concept shown is the only concept the team can define. No proof of other concepts at all.	No cascade can be shown.	Component scorecard is complete with predictions for critical component features that have been identified by the transfer functions and variation analysis.	No scorecard is shown.

number of years ago. As you create the structure and implement the change to DFSS, gauge the acceptance level in your organization.

There are two main elements to consider when predicting the acceptance of change. Leadership commitment is the most critical element, followed by the tolerance of and motivation for change.

LEADERSHIP COMMITMENT

It takes more than one senior leader to drive DFSS (even if that senior leader is someone in a position like Jack Welch at General Electric). You must gauge the commitment of each leader in the organization. Some leaders may just need to be verbally supportive of DFSS, while others will need to actually make things happen in their departments.

Note that we're using the term *leader* here, not *manager*. Not all managers are leaders, and not all leaders are managers. Who do your people really look to when leadership is needed? Of approximately 20 managers in FPL's Power Plant Engineering department during the 1980s, we'd count only two as leaders. Some of these managers were even anti-leaders, resisting change from any direction. There were, however, another six or seven engineers in the department who were truly leaders, even though they did not have the word *manager* in their titles.

Deploying DFSS takes strong leadership at all levels of the organization. You should assess each leader's position as a stakeholder and determine whether they are 100% behind the drive for DFSS, whether they are merely passively supportive of the change, or whether they may work to torpedo DFSS. In addition, you should consider where they need to be for the change to be successful.

Table 5.3 is an example of a *stakeholder analysis*. Your DFSS implementation team can use it to analyze and track the commitment of your leadership. They can also use it to develop a plan to move each leader to the necessary level of commitment.

This example shows just a subset of stakeholders you will actually need to evaluate. Presidents, vice presidents, directors, and other managers who have strong influence across the business should be interviewed to explore their concerns and commitment to this important change. Also include the informal leaders in your business. Are there external stakeholders you need to include? For example, some regulatory bodies, such as the Food and Drug Administration, are very interested in the new product development process. Some of their regulations promote DFSS thinking; others do not. After an

Table 5.3 Example of stakeholder analysis.

Key: X = Stakeholder is here   O = Stakeholder needs to be here

Stakeholder VPs	Against	Neutral	For	Concerns/Details	Actions	Responsible
Mark Martin, VP of R&D		X	O	Understands the worth of DFSS, but is concerned about the resources/commitment needed.	Share success stories from other organizations. Let Mary Jones tell the story herself. Calculate the cost to deploy DFSS and estimate the savings to show return on investment.	Mathews
Kim Reynolds, VP of marketing		X	O	Concerned that it is just another "flavor of the month."	Share success stories from other organizations. Let Mary Jones tell the story herself.	Chen
Mary Jones, VP of operations			X O	Has seen it work in prior companies.	Get details/success stories from Mary Jones to share.	Connor
Joe Patel, director of X franchise	X		O	Thinks his organization is already stretched with the recent changes and upcoming launches.	Share success stories from other organizations, and estimate the cost of not deploying DFSS, in both time and money.	Thomas

introduction to Six Sigma, a chemist from a pharmaceutical company told us point-blank that the organization would never be able to achieve Six Sigma performance. When we asked a cautious *why,* she explained that they set their specification limits for the process by producing three registration batches of product, calculating the mean and standard deviation, and then setting the specs at $+/-$ 3 standard deviations. If they reduced the variation in the process, that would result only in a tightening of the spec limits! She stated that this was the way the FDA forced them to do business!

Keep in mind that not every leader will need to be moved to the "for" box on the stakeholder chart. Some leaders with minimal influence may be fine in the "neutral" box. Others may not need to be moved from the "against" box.

For example, one vice president might be assessed as "against" the change right now, but you know that the vice president is retiring in three months. You know you will take the next four to six months creating the DFSS structure before you even roll out the change. While this organizational role might be critical, your energy will best be used in communicating with the executive who will take that vice president's place.

If you complete your stakeholder analysis and find that fewer than half of the leaders are "for" the DFSS drive, you may want to rethink your timeline for implementation. As you will read in the "Don'ts to Avoid" section of Chapter 6, a grass-roots approach to a change this great in scale is not likely to work. Your team's time would be better spent bringing the critical subset of leaders further up the commitment curve before embarking on the wider DFSS implementation strategy.

Make sure you spend time understanding why people are for or against the change represented by DFSS. During Florida Power & Light's quality journey, John went through his own roller-coaster-like change experience. In late 1985, he was sent to FPL's team leader training, a one-week course that today would be equivalent to a Green Belt Lite course. Leaving the course, he was excited by the idea of using facts and data to solve business problems. If you asked him to help you implement DFSS when the course ended that Friday, he would have given you an enthusiastic "yes!"

The following Monday, though, he was assigned by his manager to lead a team. Unfortunately, instead of providing a *problem* to solve, his manager gave their team a *solution* to investigate. The team was quickly frustrated; they didn't even know what the problem was! And John was caught in the middle. The manager kept demanding progress on the solution while the quality improvement folks kept demanding that he and his team follow the problem-solving method—a no-win situation. Eventually, the team was disbanded as a failure. After this experience, John wanted nothing to do with the quality improvement program. If you asked him to help you implement DFSS then, you would have gotten a very negative response.

A turnaround occurred when he was selected to be one of FPL's 13 statistical specialists (today, a Master Black Belt). At first he resisted, but fortunately (for John), there was no choice in the matter. He was then exposed to people in FPL who were using the quality process to solve problems and achieve better business results. Slowly, his attitude changed and he became a born-again promoter of the quality process, and today it is his passion. Today, once again, your request for help would get an enthusiastic "Yes!" So, we hope the lesson is clear: Make sure you understand "why."

What should you expect in terms of leadership behaviors? Here are some examples of good behaviors:

- *Resourcing the DFSS implementation*—Leadership will send a strong signal about their DFSS support when they select the DFSS implementation team members and resource this team. This behavior applies in general to how the DFSS initiative is resourced. For example, when one team leader became excited about the benefits of variation prediction, he ordered 15 copies of a Monte Carlo simulation software package, one for each of his development engineers.

- *Personal involvement in the change*—This can take many forms. We've mentioned the R&D leader who scheduled charter review sessions that represented about one day per month of involvement for him and his team. One R&D leadership team conducted periodic DFSS assessments of each development team; this helped them both gauge team progress and learn the DMADVI process. Even having a senior leader kick off DFSS training sessions is appreciated.

- *Willingness to change their habits*—Let's face it, many of the *gaps* you're trying to improve were created because of the design system set up by current and past leaders. A big A-side win will involve leaders changing their expectations. For example, one organization's leadership expected to see early physical prototypes of new products. The DMADVI method adopted by this company now focuses on obtaining product requirements first, and then developing and optimizing virtual concepts. This organization's leaders fortunately developed the patience to let the teams follow the process. Now the team can show up at the charter review without a prototype. In another case, an organization overloaded itself with product development projects numbered in the hundreds! Here, a new leader diagnosed this as a key gap. He soon decreed that the organization was not allowed to have more than 30 development projects on the books at any one time. He also was clear about his strategy for the organization, including revenue and profit goals for new product launches. This resulted in a portfolio of projects that had a much higher value per project. Many of the low-revenue line-extension projects were canceled, freeing up resources to work on fewer but better projects. Although this action could be considered a bit draconian, the message was certainly clear.

- *Willingness to lead the change*—It's often perceived as risky to change what we're asking subordinates to do, especially if we're not quite sure of the benefits. A while back, John was the guinea pig for a change to Florida Power & Light's engineering scoping process. Sid, the project manager, came to John's office, explained the change and why he was asking for the change. Although John was a bit dubious of the benefits of the change, Sid convinced him to give it a try. John struggled a bit with the new scope form but completed a draft. Sid then helped John make a few corrections, approved the form, and sent it along to the customer. A few days later, the customer gave Sid positive feedback on the new scoping form, which Sid passed on to John. Word got around, and pretty soon other engineers were stopping by John's office to get help completing the form. In this case, Sid had not only personally led the change, but he had also co-opted John for help and support in rolling the change out to the whole organization. Sid could have saved some of his time by just writing a memo telling the organization that the new form was required, but that would have been an ineffective change method (remember, $Q \times A = E$).

- *Playing nicely together*—We've seen situations where the heads of R&D and manufacturing are solidly behind the DFSS initiative, but marketing is missing in action. This may be the most difficult good behavior, but these three functions should all be supporting DFSS. Leadership signing up to review and agree on the results teams achieve in each DMADVI phase can be evidence of good behavior. At the beginning of each phase, the triad of marketing, R&D, and operations agree on the development team's deliverables and also on the path going forward.

TOLERANCE AND MOTIVATION FOR CHANGE

Your organization's tolerance and motivation for change is the other key A-side issue you will have to face. One of your key risks to address is *low commitment* to your DFSS initiative. This can occur either because of flaws inherent in the DFSS implementation plan or as a side effect of other poorly planned or executed changes. We'll help you as much as we can with the former, but, whatever you do, don't underestimate the latter! It may not be your initiative the organization is apathetic toward, or fighting against, it's that DFSS is *another* change in an already change-overloaded world.

We'll freely admit that, when younger and a bit more immature in the ways of organizations, we either ignored or didn't pay appropriate attention to the tolerance and motivation factor. Even Dr. Joseph Juran notes that he didn't understand this factor until he read Margaret Mead's *Cultural Pattern and Technical Change*. He drew a parallel between the resistance that United Nations teams faced working with developing countries and the resistance he saw between management and labor, or between consultants and clients.

Has your organization been "doing all right" for a number of years? Is there a motivation to change? Or is your organization so threatened by competition that everyone is running scared seven days a week? What is the fear level in your group? The motivation may be there, but fear can paralyze the very people you need to help implement DFSS. These are just a few of the many questions you need to ask as you assess the readiness and tolerance for change in your organization.

Start your assessment of this factor by looking back at some of the change efforts that your organization has promoted over the last few years. We know that with all the stresses to improve the bottom line, almost all companies have been going through a tremendous amount of change turmoil.

Total quality, reengineering, outsourcing, Y2K, downsizing, SAP implementations, Six Sigma, and never-ending reorganizations are a few to which we've been exposed. What were your last few major changes? How were they implemented? How were they received? Has your organization been through a major change every year for several years? Are the associates still complaining about the past changes? Do their heads still spin from the last change?

Some of these changes may have gone well, others not. Question and research how well the changes were planned and implemented. Survey the associates in your organization. Ask them what they thought of a few of the most recent changes. Ask them whether they think the changes were critical to the success of the business, or just change for the sake of change (we know one R&D organization that seems to reorganize about every six months, whether they need it or not). Ask them whether they think the changes were well planned and implemented, or just hurriedly implemented as if to check a to-do box.

Take a close look at the associates in your organization. Are they exhausted from their efforts to follow the latest change? Have the changes in the past been followed up with data to show their successes? Have these changes even stuck? Or did the organization revert back to the old way after facing too much resistance in the last attempts to change the organization? Ask the leaders of the previous changes to articulate their successes, as well as their lessons learned. Take advice from the old song and accentuate the positive learnings and eliminate the negative learnings. Table 5.4 shows a simple template you can use to evaluate past initiatives.

Try to gauge whether your organization is ready for the changes associated with DFSS. We worked with one company whose board brought in a slash and burn CEO. In his first year, all employees were told that they were fired (the only one who had a job was the CEO). The CEO then picked his direct reports, who picked their staff and so on based on a new organizational structure designed by the CEO's consultant. The remaining employees were put in a pool, where they were given a month to see if they could find a job in the company. If they couldn't, they were laid off. One of the managers told us that it took two years before his engineers got the courage to try new things; they had all become extremely risk averse. These two years would not have been a good time to try to implement DFSS.

Learn from the mistakes of previous changes so that your implementation team can create a change model that really works.

Table 5.4 Change initiative assessment form.

Change Initiative	
Purpose of Initiative	
What Worked	What Didn't Work
Why?	Why?
Learnings for DFSS Initiative	

Evaluate the weaknesses of your organization and either strengthen them or build around them to ensure that your change doesn't crumble atop those weak pillars. The effort needed to implement and sustain a culture of DFSS is much too great to ignore the resistance.

PLANNING FOR CHANGE

Once you learn how your organization has adjusted (or not) to recent changes, you can make the plans appropriate for your DFSS implementation. If you ignore the history of the organization, the pain it has seen in recent years of change, you are destined to repeat the same mistakes. Take the time to interview a cross-section of folks in the organization. Ask them about recent changes they have seen or implemented (be sure to ask leaders of previously implemented changes for their honest hindsight). Take note of the reasons behind any changes that didn't stick. Then make a plan for your project to counter those influences. Table 5.5 is an example of a change-management analysis. It shows how recent changes failed and what the implementation team will plan to do to make sure this DFSS deployment doesn't fail.

Once you interview a representative cross-section of your organization, you can complete a similar change-management analysis and make the appropriate plans to make the new DFSS process truly stick. A bonus you will get from interviewing people from across your organization is that these folks will get a positive feeling because you are listening to them. They will talk within their subgroups about the impending change, and you get a lot of free advertisement.

Table 5.5 Change-management analysis example.

Top reasons for recent failures (from interviews across the organization)	Steps to avoid failure in this implementation	Responsible team member
It wasn't on my performance plan to change how I did things.	Work with leaders to include new behaviors on performance plans.	Mathews
Some sponsors still wanted to see things the old way.	Educate sponsors first; show them what to expect differently, and show the benefits of the change.	Chen
The policies tell me to do things the old way, and they *have* to be followed, so I don't do things the new way.	Change the policies and procedures to reflect the new process we're putting in place. Train all levels on the new procedures.	Chen
It is just extra work for me, and I don't see any benefit! So why would I waste my time?	Communicate each team's success and benefit (for example, one team that saves $70,000 on prototyping costs; another saves two months in development time).	Connor
I did not have the right people on my team to truly make the change stick. I just did the best I could before I closed out the project.	Ensure a project charter with timeline and team members who will be on the project through completion.	Thomas
My leaders were eager to move me on to the next project, so I left as soon as I could.	Identify metrics that will indicate when the DFSS implementation project can be considered complete.	Mathews

KEY POINTS: DFSS GAP ANALYSIS

This chapter takes you through DMAIEC's Define, Measure, and Analyze steps for your DFSS implementation. By now, you should understand why you want to pursue DFSS, you understand the current development processes in use, and you have performed a gap analysis that tells you which are the most pressing gaps in your organizational structure or your product development process and why these exist.

Your next steps will be to identify, plan, and execute process/structural changes to close these important gaps. Chapter 6 will guide you through the Identify and Execute steps, where you can develop the best DFSS deployment plan and design it to fit your culture. Chapters 7 and 8 will help you complete the Execute step and move into Control phase so you can measure your success and transfer the processes to a sustaining team or structure.

6

Planning, Leading, and Implementing DFSS

INTRODUCTION

Now that you have a good idea of the *gaps* between your current and a DFSS-enabled product development process, it's time to develop your DFSS implementation plan. Because Chapter 5 is dedicated to effective change management (remember, Effectiveness = Quality × Acceptance), let's keep those thoughts fresh as we work through building the specific DFSS plans for your organization.

Unfortunately, we've seen DFSS implementation failures in organizations that thought all they had to do was put up a website, buy everybody a book, or buy some software tools for DFSS to be successful. Giving everyone a hammer and nails won't build you a house. You have to assess the skill level of the organization, understand where those skills need to be, and develop a plan to improve those skills.

Follow the steps outlined here to plan and execute the DFSS implementation in your organization. These steps will drive you to improve the most important gaps first, develop a plan to drive process and structural changes through the organization, and execute against that plan.

PLANNING THE DEPLOYMENT

Based on the gap analysis you developed in Chapter 5, the improvements you need to make to your development process can range over a broad spectrum. You may find that the most important thing you can do is to put a basic development process in place with a disciplined *gate* process. Or, you may find that your basic development

| Step 1: Define DFSS goals & charter DFSS team | Step 2: Understand gaps & prioritize changes; align the organization on need for change | Step 3: Plan the changes, including training plan, intergration plan, and timeline | Step 4: Pilot DFSS process & structural changes, measure results, roll out full-scale changes | Step 5: Monitor & improve the DFSS process | Step 6: Intergrate & sustain the gains |

Figure 6.1 Steps to DFSS implementation.

process is sound, but you need to "install" a better voice of customer process, or include predictions of how manufacturing variation will affect the product CTQs.

Regardless of the scope of your changes, follow a basic change roadmap like the one shown in Figure 6.1 to take the guesswork out of the deployment process steps and focus your efforts on the process and cultural changes needed.

STEP 1. DEFINE DFSS GOALS AND CHARTER YOUR DFSS TEAM

Fully implementing DFSS can be a long journey, one that sometimes doesn't show the first full-project payback for two years. Don't worry; we'll make sure you see some DFSS victories before that—few organizations have the patience to wait more than a few months before seeing that things are getting better.

It is imperative that your leadership demonstrates full support for the implementation of DFSS. To ensure that this support is in place and that everybody is crystal clear about why you're heading down the DFSS path, we strongly recommend that you develop a project charter, with clear timelines and deliverables that your leaders can support. Get the appropriate leadership signatures on your charter. Be sure that everyone understands the commitment of time, money, and resources that will be necessary for DFSS to be implemented.

Show the gains that can be made by implementing DFSS, and refer to those gains often.

The basic elements of your DFSS implementation charter should include:

Problem statement—This should describe what's wrong (that is, the gaps) with the current development process. If this sounds too negative, call it an *opportunity statement*—and focus on which gaps are preventing you from "being all you can be."

Project scope—Using your gap analysis, you've identified and prioritized problems and the changes you need to make. This scope section should include what your implementation team will do—what you will deliver to the organization. Some implementation teams also include an out-of-scope section—things/areas that they aren't going to address.

Metrics/goals—How will you measure the success of your effort? Your gap analysis should give you some clues here. Examples of metrics/goals include reducing product recalls by 90%, reducing stabilization time by 80%, and so on. We'll also address this aspect in detail in Chapter 7.

Project plan/timeline—What are the major milestones in your plan? Five to eight key milestones should be identified. For example, if you decide to use consultants to help you, the last milestone is *DFSS Independence*—that's when you can sustain DFSS processes and performance on your own.

Just include the major milestones here in the charter; you'll develop and use a more detailed plan for day-to-day activities. It's also a good idea to include the resources required to achieve the milestones, both staff and dollars. Think through the resources along the timeline. Examples of milestones may include:

- When you will begin to train associates in DFSS
- When you will deploy software for simulation and requirements management
- When you expect to see the first teams launching new products using the new development process

In your detailed plan, you'll break out what's required to achieve each milestone.

Team members—Your charter should include the members of the implementation team and the time commitment needed for each of those members. We recommend at least one dedicated team member to lead the implementation, and any other team members to be at least 50% dedicated. In our experience, anybody who is dedicated less than 25% of their time quickly turns into a reality of 0% dedicated.

The time it takes to implement DFSS can vary from 6 months to 2 years or more, depending upon how "broken" the organization is to start with and how dedicated the implementation team is. The time it takes to implement DFSS also depends on your definitions of "complete." Your charter's scope should define what "complete" looks like.

Champions and sponsors—The charter should include who will *champion* the effort (champions bring passion to the table) and sponsor the DFSS effort (sponsors bring dollars and resources). If you have trouble gaining this support, stop right now! Do not proceed until this issue is resolved! As part of the chartering process, you should spell out what your needs and expectations are of your champion's and sponsor's behaviors. Just as your team needs to know what's expected of them, champions and sponsors need to know their roles.

Your charter may go a few rounds of catch-ball before its ready to sign. *Catch-ball* is simply the process of negotiation that will occur among you, your team, and your sponsors/champions to agree on the goals, scope, timeline, and resources associated with DFSS implementation. When everybody is comfortable with the charter, have a signing ceremony—and record it with pictures/video so you've got evidence.

Table 6.1 shows an example project charter for a DFSS implementation team. It is important to properly scope the charter and identify who is on the team, how much time they are dedicated to give, and what your results are expected to be.

Table 6.1 DFSS implementation team charter.

Company X—DFSS implementation project charter	
Problem statement	**Project scope**
New product development teams need consistent tools and roadmap to follow to optimize the new product development process at Company X. Developing and deploying a robust New Product Development Process, training structure, and integration plan will reduce start-up time and scrap and will enable associates to adopt and use the DFSS process quickly.	Integrate DFSS with existing quality system. Develop and implement metrics to assess teams' ability to follow the DFSS process. Develop and implement training material, training plan, and structure for sustainability.
Metrics/benefits	**Project plan/timeline**
Process Utilization • Number of people trained • NPD "independence" survey results • NPD assessment results Process efficiency • Reduce stabilization time from 1 month average to 1 week average Process effectiveness • Reduce scrap rate from 2% average to 0.5% average	Define: December 20XX Measure: January 20XX Analyze: February 20XX Identify: March 20XX Execute: March 20XX through July 20XX Control: October 20XX
Team members Jane Mathews, R&D—Full-time project lead Joe Thomas, operations—Full-time project member Tom Connor, process excellence—Part-time member (50%) Amy Chen, marketing—Part-time member (50%) Dan Patel, communications liaison	**Champion** Mark Martin, vice president R&D **Project sponsors** Mary Jones, VP operations Kim Reynolds, VP marketing Duane Thomas, VP human resources

STEP 2. UNDERSTAND GAPS AND PRIORITIZE CHANGES; ALIGN THE ORGANIZATION

We devoted Chapter 5 to this subject, conducting a gap analysis and identifying the most pressing needs to focus on now. It is hard to imagine any organization that can dedicate sufficient resources to attack all of the areas needed at once.

In Chapter 5 you conducted an objective gap analysis within your organization. You know the process and structural changes that need to be made. You also conducted a *stakeholder analysis*—identifying who's supportive and who's resistive to the changes.

As far as aligning the organization goes, there are three "market segments" to consider. First, we'll address the senior leadership segment. With a signed-off charter, you've already got a core group of senior leaders engaged. They already know your team's goals and scope. Make sure you remind them of this often—communicate with them frequently about what's going on in the world of DFSS. (Two strategies are to use an existing management meeting—for example, get on the agenda for their monthly meeting—or *charter* the senior leaders as your DFSS steering committee).

The second segment includes the other leaders/managers in your organization. If the number of these is large, you may schedule a series of meetings to present your case (these must be either conducted by your champion/sponsorship team or at least kicked-off and closed by them).

For one organization, we found that a four-hour DFSS leadership session was enough to present the *case* for DFSS, the *plans* for bringing DFSS into the development processes, and the *answers* to participants' questions. The high-level objectives for this session included:

- Discuss and identify the DFSS business case for the organization.
- Describe DFSS, including the DMADVI roadmap.
- Know when to use DFSS vs. DMAIEC vs. lean thinking.
- Identify the DFSS methodology by phase with key inputs, tools, and outputs.
- Describe the leaders' roles for successful deployment.

The third segment includes the rest of the organization: development staff, engineers, designers, and support staff (quality, regulatory, configuration control, and others). Don't think that you have to convince everybody that DFSS is the best thing since sliced bread. Use the idea of a *change distribution,* shown in Figure 6.2.

You probably recognize this basic model. Some of us are *innovators;* we'll adopt the newest electronic widget the day it's released. The *early adopters* among us are quick to adopt change, but we aren't quite willing to be on the bleeding edge of change. *Late adopters* will come along eventually, but they need to see a lot of evidence that "it" works. Finally, there are some *resistors,* who will never get on the train.

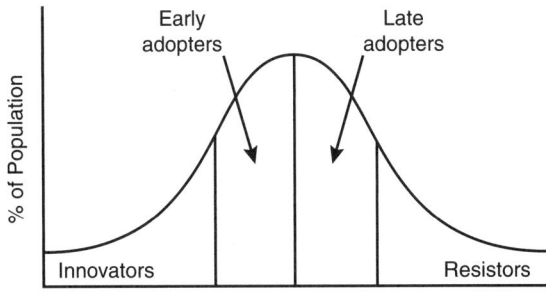

Figure 6.2 Change distribution.

Applying this idea of *change distribution,* focus your alignment efforts. Find the innovators and solicit their support first. They may already be allies and be willing to be the first to try the changes that DFSS will bring to the development process. As a start, remember who was excited about improving the development process when you did the gap analysis interviews. If these individuals are respected in the organization and are willing to help, you've taken a solid first step toward aligning this third segment.

STEP 3. PLAN THE CHANGES

There's a very old saying in woodworking: *Measure twice, cut once.* You're not going to be cutting any wood, but you will be asking people to change the way they do things. You'll likely get some leeway from the organization to redirect your efforts when (not if) you make implementation mistakes, but if there are too many missteps, then the sharks in your organization will start to circle. It is vital to your deployment team's success that you plan the implementation well and even do some contingency planning. Let's look at the typical implementation plan components.

Integration Plan

The integration plan includes the process and structural changes that you've identified in your gap analysis. We call this an integration plan because we're challenging you to integrate these changes into the day-to-day work of the development teams. For example, after a successful pilot of charters, all development teams at one company were required to create project charters before proceeding further into development.

A large conglomerate promoted DFSS in its divisions. After about two years of work, a progress audit by the corporate DFSS promotion group found a distinct lack of integration. For the divisions that were not regulated (by the Food and Drug Administration in this case), most development groups were trying to balance two processes—the normal development processes and DFSS. For the regulated divisions, they had not only the first two, but also the quality system demanded by the FDA, You can imagine the confusion! In this organization, there were only two divisions that *got it* – meaning that they had done the up-front work to integrate DFSS into their development processes. The development teams in these divisions could then focus on learning and applying one process.

Think through all that's needed to implement a process or structural change. For example, one of the key DFSS process changes often involves predicting how manufacturing variation transmits up to the CTQs.

The first part of making this change involves deciding where in the design process to include this prediction. Generally, the team will need to know something about the product's parts, along with their fabrication and assembly processes. Typically, this prediction activity will fall in DMADVI's Design step.

Second, these predictions require knowledge of a *transfer function*—the $Y = f(X)$ relationship from parts and process to the CTQ. Even though a transfer function seems like something every engineer should know how to develop, we've found that teams need help, at least the first couple of times. So your change plan should include an *intervention* with teams to help them develop their cascade and associated transfer functions. Building these transfer functions will start in the Analyze step and continue *maturing* in the Design step.

Third, to move variation from the Xs to the CTQ will often require Monte Carlo simulation. For example, we've used both Decisioneering's Crystal Ball and Cognition's Mechanical Advantage software to perform these simulations. Your implementation plan must then include the software selection process, training, and application support for the chosen Monte Carlo tool.

Fourth, the simulations will require data on fabrication and assembly *variation.* Who "owns" this data in your organization? Is it even being collected today? Your implementation plan may take a phased approach here. Phase 1, for example, may use generic variation data for predictions. For example, the Society for Plastics Engineers publishes information on tolerances one can expect when molding different plastics and Todd, Allen, and Alting's *Manufacturing Processes Reference Guide* provides tolerance information for wide variety of mechanical, thermal, chemical, and other processes. While your development teams are becoming proficient at variation prediction, a DFSS infrastructure project will have developed a database of variation data specific to your fabrication/assembly processes. Phase 2 will transition from generic to specific data.

Finally, what should the teams do with the results of the predictions? What's the decision process? For example, if the design scorecard has a value of 6 for the targeted Sigma Level of a particular CTQ, what happens if the prediction results in a value of 5.8? Is this close enough?

Your integration plan needs to consider all of these change elements.

Training and Pilot Plan

Skill building will be required. You need to think through who needs training and what they need to know, when they need to know it, and how those skill sets will be gained and then applied. Table 6.2 provides a sample training strategy that considers *who, what,* and *how.*

Apply *adult learning principles* to your training plan. One of the principles that we learned at GE is to make DFSS training action oriented. For example, the price of admission to the Green Belt training shown in Table 6.2 is a DFSS project charter. Each participant is expected to apply the tools and methods to a real development project. No charter, no training! People aren't trained by going to a lecture. They are trained by learning and immediately applying the process.

For companies with a short development cycle time, this project can be an end-to-end product development (charter to product launch). For those with longer development cycle times, candidate Green Belts may carve out a piece of the project, for example a subsystem, subassembly, or part design. Some of the project charters have focused on designing key steps in the production process or even measurement systems that were needed by the development team.

Another learning principle we apply is *mentorship.* Each Green Belt candidate will have a sponsor who cares about the project from a business perspective. For example, the product development team leader will typically sponsor a Green Belt's design project. In addition, the Green Belt candidate will have a mentor who can help guide him or her through the DFSS process after the training session. Typically, these mentors are DFSS Black or Master Black Belts, who

Table 6.2 Example of DFSS training strategy.

Who	What	How
Senior leaders (sponsors and champions)	Overview of DFSS/DMADVI process	DFSS executive briefing (4 hours)
	DFSS-specific tools and methods	Monthly tool briefings (20 minutes/briefing)
	Reviewing DFSS team output	DFSS Master Black Belt partnering
Product development team leaders	Overview of DFSS/DMADVI process	DFSS team leader briefing (4 hours)
	"Just-in-time" application to development project	Individual DMADVI step workouts for individual teams (3–4 hours/workout)
Product developers (including support staff—packaging, regulatory, others)	Details of DFSS/DMADVI process and associated methods (chartering, VOC, concepting, cascade, design of experiments, variation transmission, Design for X, reliability management, verification and validation methods)	DFSS Green Belt training (10 days)
Product designers	Overview of DFSS/DMADVI process and designers' role in DFSS	DMADVI for designers overview (2 days)
Suppliers	Overview of DFSS/DMADVI process	DMADVI for suppliers (1 day overview)
	Specific DFSS tools and methods	DFSS modules (delivered by Master Black Belts, 2–3 hours/module)

have demonstrated their DFSS capabilities. Early in your implementation, you may need to contract externally for these services.

DFSS is both a broad and a deep body of knowledge. Expect your Black Belts and Master Black Belts to develop a broad view of DFSS— that is, their main function is to help teams and training participants work through the process. Deep knowledge of particular tools/methods can reside with the Black and Master Black Belts, but you may also enlist the help of subject matter experts (SME). We often find that these deep skills already exist in the organization (a benefit from all the other improvement initiatives your company has embraced!). A few SMEs that we'd like to have in our organization include:

- Voice of customer gathering/requirements translation (for example, QFD)

- Advanced concepting tools (for example, theory of inventive problem-solving, or TRIZ)
- Measurement systems
- Statistical analysis (for example, design of experiments)
- Industrial design/human factors
- Reliability prediction and testing
- Simulation (for example, finite element analysis)
- Process control system planning
- Verification and validation testing
- Project planning and control
- Risk assessment and mitigation planning (for example, failure mode and effects analyses, fault tree analysis)

Look around and see if you can find these SMEs in your company. Ask them whether they are willing to support the DFSS effort and then make sure their management agrees. There should be some sort of *win* for both the SME and his or her manager here. Make sure people are aware that these SMEs exist and are available to help. For example, one organization's SMEs have plaques outside their offices, noting that they are DFSS SMEs and where their skills lie. Another organization includes the SMEs as "guest" trainers on their specific topic.

You may have to engage external support if SMEs don't exist in your company (or can't support you). It's generally not hard to find consultants who are specialists in this or that tool. Be careful, though, in how you ask them to deliver their message. For example, one consultant in voice of customer methods had been told by a company's DFSS implementation group that the existing VOC process was very broken. When she presented her approach to the market research group, she assumed that they knew the process was broken, too! Her presentation, then, focused on completely replacing the existing process with hers. The market research group was completely alienated by her seemingly arrogant attitude. Even though her VOC method was considered a best practice, DFSS implementation team had significant damage control to do after her visit. Lesson learned: Be careful and don't assume.

Consider *flexibility* and *customization* in your training plan. Many of the DFSS tools have been around for a while. You may find that people already know how to use tools such as design of experiments.

For one organization, we designed the training curriculum so that people could decide which topics they needed, based on their previous skills and experience. While this strategy can work in a mature Six Sigma company, we found in another case that some of the associates just thought they knew the topic and would encourage the instructor to move quickly through the material. However, the implementation team saw that the know-it-alls were actually applying the tools poorly in practice. The implementation team constantly reminded the DFSS instructor of this fact.

You might also consider DFSS skill development as a growth path from elementary DFSS skills through graduate-level skills. Junior engineers should master certain skills, senior engineers others, and product development leaders still others.

Consider whether you want to certify your staff after they've completed the DFSS training and demonstrated competency. Six Sigma initiatives generally include certification as a Green, Black, or Master Black Belt. These same skill and leadership levels have been applied to DFSS. One company's DFSS Belt certification standards are listed in Table 6.3.

Green Belt training provides core DFSS skills. Here, participants learn the overall DFSS/DMADVI method and associated tools that they will apply in product development. Tables 6.4 through 6.6 show you the agendas for a nine-day Green Belt DFSS program. This agenda assumes that the participants have either taken the organization's Six Sigma Green Belt course or a "primer," which provides basic Six Sigma concepts and tools. Notice that the second and third sessions include project presentations so participants can share progress on their projects.

Even though DFSS is a mature development method, you'll want to gain some company-specific experience through a pilot test of your changes. Who will you use as a pilot team? This team should have strong, open-minded engineers, and maybe one or two outspoken DFSS critics that can be turned into early advocates once they see the process work. The team should have a strong leader who supports the DFSS efforts and will demonstrate that support at all times during the learning process.

As you work through the pilot or lead DFSS teams, you'll develop a timeline for training the other development teams in your organization. This, in turn, will help you identify the resources needed to support the full-scale training and mentoring. While filling out the full-scale training spreadsheet is needed for scheduling purposes, there are a number of additional benefits. The spreadsheet also becomes a communication tool for teams. Team A can see where

Table 6.3 Example of DFSS certification requirements.

DFSS certification	Requirements
Green Belt	• Attend Six Sigma *Primer* or Six Sigma Green Belt *Training* • Attend DFSS Green Belt *Training* (score minimum of 70% in each session's quiz) • Complete DFSS Project (may be a subset of a product development effort), demonstrate application of required tools and agreed-to validation tools) • Demonstrate technical competency (review panel includes project sponsor and mentor)
Black Belt	• Attend Six Sigma Green Belt training (score minimum of 70% in each session's quiz) • Attend DFSS Green Belt training (score minimum of 70% in each session's quiz) • Lead and complete DFSS project (may be a subset of a product development effort), demonstrate application of required tools and agreed-to validation tools) • Demonstrate technical and leadership competency (local review panel includes project sponsor, mentor, and Master Black Belt, followed by corporate review panel)
Master Black Belt	• DFSS Black Belt certified • Mentor at least 10 DFSS Green (or Black) Belt projects • Make a significant contribution to advancing DFSS state of the art for the division • Demonstrate DFSS technical and leadership mastery (corporate review panel)

they are relative to Team B. Team E can see that Team D is ahead of them slightly, so their team members might wander over and talk to Team D's members to get some help or advice.

You also get a communication tool for management. We have yet to see an organization whose management wasn't concerned with the pace of deployment. For the most part, they want to see as

Table 6.4 Design for Six Sigma Green Belt course agenda—session 1.

Session 1	Day 1	Day 2	Day 3
8:00–10:00	• 0.1 Course introduction and overview • Participant introductions and case study selection	• Review • 2.1 Gather VOC (continued—interviewing) • 2.2 Translate to product requirements	• Review • 2.3 Managing critical parameters and design scorecards (continued) • 2.4 Measure review
10:00–10:15	Break	Break	Break
10:15–12:00	• **1.0 Define intro** • 1.1 Product planning and charter development	• 2.2 Translate to product requirements (continued—QFD)	• **3.0 Analyze intro** • 3.1 Concept generation and selection
12:00–1:00	Lunch	Lunch	Lunch
1:00–3:00	• 1.2 Generational planning • 1.3 Project planning and controls • 1.4 Define phase review	• 2.2 Translate to product requirements (continued—QFD, image diagrams)	• 3.1 Concept generation and selection (continued) • Individual/team—organize session work/planning for next session
3:00–3:15	Break	Break	Break
3:15–4:20	• **2.0 Measure intro** • 2.1 Gather VOC (quality function deployment process overview and customer identification)	• 2.3 Managing critical parameters and design scorecards	• Summary and going forward • Session 1 quiz • Evaluation
4:20–4:30	Summary and evaluation	Summary and evaluation	

Table 6.5 Design for Six Sigma Green Belt course agenda—session 2.

Session 2	Day 1	Day 2	Day 3
8:00–10:00	• Review and agenda • 3.1 Concept generation and selection (continued) • 3.1 Design for "X" presentations	• Review • 3.3d Feasibility–advanced DOE (robust design and response surface methods)	• Review • 3.4 Reliability-analyze phase
10:00–10:15	Break	Break	Break
10:15–12:00	• 3.2 Cascade and flowdown • 3.3 Feasibility overview	• 3.3d Feasibility–advanced DOE (response surface methods)	• 3.5 Risk management (process and hazard analysis)
12:00–1:00	Lunch	Lunch	Lunch
1:00–3:00	• Project presentations (1/3) • 3.3a Feasibility-analytic • 3.3b Feasibility-simulation	• Project presentations (1/3) • 3.3d Feasibility–advanced DOE (response surface designs)	• Project presentations (1/3) • Individual/team—organize session work/planning for next session
3:00–3:15	Break	Break	Break
3:15–4:20	• 3.3c Feasibility—DOE • 3.3d Feasibility-advanced DOE (screening designs)	• 3.3d Feasibility—advanced DOE (response surface designs and mixture overview)	• Going forward • Session 2 quiz • Evaluation
4:20–4:30	Summary and evaluation	Summary and evaluation	

Table 6.6 Design for Six Sigma Green Belt course agenda—session 3.

Session 3	Day 1	Day 2	Day 3
8:00–10:00	• Review and agenda • 3.5 Risk management (FMEA and fault trees)	• Review • 4.2 Variation transmission (continued) • 4.3 Proactive reliability—design	• Review • 4.5 Process simulation • 4.6 Process controls
10:00–10:15	Break	Break	Break
10:15–12:00	• 3.6 Analyze review • **4.0 Design intro** • 4.1 Product design-cascade	• 4.3 Proactive reliability—design (continued) • 4.4 Process development	• 4.7 Process reliability • 4.8 Design review • **5.0 Verify—big picture**
12:00–1:00	Lunch	Lunch	Lunch
1:00–3:00	• Project presentations (1/3) • 4.2 Variation transmission	• Project presentations (1/3) • 4.4 Process development (continued)	• Project presentations (1/3) • 5.1 Verify and validate
3:00–3:15	Break	Break	Break
3:15–4:20	• 4.2 Variation transmission (continued)	• 4.4 Process development (continued)	• Going forward planning graduation • Session 3 quiz • Evaluation
4:20–4:30	Summary and evaluation	Summary and evaluation	

many people trained as possible. You now have a communication tool that shows management the training schedule in black and white. There is nothing to argue over once you show this schedule. If you are delivering workshops just-in-time, you can deliver each phase workshop only when a team is in that phase. Table 6.7 shows an example of a training schedule, showing both when the teams were actually trained and when the teams are due to be trained. Note that this is not intended to show the slippage of a training schedule; rather, it is meant to provide the planning tool for your trainers to see when resources are needed for training. Because the just-in-time training concept works best in our experiences, you can schedule training around teams' project plans. In our experiences, leaders have focused on training as a measurement in the short term, as there is little else to measure early on. A table like this will help at least show the progress of training for those eager to see something measurable out of the DFSS deployment.

Going Live with DFSS

How will you integrate the new DFSS processes into an existing development pipeline? It's easy for new development projects; they can follow the DFSS process from the beginning. But what about the teams who are in the middle of product development? We faced this issue with one organization and adopted a *grandfathering* approach. Because this organization was regulated and followed a design control process, the designs-in-progress continued to use the existing development process. We met with the teams, though, and discussed how they might take advantage of DFSS processes moving forward. Nobody was forced to go back and redo development work, but some teams chose to do so.

For example, one team that was close to ordering tools got excited about the idea of predicting variation. Although they really didn't have a good set of CTQs, they used the design requirements that they were going to verify through testing. During a two-day workout, the team built transfer functions and predicted how manufacturing variation would affect their requirements. From a risk perspective, some of the requirements' predictions came out *green*, some *yellow*, and some *red*. The team revised the design, addressing all of the *red* issues and as many of the *yellow* as possible. The team then ordered tools with a much higher confidence in their design and actually saved development time, because the tools came in right the first time.

Two outcomes of this example are worth noting. First, by applying pieces of the DFSS process, this organization gained experience,

Table 6.7 DFSS training timeline.

Team Training Schedule

Phase	Define	Measure	Analyze	Design Transfer	Design	Verify/Implement
Workshop	NPD	CTQs	Concept selection	Transfer Functions	CTQ scorecard	CTQ scorecard
Project	Charter	Defined	CTQs, cascade		Predicted capability	Actual capability
A	Dec-05	Feb-06	May-06	Jun-06	due Aug 06	due Dec 06
B	Dec-05	Feb-06	May-06	due Jul 06	due Sept 06	due Dec 06
C	none	Nov-05	Dec-05	Jan-06	Mar-06	Jun-06
D	none	Oct-05	Dec-05	Feb-06	May-06	Jul-06
E	Nov-05	Jan-06	Feb-06	Apr-06	Jun-06	due Sept 06
F	Jan-06	Mar-06	Apr-06	Jun-06	due Aug 06	due Oct 06
G	none	Oct-05	Dec-05	Feb-06	Apr-06	Jul-06
H	none	Oct-05	Jan-06	Mar-06	May-06	Jul-06
I	none	Nov-05	Jan-06	Jan-06	May-06	Jul-06
J	Oct-05	Dec-05	Feb-06	May-06	Jun-06	due Sept 06
K	Mar-06	Jun-06	due Sept 06	due Nov 06	due Dec 06	due Feb 07
L	May-06	due Jul 06	due Oct 06	due Dec 06	due Jan 07	due Mar 07
M	Nov-05	Dec-05	Feb-06	Apr-06	Jun-06	due Sept 06
Leadership	Oct-05	Dec-05	Jan-06	Jan-06	Jan-06	Feb-06

Those with "none" were too far past the phase to receive workshop training.
Others might have had the first workshop training in the middle or toward the end of the phase, so the benefit of the training may not be as strong as if they would have gone through the workshop at an earlier point in that phase.

confidence and, most importantly, early results! Second, because of the organizational buzz that resulted from the workout, other teams started talking about doing their own prediction workouts. In fact, the manufacturing staff who attended the workout went back to their plant and told their friends about the workout. The very next week, other teams were getting calls from their manufacturing team members with the question, "When do we get to do our predictions?"

Success Measures

As you develop your implementation plans, consider how you will measure DFSS success. Review your charter goals and metrics—these are the outputs or Ys you are trying to accomplish. Make sure there are measurement systems in place for these. Consider also early or in-process measures—your organization will see *movement* of these indicators much sooner (Chapter 7 will cover this metrics topic in more detail). How will you communicate the success? What else does it take for your organization to internalize DFSS? Now you see why the deployment team can't be a one-man band.

DFSS Drivers and Accountability

In most organizations where we've seen DFSS successfully implemented, the implementation plan was divided into deployment elements (the drivers of DFSS internalization) and these, in turn, were assigned to the deployment team members. An example of the drivers of success and their division is shown in the X–Y chart in Figure 6.3. Your X–Y chart may look very different than this example, depending on the exact needs of your organization.

It is a helpful exercise for your deployment team to identify the success drivers (the little y's) early in your process, and then revisit them as you know more about the specific needs in your organization, allowing you to fill in the details contributing factors (the x's). Identifying the "owner" of each driver is also a critical success factor. Each team member should wake up every morning with a sharp focus on the driver for which he or she is responsible.

DFSS Budget

As you develop your plan, somebody in your company will likely ask, "What will this cost?" Table 6.8 provides the basic elements you'll include in the DFSS implementation budget.

126 Chapter Six

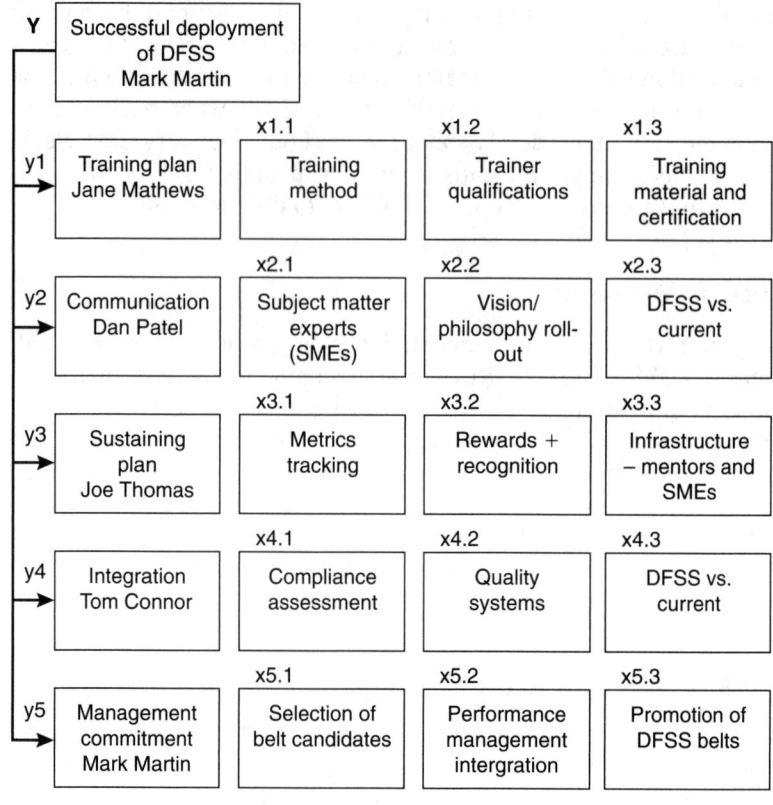

Figure 6.3 Examples of DFSS success drivers and owners.

Consultant Support

By now, you may be a bit overwhelmed by all that's needed. First, remember to prioritize your DFSS changes. It may take a bit longer to get there, but we've found that it's much better to learn to do a few things well rather than try to do all things poorly. You may, though, decide that you need some external help. Think through this carefully, before you pull the consultant trigger! What do you want them to help you with? How will you manage their interaction with your organization?

For example, while working with General Electric, we observed that the company used consultants to help develop the Six Sigma training materials, to work with early teams (quickly achieving success),

Table 6.8 DFSS implementation plan budget elements.

Budget Item	Description	Cost Basis
Implementation team	Internal costs associated with the time spent by the DFSS implementation team. External costs if a consultant's support is necessary.	Number of team members multiplied by time dedicated to implementation activities, consultant fees, and travel and living expenses. Supporting resource costs (policies and procedures group, IT staff costs, human resources staff costs).
Education and training	Costs to develop or license DFSS training materials, delivery costs including instructor, facility, travel (if necessary) and logistics (training material reproduction, flipcharts, certificates, other materials). Cost to maintain DFSS materials (as your development process matures). Costs associated with "Belt" certification (time, travel). Include labor/cost of trainers as well as associates being trained. Cost to purchase DFSS books and other materials.	Development or license cost. Instructor cost/session (include travel and living expense if external) Facility rental (include room, lunch, breaks). Material costs (include books, binders, or CDs and other support materials). Number of "Belts" to certify times the certification cost per belt.
DFSS support software	Costs to license or purchase software (examples include QFD, statistical analysis, Monte Carlo simulation, finite element, requirements management, parts capability database, materials database, mold fill analysis).	Cost per software license or volume cost of licenses. Training costs for software (may overlap with training budget). Computer hardware (if necessary). IT staff support.
Mentoring/consulting	Internal costs of DFSS Black or Master Black Belts hired/assigned to coach teams. Internal costs of subject matter experts' time. External costs if a consultant's support is necessary.	X mentors multiplied by time dedicated to implementation activities, consultant fees, and travel and living expenses (this may overlap with implementation team costs).
Promotion and communication	Costs to promote DFSS within the organization (wall posters, DFSS contest prizes, booklets, DFSS trinkets) and communicate DFSS (website development and maintenance, newsletter production).	Production or purchase costs.

and to do the heavy lifting of training as Six Sigma was rolled out through the company. After this initial implementation period, the consultants were phased out and GE Master Black Belts (MBBs) assumed the training role.

On the other hand, some organizations we've seen continue to employ external consultants for DFSS training. Their view is that the MBBs should devote their time to team coaching and, because DFSS training doesn't occur that frequently, the consultant can be a more effective delivery mechanism.

STEP 4. PILOT DFSS CHANGES, MEASURE RESULTS, ROLL OUT FULL-SCALE CHANGES

By now, you've identified the success drivers and the plan to get you there, so it's time to go implement. Starting with your pilot team, explain the new process to the organization. Don't forget to train your leadership. They need to be armed with the knowledge of what is different. They need to see the key differences to expect in their teams' behaviors as they pass through each new DFSS phase. Leaders need to be asking the right questions of the teams, and they need to know the difference between right and wrong answers.

One element of General Electric's Six Sigma success is the knowledge possessed by the senior leadership. When senior leaders made visits, they asked all the right questions, not because they were spoon-fed key questions to ask, but because they were trained on what Six Sigma success looked like. They asked probing questions of Green and Black Belts and listened for the right answers. If they heard wrong answers, associates were quickly made aware of the observed gaps.

On the other hand, we had the unfortunate experience of training another company's teams in DFSS. Although we offered many times, the responsible manager refused our help in coaching the teams through their projects. One day, we received a call from the manager asking whether we could certify the team members as Green Belts. When we took a look at their projects, we found that there was no voice of customer, the design solutions hadn't changed since the day that they walked into class, one of the projects included a half-finished FMEA (that was done during the class), and there was no data that the designs did what they were intended to do—that is, no verification work. When we asked whether they could at least collect some data on how well the designs performed, the manager stated that they didn't have time. The discussion got a bit heated (on the manager's side), but we could not certify these individuals.

You've no doubt heard the phrase "what gets measured gets done." This holds true when senior leaders engage in "measuring" the success of their teams. Teams that know their leadership is advocating use of the DFSS roadmap and tools will follow that roadmap and use the tools. Teams that think leadership is just spoon-fed representative questions will soon learn those questions and the "right" answers. So do your organization a favor and train your leadership so the questions come from knowledge rather than a script!

STEP 5. MONITOR AND IMPROVE THE DFSS PROCESS

You can develop a well-thought-out plan before you roll out the new DFSS process, but always expect it to need a few course corrections. As you implement the training, listen to feedback from the workshops. Are you focusing on the right things in the workshops? Are you going too quickly or slowly? Are you taking teams through workshops at the wrong time? What are people saying about the workshops as a whole?

What about the mentoring that is being done outside of the workshops? Do you have enough mentors? Are those mentors trained? Are people hearing too many different answers? In one organization, we found that teams were hearing different answers from different mentors and leaders. It turned out that we were not training the mentors and leaders fast enough. So the mentors and leaders were left to guess at some of the answers. We made an immediate course correction and trained the mentors and leadership on the entire process, also developing a guide that eliminated some of the guesswork. We published the guide on the company's intranet so anyone who needed it could get answers quickly.

Keep your eyes and ears open! Even when you think the organization is starting to *get it,* you'll find examples of old ways creeping back in and misunderstandings about how the process works. For example, one organization spent a significant amount of energy changing the VOC/requirements definition process. The training was clear about how to develop a "solution-open" requirement—it should be stated in terms of a product function (not a solution or feature), with an associated metric that defined how well the function needed to be performed. Mentors skilled in the process worked with teams to help them through the requirements definition process.

One day, though, we were discussing a product's CTQs with a couple of team members. They initially approached us because they were struggling with the idea of design cascade. When we looked at their design scorecard, we quickly realized that they had gotten off track. One of their CTQs was really a product feature and another was stated in go/no-go terms. No wonder cascade was difficult for them; it's hard to write a transfer function for a feature.

We'll spend a lot more time on measuring success and improving the DFSS process in Chapter 7.

STEP 6. INTEGRATE AND SUSTAIN THE GAINS

Once you have reached a level of success in the pilot deployment of DFSS, you are ready to integrate the necessary elements into your organization's framework. Do you follow a quality system like ISO-9000, or are you subject to a design control process from a regulator such as the U.S. Food and Drug Administration or the Nuclear Regulatory Commission? If so, get your policies and procedures out and be sure they are rewritten to incorporate DFSS into the new product development process. If DFSS is something on the side, it will never become part of your DNA! Here, as the DFSS expert, you will partner with the design control expert to integrate the methods. You don't want to wind up with a great DFSS process and then be cited because you missed an important design control issue that your regulator cares about.

What do your rewards and recognition programs look like? Be sure they include proper reward and recognition for following the DFSS process and achieving business results through DFSS. Some organizations reward their Green and Black Belts upon certification; others have a formal recognition process and an understanding that future leaders will be trained as Green or Black Belts.

Chapter 8 is dedicated to integrating the DFSS process into your culture and sustaining the gains made.

DOs AND DON'TS TO SUCCESSFUL DFSS IMPLEMENTATION

Simply following the steps to make a change happen will not guarantee you a successful implementation. In our work with and on DFSS deployment teams, we have found some factors that have contributed to success, as well as a few things that haven't led to success (putting the latter nicely). We'll share both with you here.

DOs TO SUCCESSFUL DFSS IMPLEMENTATION

We have identified four keys to successful DFSS implementation into any organization:

1. Do use Six Sigma thinking and methods to develop and design your deployment process and structure.
2. Do look at the cultural needs of your organization and design the processes and structures to fit your culture and your business needs.
3. Do use a cross-functional implementation team for maximum and quickest results.
4. Do use a "pilot team" to focus your early efforts and receive immediate and direct feedback.

Let's look at each of these elements in detail.

1. Do use Six Sigma thinking and methods to develop your deployment process and structure. Put as much rigor into the development of the DFSS structure as you would any other "product" you develop. DFSS implementation is your chance to make a critical change to the organization; plan it well and implement it with rigor and purpose. The best chance you have to make this work is to charter your own implementation team as a Six Sigma project. Starting with the gap analysis of Chapter 5, we've been leading you through DMAIEC's Define, Measure and Analyze steps—applied to your current new product development process. This chapter has focused on the Identify (changes) step and the "doing" part of the Execute step. Chapters 7 and 8 will help you complete the Execute step and move into the Control phase for your process improvements.

Starting with the appropriate project charter and support from your DFSS champions, make sure that you gather the voice of the customer (your organization in this case) and measure where your organization is along the way to DFSS maturity. Before you make changes, ensure that you understand the root causes of why your development process is not performing well today and design, test, and implement process changes that address these root causes. Finally, make sure that you measure the results of your changes and that the effective changes become part of your organization's DNA.

2. Do look at the cultural needs of your organization and design the processes and structures to fit your culture and your business needs. DFSS has a core roadmap and tools that are helpful and that have been applied "out of the box," but don't just try to copy what others have done or become a slave to any terminology, method, or tools you find in this book or any other source. Some people find comfort or security in being able to refer to some industry standard process or by following some published methodology. However, if this doesn't work for your organization, design your process to make it work for you. If your product development process has four or six phases instead of five, and the milestones are clearly marked, continue to use your phases. If, on the other hand, each team's interpretation of the milestones is different, you may want to force the radical change to new names and phases. In one organization, that is exactly what we did.

We've seen teams in one organization follow a very document-centric process. Doing so, they became so bogged down in the bureaucracy of the process that they forgot the number one purpose of product development is to get the right product to the customer and make money. It turned out that, in order to make any development process work in that organization, we had to destroy the old product development process and replace it with a brand new one, "shocking" the system back to life.

Another key cultural element is your organization's need for direction. If your culture needs every step detailed, then you should follow that level of detail through as you design your DFSS process. If your culture thrives on flexibility, allow for that flexibility in the DFSS process. There is a common misconception that you can't have a defined process if you want to remain flexible. We submit that you can indeed be flexible *and* have a process. Think of what it takes to build a house. You need the architectural structure rigorous enough to withstand the elements of weight, wind, and wear. But there can be flexibility on where the walls are built and how high the ceilings will be. The builder's solid structural base and rules for construction allow for ease of customization for each homeowner. Now there are some plans that may have every last detail, down to the faucet color and cupboard handles detailed out, allowing the builder to blanket-order materials, do exactly the same thing on every single house, and not even have to think. Other builders simply start with a blank sheet of paper and start asking the homeowner what they want; one story or two, vaulted ceilings, big rooms or little rooms. You have to determine where your organization falls within that spectrum.

Our final advice on this topic concerns the DFSS tools you bring into your organization's development toolkit. Many of our clients, for example, use quality function deployment to provide the structure and method of gathering customer needs and translating them to requirements. One of our favorite little measure step "jingles" is "You take the VOC and use QFD to get your CTQs!" There's no law, though, that says you have to use QFD in DFSS. After several years of use, one organization abandoned QFD in favor of a better approach (for their business needs!). They kept the function of gathering customer voices and translating them into product requirements, but they changed the method by which that function was performed.

3. Do use a cross-functional implementation team. The use of a cross-functional implementation team is *not* an option if you want a sustainable DFSS process. We've seen organizations assign one Black Belt or Master Black Belt to implement DFSS by themselves, only to see that almost nothing is different a year later or even two years later. The implementation team does not need to be 10 or 15 people; it just needs to have fair representation from the key elements of the organization. Look at your stakeholder analysis you performed in Chapter 5. Your engineering, research and development, manufacturing/operations, and marketing groups should have voices in the process. The best way to ensure that voice is heard is to have a representative from these areas on your implementation team. In the end, the DFSS process you put into place has to satisfy the needs of all of these areas, so take the shortest route to success, by putting all the right people on your team.

This can prove to be quite a challenge, as you want each team member to have the respect of his or her peers. But everyone wants the top players to be on *their* special project. That is one more reason why the change-management aspect of this implementation is so important. The most important stakeholders need to be so committed to this implementation that they are willing to release their best resources to be on your team. We have seen organizations where this has worked, and we have seen organizations that have not allowed it to work this way. Inevitably, the companies that succeeded in their implementation gave up their best resources for a year or more to focus on deploying DFSS. It was quite a short-term sacrifice for some of the leaders. But they showed their commitment to DFSS by making that sacrifice, and it paid off in every instance. In organizations where leaders did not make such a commitment, the DFSS deployment team (or single person, in some cases) seemed to hit resistance in every direction.

Of course it is hard to determine the root cause of that resistance. Whether the resistance was caused by the lack of representation in given departments, or whether the lack of representation was just another indication of lack of commitment and resistance, we can't say for sure. But the bottom line is this: Get representation from all of the critical areas in your organization, and your team will be able to withstand any resistance you come across. Remember that the team members do not need to give 100% of their time to your implementation project. If one or two full-time team members are leading the change, and one or two other members are committing half of their time toward the implementation, then success can be achieved.

4. Do use a "pilot team" to focus your early efforts and receive direct feedback. We have never seen an organization put so many resources into DFSS implementation that it could simply "release" the process across the board. Even the most heavily staffed DFSS implementation team will need to roll out the new process in pieces. The most successful implementations we have seen were those where the organization designated one pilot product development team to take the time to learn and apply the new process and give feedback to the DFSS leaders. In these successful cases, the teams were aware of their responsibilities to follow the DFSS process and to give honest feedback to improve the process before the implementation team rolled it out to the rest of the organization. The DFSS leaders could then make any modifications to the process based on the real-world experience of the product development team.

One example of a pilot team's value occurred at a company that struggled in the beginning of their DFSS process. Early on, the company deployed a plan it thought would satisfy the product development teams. The leaders of the organization wanted as many people trained on the process as possible in as little time as possible. Our implementation charter identified the number trained as a primary metric. The organization wanted as many people trained as thoroughly as possible, so it identified two pilot teams instead of one. The implementation team agreed to this expectation, even though they expected it would present some unique challenges. Both product development teams were at very similar points in the product development process, so they were looked at in many respects as one pilot team. The two pilot teams were set up in a room to train them on the DFSS process together.

But the culture of this organization is very team oriented and exclusive. Having two teams in the same room proved to be an absolute disaster. Team members could share their questions, concerns, and weaknesses among themselves, but they could not imagine "opening up" with another team! It became painfully evident that these two teams should not be treated as one big team.

From that day forward, we broke our pilot team training plan into two, so that each team could learn privately and share their concerns and issues only among themselves. From that point forward, our roll-out plan stated that any team who needs a workshop gets a workshop all to themselves, with full attention from the facilitator. We budgeted accordingly, and we were able to sell the new budget to management with this strong example of how we would fail otherwise. Things like this can be learned with one or two teams, especially if they know they are given the responsibility to give feedback.

DON'TS TO AVOID IN IMPLEMENTING DFSS

We have seen many success stories in implementing DFSS, but we have also come across approaches that have failed, causing companies to spend extra resources on damage control or simply failing to sustain the DFSS improvement. We have summed up the five most damaging approaches we have seen in organizations as they have tried to implement DFSS, so that you can learn from others' mistakes.

1. Don't count the number of people trained as your primary metric.
2. Don't put too much focus on the tools in DFSS and not enough emphasis on the process and roadmap.
3. Don't define your implementation team as "here to save the day" heroes.
4. Don't take a grass-roots approach when management has not declared buy-in.
5. Don't give everyone a DFSS book and expect a miraculous turnaround.

1. Don't count the number of people trained as your primary metric. After seeing countless organizations attempt to implement changes, we have concluded that one of the biggest reasons initiatives fail is putting too much emphasis on traditional classroom training. If we only needed classroom training to instill a lesson, your 8-year-old would never have any homework or projects, ever! Think of every class you have ever taken, every lesson you have ever learned. What were the lessons that stuck with you the longest? The lessons that stick the best are those that allow you to put into practice what you have learned. This is the biggest reason Six Sigma and Design for Six Sigma have outlasted other quality movements. The premise behind Six Sigma and DFSS implementation is the basic apprentice/expert approach to learning and becoming proficient.

People don't go to karate classes or carpentry classes, watch the experts perform in class, then go back home and say they were trained. In these cases, they learn the process and tools to use, and then they are paired up with an expert practitioner to learn by doing. The expert teaches the apprentice and then lets the apprentice demonstrate his or her skills until the point he or she can be considered proficient. The primary way to measure how much DFSS has stuck in your organization should be around the use of the right tools at the right time, or the outcome of the process (saving time, improving quality, or reducing product cost).

You know the old expression "be careful what you wish for." Well, organizations that have pressed their deployment teams for "students-in-seats" metrics have gotten just what they wished for. Everybody gets sheep-dipped, but the organization has nothing to show for it besides a lot of training certificates hanging on employees' walls. Even in organizations that don't use this as a primary metric, we are still constantly asked by people who want to go through training, "Can I go through training without a project? I don't really have a good project right now to apply, but I really need the training." Here are our three favorite responses:

- "Why do you think you need the training if you have nothing to apply it to?"
- "Why don't you have anything to apply the training to? Aren't you an active member on any project?"
- "You don't need the training until you have something to apply it to, so come back when you are on a project."

2. Don't put too much focus on the tools in DFSS and not enough emphasis on the process and roadmap. We have also seen companies put too much emphasis on the tools in the DFSS toolkit. Let's go back to the home-building analogy. People don't go to learn how to use a miter saw or cordless drill and then claim to be a carpenter. They may need to know how to use the saw and drill, but the real skill comes in learning to measure the wood, lay it out just the right way, and verify that it is plumb and even. Sure, the tools will enable you to get more carpentry done in less time, but only if you know the process. If you know only how to use the tools, you'll be cutting an awful lot of wood for the second and third time, wasting time and money with each mistaken use of the tool.

We saw an organization put a lot of emphasis on the tools, keeping track of each tool training session each engineer went through. In the end, no engineer could articulate when or why he or she would use any given tool, but felt he or she knew how to use it. As it turned out, even the tools weren't used consistently then, because the tools training did not give anyone an opportunity to actually apply the tools to their current project. So by the time the engineers began to use the tools on their projects, it had been so long since the training that their application was all over the map.

3. Don't define your implementation team as "here to save the day" heroes. One organization brought a new president on board from a leading Six Sigma company. That president's first priority was to deploy Six Sigma in this new organization. He called up folks from his prior company, hired a handful of great executers, and tasked them to "deploy Six Sigma in eight months." These individuals were so flattered to have been handpicked by the president that they forgot the major elements of change management.

For the most part, they simply began to execute the president's wishes, putting in place exactly what they had seen in their successful last company. They felt empowered to "save the day" for this new company. Unfortunately, this "new company" was not really new; it was just new to these five individuals. To the other 1100 employees, the company had a hundred-year history rich with skills, energy, and desire to do the right thing. If these "outsiders" had taken the time to understand the history, culture, and *heart* they were dealing with, they might have actually gained 1100 supporters. Instead, they were met with resistance from people who overheard them talking to each other about "how much of a mess they have to clean up at this place."

The most outspoken person (we'll call him "Dave") made the most negative impact as he tried to show everyone how he was saving the day. Dave made sure everyone knew how bad he thought the place was. Dave made sure everyone knew how closely he worked with the president and how often he told him what he thought of this place. But when the president resigned less than a year later,

Dave wished he had made a few more allies at this new company. In less than 12 months, Dave came, tried to conquer, failed to conquer, and finally left to follow the president to the next "new" place. We were left to truly clean up the mess with our 1100 friends and coworkers.

In sharp contrast, another member of this five-person hand-picked team, Ed, had a totally different approach. Ed came in, put his heart into learning the culture, understanding the past heartaches, and letting people tell him what *they* thought was wrong with the organization. He worked together with these folks to list the things that needed to be improved and assigned them to key positions to make the improvements and make them stick. He continually rewarded the folks for their improvement work, and within six months people stopped thinking of him as an outsider at all. He showed respect for the culture in that organization, and had earned the respect of the 1100 people who now considered him an ally. For five great years, Ed showed true leadership and gained more and more respect as he helped people improve department after department. The folks saw him as their ally, their advocate for improvement. They looked forward to his visits, whether they were for one day or for a year of focused effort.

After five years, when entirely new management came on board with their own agendas and a need to make their own "mark" on the organization, they asked Ed to step aside so they could be the new "stars." When Ed left, his send-off included 1100 people with tears in their eyes and heartfelt thanks for helping get the organization as far as they got. Years after Ed is gone, we still hear people in that organization talk about what an influence he had been and how they wish Ed were still there to help lead them to success.

4. Don't take a grass-roots approach when management has not declared buy-in. Taking a grass-roots approach to implementing DFSS is definitely the most painful road you could take. When the associates know the right thing to do but management has not yet bought in, it is understandable to want to "just go do the right thing." In rare instances, a grass-roots approach can be the catalyst that management needs to see early successes and then give their full backing. But mostly, it is an effort that can wear everyone down, as they work doubly hard doing work for two causes. First, they are expected to do things the same way as management expects. But on top of their normal work, they are spending energy to implement the changes to make DFSS part of their process. They risk getting physically and emotionally burned out if their efforts do not get noticed.

The physical burnout is one thing, as they may stop their DFSS efforts after a certain length of time goes by without management buy-in. But their emotional burnout goes way beyond that, as they are torn between continuing down the DFSS path without support and stopping the efforts to gain some work-life balance. These folks usually can see the benefit of the DFSS processes, but they know that without management support their efforts will all be for naught.

As an example, consider the organization we discussed in the third "don't." Here, new management came in to make their mark on an organization that had already experienced five years of success through Six Sigma. Naturally, the folks at the working level still wanted to use the Six Sigma methods. But it became harder and harder for the folks in this organization to continue to apply Six Sigma without management support. For a while, the Black Belts and Master Black Belts continued to work toward mentoring and certifying Green Belts and more Black Belts. However, a trend soon appeared. Without management support, many Green and Black Belts' first postcertification action was to submit their resignation letters. Because management didn't value these people's skills and achievements, they voted with their feet and went to another company that would.

5. Don't give everyone a DFSS book and expect a miraculous turnaround. There are quite a few DFSS how-to books on the market. As constrained as organizational resources are, it seems like an easy shortcut could be to surf to Amazon.com, order everyone a DFSS book, and have them read it. Surely the bright folks in the organization will simply read the book and "get it." The next day, all the development teams will be practicing DFSS!

Unfortunately, most DFSS books focus mainly on tools and are much too generic to provide the direction an entire organization needs to change.

Taking the house-building analogy again, imagine giving everyone a book on how to build a deck. You'd expect the book to explain what tools you need (saw, brackets, fasteners, plumb bob, tape measure, etc.). If you let everyone start to build your deck after reading that book, what would it look like? How do you tell them that you are building a deck that fits *your* environment? The book surely couldn't tell you that for your environment there are certain keys to building a deck, whether you live in a flood zone and require a certain depth of reinforced post, or a heat-intensive zone where synthetic decking material is a better choice than pressure-treated wood, or a waterfront restaurant where the deck must withstand the weight of patrons, staff, tables, and chairs. Someone has to convert the generic information from the book into the reality of your culture! That someone should be a dedicated DFSS implementation team.

While some DFSS books provide great help in describing how this or that tool works, it is critical to have a support structure in place to guide the team members and Green or Black Belt candidates through the proper tool *usage*. At one organization that focused very strongly on the tools in a DFSS book, we were helping a Green Belt candidate get certified. This person went through the very first DFSS training held in the organization some years back and checked off all the tools that applied to her project. She was learning along with the rest of the organization, even the Black Belts. Her first Black Belt mentor helped her with some of the tools as she worked her project. But that mentor left before she completed the project. Her second Black Belt mentor picked up her project about a year later and recommended that the Green Belt use some tools that this mentor liked to use. Because each Black Belt was so tools focused, each of them told this poor Green Belt candidate to use different tools to accomplish the same outcome.

By the time we saw her project three years later, this Green Belt had used about three tools to get to every conclusion she needed. Instead of walking her through the best tools to use, each of her mentors looked for tools that they were accustomed to seeing or were most comfortable with themselves. The happy ending of the story is that this Green Belt shared her lessons learned in her report to her sponsors, showing only the tools that got her there the most effectively, and then listed the tools she felt she wasted time doing. It was with great pride that we certified her, knowing the valuable lesson she had learned along the way.

KEY POINTS: USING THIS BOOK TO HELP YOU ALONG IN YOUR IMPLEMENTATION

While this chapter outlines the general roadmap you will follow to plan and implement DFSS in your organization, each of the other chapters provides a deeper focus on each of the steps. We encourage you to read all chapters of this book as you begin to plan your DFSS implementation. But we also encourage you to reread the appropriate chapters as you progress through your implementation. Reread the following chapters to guide you through each phase of your implementation:

Define/measure

- Gap analysis: Chapter 5

Analyze

- Planning your DFSS strategy: Chapter 6

Implement and measure success

- Implementing the strategy and measuring your success: Chapter 7

- Validating the DFSS process and beginning your team's exit strategy: Chapter 8

Control

- Integrating into your culture and turning the project over to a sustaining group in your organization: Chapter 9

7
Measuring Success

INTRODUCTION

Here are two quotes to start and motivate this chapter:

What gets measured (and rewarded) gets done—Unknown

When you measure what you are speaking about and express it in numbers, you know something about it, but when you cannot express it in numbers your knowledge about it is of a meager and unsatisfactory kind—Lord Kelvin

The first quote is intended to remind you that *measurement* (tied to rewards and recognition) can be a powerful change motivator. Nobody likes to "look bad" on the monthly new product development scorecard that's reviewed by senior leadership!

The second is intended as a weapon for you to use with your scientists and engineers. A few of the objections you'll hear to DFSS metrics are: "You can't measure creativity," "Putting a target on a creative process just isn't realistic," and "What good is measurement?—all our product development projects are different."

Let's dive into the *what, when, who,* and *how* of measuring the success of your DFSS transformation.

WHAT AND WHEN TO MEASURE

The "what" to measure is a function of your DFSS implementation strategy. Let's take the case where you are working to transform your product development organization over a relatively short period of time (24–36 months). We'll assume your strategy includes three phases: Introduction, Implementation, and Independence.

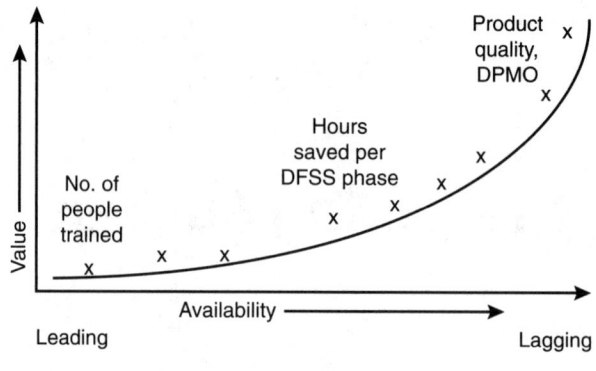

Figure 7.1 DFSS success indicators.

During DFSS Introduction and the very early phase of deployment, *leading* metrics should be in place. These will primarily help you measure *activity*—for example, how many teams are using DFSS, what tools are being applied, and how the training plan is progressing.

As you proceed into Implementation, you should expect to see tangible results. At first, these will be in-process results. You'll see, for example, the use of a DFSS tool here or there to make a better (or faster) design decision. Note that these are "victories" and should be communicated and celebrated.

This phase is probably the hardest from a metrics perspective, because you will walk a fine line between the leading, activity-based indicators and the lagging, performance-based indicators. The performance-based indicators will, of course, be tied directly to your organization's bottom line. An example of that trade-off is shown in Figure 7.1.

As you move to DFSS Independence (the sustaining, continuous improvement phase), you'll add a third type of indicator: the improvement variety. After the initial DFSS transformation, you will identify further development process improvement opportunities. The improvement projects chartered here will likely focus on select areas of the development process—for example, reducing the cycle time required to assess concept feasibility.

DFSS LEADING, OR EARLY DEPLOYMENT, METRICS

You should be measuring and communicating the success of your DFSS deployment as early as possible. In the first few months, though, what can you expect to see? Well, mainly the results of your deployment activities. Some early indicators will include:

- Number or percentage of people trained
- Number (or dollar value—in expected sales) of DFSS pilot teams
- Number or percentage of teams using the tools
- Changes made to the product development process

We recognize that the number of people who attend a class or workshop is at best an indirect measurement of success. What you ultimately want to measure is the dollars saved on a project, the time or man-hours saved during a launch, or the additional sales of product as a result of designing a robust product that meets the customer's needs.

However, this early in the deployment, it will be tough to find tangible results that directly link to schedule, cost, or quality. It is so important to show progress in this long deployment road that we should at least track the training and pilot progress. While it does not directly link to cost, time, or quality improvement, it does directly link to the commitment the organization has made to the DFSS deployment.

Don't underestimate that commitment! If the commitment isn't there, the organization won't wait for the later, more tangible results. So show these results early and often. Keep track, show the success of teams that took the time out of their development schedule to go through a workshop, and spread the word about what that team predicts it will save as a result. Even if it is just a prediction now, that linkage between the training and what might be saved down the line starts *correlation thinking*—teams will predict how this new process will help them. Keep communicating to the organization these teams' predictions, real outcomes, and overall commitment; team after team will start to make the connection.

You will also pick up some early warning signs with these metrics. Stratify the results—how many personnel from marketing, R&D, and operations are showing up at the training sessions (vs. the plan)? If your R&D division is organized by product lines or franchises, stratify and report the results this way, too. Stratify the data by organizational level. Are the "troops" going to workshops, but product development managers and senior leadership are opting out of these sessions, saying they don't have time for them?

Measure and communicate the intangible, too. After people have been trained, what are they doing differently? For example, after going through a DFSS exposure session, one R&D director immediately began to require and schedule reviews of project team charters. That behavior change was a powerful message to the organization—you don't get your project resources and funding until you've got agreement on your charter!

Note: As an implementation leader, be prepared for these "lightning bolts." As a result of the director's action, virtually all of the product development teams demanded charter training. The DFSS implementation team had to quickly create and staff a one-day charter workshop; it was a necessary distraction from the rest of their implementation work.

DFSS MID-DEPLOYMENT, OR IN-PROCESS, METRICS

As application of the DFSS tools and methods begins to pick up, the *middle* metrics should pick up on *in-process* successes and failures. For example, if the members of a development team predict the performance of their design in the face of manufacturing variation and reduce several design risks, that activity would be counted as a "victory" and should be measured. Another measurable victory occurs when a project is *killed early* (appropriately), because the development resources can be reassigned to another project with a better business case.

Some mid-deployment/in-process indicators include:

- All of the leading/early indicators

- Time saved in iterations of designs because of robust VOC collection

- Time saved in prototyping iterations because of predictive designing

- Reduction in money spent on prototype tooling because of predictive designing

- Reduction in money spent on tooling changes because of robust design-for-manufacturability and predictive designing

- Number of projects killed early (before the beginning of the Design phase)

- Resources (time and money) saved by killing appropriate projects early

One way we've seen these metrics applied before a product launch was in a phase-by-phase comparison. One of our teams used the Design phase tools on their product design and dimensions. They went over the critical dimensions, evaluated the worst-case scenarios with dimension stack-ups as well as stand-alone material dimensions. They were able to simulate a distribution of dimensions and failure rates that drove them to redesign two elements of their product. These design changes were simple, because they had not yet cut tooling. If they had cut tooling, verification testing might have revealed the design weaknesses. The subsequent need to redesign the product would have been costly both in dollars and time waiting for new tooling. If the verification testing did not reveal the design weakness (and it might not have), a more costly finding in the field later would have resulted in a product recall, the most costly of all failures in terms of money and goodwill lost.

This team touted their success long before they launched the product. They were recognized for taking the time to dive into the Six Sigma toolkit (about a two-week project "time-out") and saved hundreds of thousands of dollars and 6 to 12 weeks of tooling changes in the end. "Pay me now or pay me later" was their mantra from then on.

These in-process metrics don't just pop up like the monthly project financials. If you take a "reactive" data collection strategy, you likely won't hear about many of them. You'll need to develop a proactive approach. Here are two suggestions:

Coaching reports (formal or informal)—The coaches you have assigned to teams should be actively identifying and reporting back on DFSS "events" such as the dimensional predictions described above. Make these reports part of your weekly DFSS implementation meeting agenda. ("OK, let's go around the table. Jorge, what happened out there last week?")

Team assessments—While the premise of the assessments in chapter 5 was to establish what needed to be fixed in the first place, now we can use those same assessments to track how we are improving team by team. The basic questions asked in the assessment are "How are you applying DFSS?" and "How is it helping (hurting) your development project?" This can be a great source of these in-process metrics. A successful model for measurement comes from a company we have worked with that assesses every team at the end of every phase. This model allows the deployment leaders to gauge the success of teams at any given phase, and it allows for the senior leadership to see those intangible results along the way. For instance, a team may be able to demonstrate in the Analyze phase that their chosen concept will deliver all customer requirements superior to all competitors. While it can't be proven with actual sales dollars until launch, leadership can begin to see the product's potential.

One of your challenges is that you will generally be able to get only before and after statistics. Although it would be fun to assign two teams the same development project, and then train one team in DFSS and not the other and measure the results, most development organizations don't have the resources for such an "experiment." Often it's possible to get meaningful comparisons with previous development projects, especially at the design task level.

For example, one team's pre-DFSS practice was to design, prototype, and test a critical part of their product. Building the prototype took about seven weeks, so if it didn't pass the test, a *minimum* of another seven weeks would be added to the development schedule (assuming the second prototype passed the test, which it often didn't). So we knew that the "before" process would take at least 14 weeks, but could often take 21 weeks.

The team decided to apply finite element analysis (FEA) to predict and optimize the part's performance *before* prototyping (building and running the FEA model took about two weeks). The prototype was built and passed its tests with flying colors. They felt comfortable claiming a net schedule savings of five weeks, but everybody on the team knew that they'd really saved 12 weeks. At a development burn rate of $1000/hour in salaries alone, guess who's become a firm believer in the value of prediction?

What about when application of DFSS doesn't work or achieve the desired outcome? Measure and communicate these events too, but explain what went wrong, why it went wrong, and how you're going to fix it!

Here is an example that's still painful to remember. One company identified 10 DFSS pilot teams. Two of the projects were just starting out, and so we decided that they would get the "full DFSS treatment." The rest would be "DFSS triaged," identifying appropriate applications of DFSS based on where the teams were in their projects (but not forcing the teams to go back and revisit previous decisions).

We arranged a full-day session for the full-treatment teams to go through the Define step of DMADVI. The agenda included chartering, multigenerational planning, project planning, and so forth. Similar workouts at other companies had gone quite well, with the teams getting a lot out of these sessions.

From the start of the session, though, the signals weren't good. The team members sat silently, with stony looks on their faces. As we presented the tools, the only responses were "We do that already" or "That's some other group's responsibility." At one point, a team member asked "Can we get back to our *real* work?"

Well, we stopped the session, retired as gracefully as we could, and held an emergency team meeting in the company's cafeteria. Through our discussions, we identified a simple root cause—we didn't match the material to where the team was in their project.

We decided that before all meetings with teams that we would meet with the team leadership and do a "gap analysis" and mutually agree on specific tools and methods that would be covered and that would add value to the team's work. Each meeting was then opened by the team leaders stating *why* they'd asked us to come and work with the team and what *they* wanted to accomplish.

Of course, the news of the disastrous team meeting had gone through the organization like wildfire, but we were able to recover because we were honest about admitting our mistakes and what we were going to do to prevent them from happening again.

As we continued to meet with more and more teams (and start to see success in the sessions), we still opened the meeting with "Well, we're sure you heard about the meeting with Projects X and Y—here's what went wrong and here's how we're doing things differently." Then we went straight back to the purpose of their session, what this team needed to accomplish and how they predicted they would benefit from the session.

DFSS LAGGING, OR INDEPENDENCE, METRICS

As new products are launched using the DFSS process, the downstream, performance-based measures become appropriate. The organization may already have some of these in place: sales and profitability of particular products, scrap or warranty rate, customer returns/satisfaction/complaints.

Some lagging indicators include:

- Customer satisfaction levels from new products
- Launch time saved on new products (difference in launch time between what previous products had taken and what new products have taken)
- Defects per million opportunities on new products
- Customer returns/complaints on new products vs. old products
- Warranty costs
- Number (and/or cost) of redesigns done to new products vs. old products

One team we worked with spent time dissecting their design, making sure each component was as robust as it needed to be, and each assembly process was reviewed for potential failures. Once the design-for-manufacturability and design-for-assembly tools were properly used, the team launched the product in record time. That product's production and quality standards were met in 1/20th of the time it took previous, similar products. It is hard to argue with numbers like that.

Also, post-DFSS Independence, you will identify continuing opportunities to improve the development process. Note: This is a side benefit of a DFSS implementation—people get used to the idea that design is a process and can/should/*must* be continually improved. The number (and value) of the improvement projects should be measured.

For example, after the initial DFSS implementation, one organization decided to apply lean principles to its development process. This improvement project's impact was measured in reductions in non-value-added development activities, reductions in duplicate design "paperwork," and the subsequent effect this had on specific phases of their DFSS development process.

This is really where any remaining doubts about the worth of the Design for Six Sigma process will be eliminated. But we can't stress enough that your organization won't wait this long to see some success stories. Very few organizations in the world have the patience to wait this long to verify that they are deploying DFSS the right way. That is why the early and midstream metrics need to be communicated to all those involved.

No one goes to a three-hour football game without watching the score along the way. You wouldn't expect an organization to have that kind of patience either. An organization wants to see leading indicators of success, and it wants to continue seeing further indicators often.

PLANNING TO MEASURE YOUR DFSS SUCCESS

As you begin to plan your deployment of DFSS, think through the metrics you will be communicating. Think through the leading metrics; the mid-deployment, in-process metrics; and the lagging metrics. Work with your deployment team on the data collection and communication plan for the metrics.

The most successful implementations we have seen were those organizations that communicated through newsletters, e-mails, and special recognitions at department or franchise meetings.

For instance, we worked with two teams as we piloted the training program and workshops. Those teams got constant recognition as "DFSS pilots" because they were the first to go through training from the beginning to end of their project. Other teams that learned and applied deep-dive simulation of their product design were given awards for saving time and money on prototyping tools. These were not financial awards, yet they were the envy of all of the other teams, who wanted to emulate them to receive similar recognition.

As new product development teams used the DFSS tools and launched the products, the lagging indicators like launch time, defects-per-million, and customer satisfaction were shared with the organization.

A sample matrix you might use to plan for your tracking and communication of metrics for DFSS deployment is shown in Figure 7.2.

DFSS DEPLOYMENT METRICS EXAMPLES

As you begin to plan your deployment, think through the triggers in your organization. Think through the key reasons you are deploying DFSS. The metrics you use should reflect these triggers and reasons. For instance, if you are deploying DFSS to improve design efficiency and save development dollars, look at all phases of DFSS and all stages of deployment for metrics that will show these changes. Engage your new product development teams to keep track of these metrics on each individual project, and communicate those wins early and often.

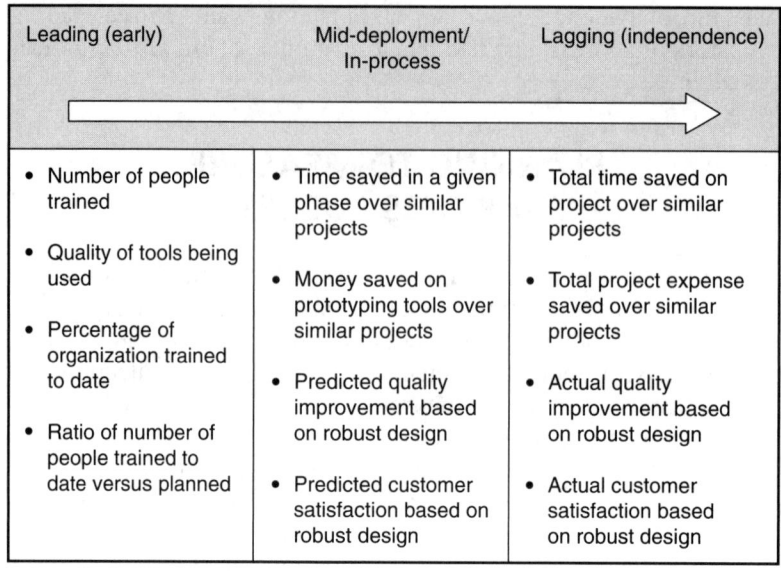

Figure 7.2 Maturing DFSS deployment metrics.

Just like showing the score during a football game, showing the successes all along the timeline of DFSS deployment will get the teams fired up about the wins and waiting for more successes.

WHO TO MEASURE

The most important thing we can say here is that *someone needs to "own" the metric!* If somebody isn't responsible and accountable for moving the metrics toward a goal or target, your measurement system is useless.

Look at your organization's structure. Think about a system of indicators like the one shown in Figure 7.3. For example, let's look at an early metric: training rate. Who owns the overall metric? Suppose we give it to the R&D director. Well, he or she may have little control over whether the marketing staff attended the training. If the vice president of product development has both marketing and R&D reporting to her, then she has the right level of responsibility and accountability for the overall metric. The R&D director, of course, owns a "piece" of the metric—the goals for training his staff in DFSS.

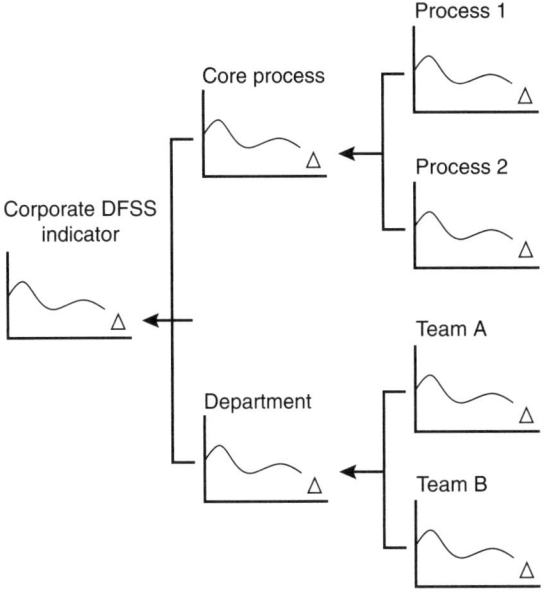

Figure 7.3 Example of a system of indicators.

HOW TO MEASURE

If you are in a large R&D organization, you will probably want to consider implementing some sort of electronic metrics system. For a global R&D organization, a web-based approach could make sense. For a small organization, a poster board divided with black tape into spaces for each metric could serve the same purpose. In either case, make sure that the metrics are visible; the entire organization should know how well it's doing. Some companies publish a DFSS magazine—an opportunity both to see both the metrics and to share implementation stories and best practices.

Your company may already report progress toward goals on a *dashboard* or *scorecard*. The idea is simple—the right information for the right person or team at the right time in the right format. Similar to the system of indicators, each organizational level should have its own dashboard. An example of dashboards is shown in Figure 7.4.

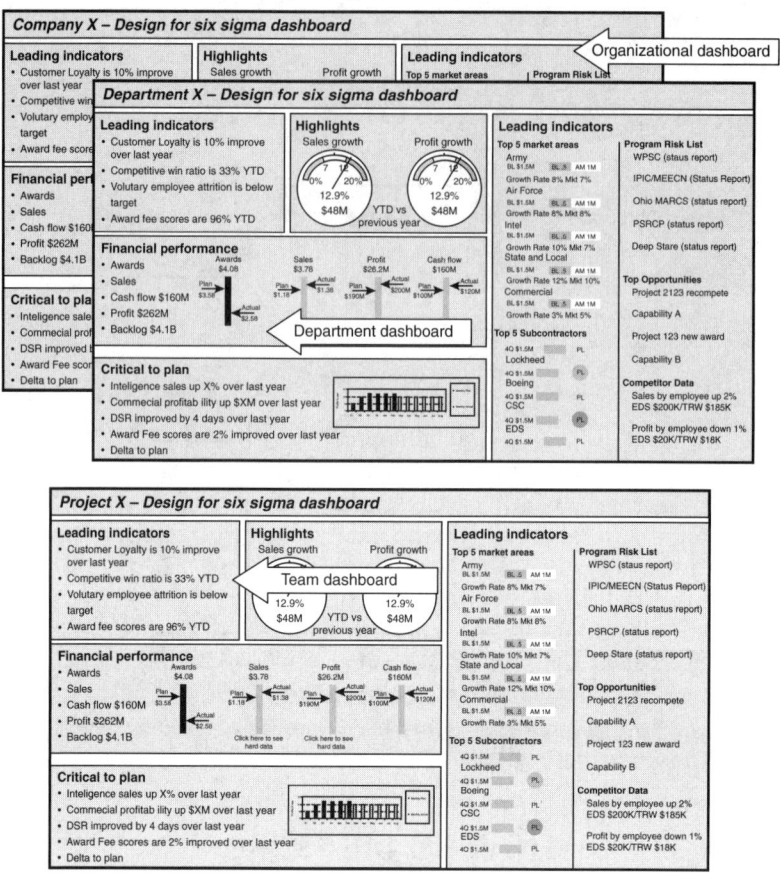

Figure 7.4 Example of a set of dashboards.

KEY POINTS: GUIDE TO MEASURING SUCCESS

- You must measure.
- Measure early and often.
- Communicate, communicate, and communicate.
- Tie metrics to accountability.
- Seek out and communicate both success and failure.

8

How to Know When the Organization "Has It"

Companies take different approaches to adopting DFSS. A "slow-burn" approach takes a patient, prioritized project approach to improving the development process. For example, a large southern U.S. utility began a design improvement journey by requiring "scope documents" for new engineering projects. A year later, a cross-functional team introduced a "standardized engineering package." During this time, improvements in drawing control processes, supplier management, and project prioritization occurred. This approach worked because competitive pressures were low and the engineering management only had a small appetite for change.

Across most industries today, a more typical approach to implementing DFSS includes a focused one- to two-year initiative in which design process improvements are made under a DFSS banner. Here, clear goals for improvement can be articulated and a *DFSS Independence Day* concept—the point at which the organization can sustain the DFSS process—can be employed.

But what does Independence Day look like? When can you disband your implementation team and consider the deployment a success? Look back to your DFSS implementation charter. What are your metrics and goals? How does your organization stack up to those goals? It is helpful for you and the deployment team to identify what the "end" of deployment looks like, what the areas of success will look like before you consider your organization independent enough to let the deployment team disband.

Every organization has a different patience level for keeping a deployment team in place. Some organizations may see the need to continue the same intensity of focus on DFSS for the long term. Those organizations will keep a deployment and training team intact for a greater length of time than organizations that are more eager to declare victory. You will need to assess where in that spectrum your organization lies.

If your organization falls closer to the eager side, this chapter will be most helpful to you as you define the "End of Deployment" and "Beginning of Sustaining" phases.

IDENTIFYING THE SUCCESS OF TRAINING

Although training is one of the softest indicators of success, it is also one of the earliest indicators. For this reason, most organizations use training metrics to measure the successful implementation at least early in the DFSS deployment.

As we mentioned in Chapter 7, the number of people trained is only an early metric. While we will advise against the typical metric of *number of people trained,* we can offer some alternative training-based metrics. One measurement that helps you understand how deeply you have engrained DFSS into your culture is how many teams have had workshops and what workshops they have had. We recommend workshops to truly allow the team members to learn the roadmap and tools and then immediately apply those tools in a just-in-time format. Look back to Table 6.4 for a way to track the training as it is completed. You can color-code the chart to show the successful workshops if that metric is important to the leadership in your organization.

What is more important is the benefit the teams get from the training. Before-and-after evaluations are good ways to show successful training. Keep in mind that you are asking the attendees whether or not they can perform the steps they were trained on. A more robust measurement is to have an outside evaluation to objectively assess whether these attendees can perform the steps now. In the short term, the easiest way is still to ask them to answer for themselves. They are likely to be honest about it, especially if questions like this are asked in the same organization that conducts more formal assessments later. Teams that are assessed at the end of each phase are most likely to be honest about the effectiveness of the training. They know they are going to have to perform those tasks and follow that roadmap, so they will make sure they get what they need out of the training.

By asking workshop attendees to identify their knowledge before and after, you are able to accomplish two things. First, you are able to measure the effectiveness of the trainer and the workshop (how far did the "after" measure from the "before"?). Second, you are able to assess areas that individuals or teams are most worried about (the subjects with the smallest improvement between "before" and "after"). This allows you to step back immediately and reassess the workshop or trainers in any given area. This just-in-time feedback is much more valuable to the organization than if you waited until the teams were completely through any given DFSS phase to find out that the gaps exists. Figure 8.1 identifies two examples of before-and-after self-assessments.

Chartering – Key elements and importance

Response	No clue	Limited knowledge about it	Can use it	Comfortable with it	Can teach it
After training ●					
Before training ○					

Before training ○ Place a red dot in the column that best describes your skill level
After training ● Place a green dot in the column that best describes your skill level

Transfer function

Response	No clue	Limited knowledge about it	Can use it	Comfortable with it	Can teach it
After training ●					
Before training ○					

Before training ○ Place a red dot in the column that best describes your skill level
After training ● Place a green dot in the column that best describes your skill level

Figure 8.1 Examples of before- and after-training assessment.

BENCHMARKING SUCCESS AGAINST OTHER ORGANIZATIONS

One way to help you identify success is to compare yourselves against similar organizations. What do other organizations look like now? Compare yourself to organizations that have deployed DFSS and have communicated their success through books or other publications. Because of the potential time difference between writing this book and your reading it and implementing DFSS, it would not be wise for us to show you current (at the time of this writing) success stories. The wiser choice would be for you to look for up-to-date publications that communicate companies' successes in the DFSS world.

We have found that companies that broadcast their success stories at conferences or in publications are fairly eager to tell their story in as much detail as their external communications departments allow. Go to a DFSS conference or a conference specific to your industry and talk to the folks who are speaking about their DFSS success. Compare what other organizations consider "good" with what yours has defined as "good." Another good source of benchmarking information is *Rath and Strong's Six Sigma Leadership Handbook*. That book presents a variety of case studies and interviews with company leaders. It is a good book to scan for examples and case studies.

VERIFYING INDEPENDENCE DAY

The best way to measure success is with finance-backed savings. What kind of success stories has your organization collected as you deployed DFSS? Look back to your charter. What were your metrics for DFSS implementation? What were the metrics around scrap rate, product launch, or start-up time? Now compare recent projects with those metrics. Be careful not to take one pilot team's success for granted. One carefully watched and mentored pilot team is not an adequate sample of the organization.

A good rule we have seen during successful deployment efforts is the 80% rule. If 80% of the teams are following the DFSS process, using the tools, and showing success stories, the other 20% can be expected to follow. The tricky part is measuring what "following the process" and "using the tools" mean. Look back to the areas of Chapter 5 that describe the deep dives into teams' NPD process. A best practice that we have seen is to incorporate this type of analysis during each NPD phase.

If you incorporate an assessment like the one shown in Chapter 5 and illustrated in Table 5.1, you will not only get an accurate measurement of how each team is performing, but you will also be sending the very important message that this DFSS process is expected to be followed. One organization continues to assess each team at each phase as a way of identifying the next gaps in the process. For instance, it was seeing great voice of customer results and great CTQ scorecards, but very little evidence of solid cascades. An investigation revealed that, in general, the engineers still didn't understand how to cascade from the customer requirements down to the component levels. The engineers knew they were "cascading" in their heads in order to make a certain component or subassembly, but they couldn't find a way to put that in writing or express it through transfer functions. That organization found that it needed to do some focused training and mentoring around systems engineering, a concept that was foreign to most of the engineers in that organization.

Every deployment will have some areas of significant success and some areas that did not live up to your expectations. It is up to you to find a way to identify those successes, show them to the organization, and identify the areas where the organization needs to focus more efforts to internalize key processes. A structured approach to assessing the organization will allow you to decipher the areas of success and the gaps that remain to be filled.

As you incorporate assessments into every phase of every project, find a way to systematize the results. If you do that, not only will you be able to identify when 80% of the teams have it, but you will also be able to identify the gaps quickly and act to correct them. An example of systematized summary of assessments is shown in Figure 8.2.

As you look at your assessment results, you should be able to easily see the biggest gaps in understanding or adoption. For instance, if you look at the results of the example assessments in Figure 8.2, you will see that there are bigger gaps in the chartering process and in the capability prediction process. In this case, leadership was presented these results and authorized an increase in efforts in these two areas.

Showing the results objectively in an assessment summary takes the pressure off the people side of the equation and puts it onto the results side, where it belongs. What the organization is looking for is results. Let the results speak for themselves. Notice how, in the preceding paragraph, we identified the gaps by looking down the columns for red trends, rather than looking across the rows for red teams.

The importance of focusing this way cannot be overstressed! If a team's members feel as if they are subject to an inquisition, they will do their best to make a smoke-and-mirrors presentation. On the

160 Chapter Eight

Phase	Define	Measure	Analyze	Design	Design	Verify
Deliverable:	NPD charter	CTQS defined	Concept selection CTQs, cascade	Transfer functions	CTQ scorecard predicted capability	CTQ scorecard actual capability
Project						
A	1	1	3	not assessed yet	not assessed yet	not assessed yet
B	1	2	2	3	4	not assessed yet
C	2	3	3	3	3	3
D	2	5	4	4	4	4
E	2	4	2	3	2	not assessed yet
F	3	5	5	5	not assessed yet	not assessed yet
G	4	5	3	4	3	3
H	5	5	4	4	5	4
I	3	4	3	3	3	3
J	2	3	3	2	2	not assessed yet
K	3	3	not assessed yet	not assessed yet	not assessed yet	not assessed yet
L	2	not assessed yet	not assessed yet	not assessed yet	not assessed yet	not assessed yet
M	3	4	4	3	2	not assessed yet
N	3	3	3	3	2	TBD

Rating scale:
1 No demonstration
2 Very little demonstration
3 Fair amount of demonstration
4 Very good demonstration
5 Could be a benchmark for other teams

Not assessed yet:
This team has not yet completed this phase

Figure 8.2 Example of an assessment summary.

other hand, if the members understand that company leadership is simply trying to identify gaps in the DFSS deployment process, they will be more honest. Whatever you do, do not send mixed messages by looking across the rows and identifying a "bad team." In one organization we saw a lot of red across one team, but there was no need at all to point it out. They can see colors too. They immediately went to their deployment leader and asked for some immediate assistance. They focused more during the next couple of months, with more mentorship than any other team. When it was time for their next assessment, that team showed an outstanding understanding and application of the DFSS process for the first time since the deployment started. They were proud of their successful implementation of DFSS as a team, and no one had to identify them as a "bad team." They were quick to identify their need for closer mentoring and training, the deployment team and leadership supported them, and in the end they were applauded for their drive to improve the process.

So, you see, the same measurement tool that was used to get a baseline of the organization can continue to be used to show progress along the way toward the end of your deployment!

COMMUNICATING INDEPENDENCE DAY

Independence Day has a certain ring to it because it symbolizes the independence from the DFSS deployment team and the beginning of a sustained culture of DFSS-driven minds. Whatever you decide to call the "end of deployment," it is critical to identify that end and communicate that with the rest of the organization, not just your deployment sponsors and leadership. The organization needs to know what will be different when your deployment team disbands. They need to know what the successes look like and why you have established these successes as "enough."

It is important to identify at the very beginning of deployment planning what success will look like so that you can objectively identify the end of the official deployment period. And as Chapter 9 describes, the end of deployment does not mean the end of DFSS; it simply means the focus will shift to sustaining the process and making continuous improvements for the good of the organization.

KEY POINTS: HOW TO MEASURE AND COMMUNICATE YOUR SUCCESS

This chapter should help you plan and communicate the end of your deployment. Your plan should include:

- Metrics for "complete enough"
- Communication of those metrics
- Plan for understanding and acting on the gaps
- Plan for transferring to the sustaining, or continuous improvement, owner

9
Keeping Up the DFSS Drive

INTRODUCTION

After DFSS Independence Day, the organization may be tempted to take a deep breath, wipe its collective brow, and bask in the glow of their achievement. "Yeah, we're done!" This chapter will focus on preventing backsliding to old design and development methods. DFSS stagnation is not acceptable—entropy will exert its influence and the changes you've worked so hard to achieve will start to unravel. It is critical to the organization's success that the improvements made are sustainable.

The team designated to shoulder the burden of the initial implementation team can be "retired," but what governance structure is now appropriate? A basic DFSS success path may be in place, but where are the opportunities to improve its application? The in-process metrics useful during the implementation phase will require rethinking. How should the development process be measured during the sustaining/continual improvement phase? How do new hires become indoctrinated to the organization's DFSS approach?

You may have heard the change-management phrase *critical mass,* the point at which enough members of the organization at the right levels have accepted and internalized the change. Only you can define critical mass for your organization and measure when you've reached it. But the hard part isn't measuring success; the hard part is sustaining the gains you've made. Like any process change, the improvement can be lost very easily if associates aren't encouraged and expected to sustain the new process. The cultural change can truly be sustained only if the necessary resources are committed to enable the teams to use the process easily and if management enforces the process by expecting nothing less than full commitment. We have seen the formula for success in organizations that have driven Six Sigma and Design for Six Sigma. We would like to share that formula with you as you plan for the sustainability of the changes you worked so hard to design and implement.

SUSTAINING DFSS: ENABLERS AND ENFORCERS

At an individual level as well as at the team level, the members of your organization have to change their behaviors. We have identified two key categories of controls meant to sustain that behavior change: enablers and enforcers. *Enablers* are controls that *help* make it easy to change one's behavior, and *enforcers* are controls that hold the person *accountable* to change his or her behavior. If you think about the diet example, these two elements play the key role in sustaining the lifestyle change as well. The enablers for a dieter are things like your gym membership and a calorie/fat counter in your PDA. The enforcers are things like a personal trainer that you contract for three days a week, tossing out the junk food in your cupboard, and throwing away the too-big clothes so that you *can't* go back up in size.

For a behavior change in the DFSS world, an enabler is something like a software tool that makes it easy for an individual or a team to predict the capability of the new product, an easy reference guide to remind you how and when to use certain tools, or a list of subject matter experts you can call to help with a new tool or process. An enforcer to hold individuals or teams accountable under the new DFSS process would be something like a quality procedure that you have no choice but to follow or a periodic review by leadership that incorporates questions around the DFSS process. A few examples of enablers and enforcers are listed in Table 9.1. Your organization may need some or all of these to sustain the improvements brought with DFSS. Your organization may also need other enablers and enforcers not on the list; you will need to assess what works in your culture.

ENABLERS

Software Tools

Software tools are the most common enablers to process changes in today's technology-driven world. But be careful! Some software tools can be very costly and should never be accepted as an easy way to change a process. Do you recall the days when enterprise resource

Table 9.1 Enablers and enforcers for DFSS sustainability.

Examples of enablers	Examples of enforcers
Software for simulation analysis, requirements management, and tolerance analysis	Individuals' performance plans identify timeline for DFSS project completion and/or certification
Training material and aids to provide easy, just-in-time reference	Project/gate reviews incorporate DFSS questions from leadership
Subject matter experts identified and expected to help teams who request guidance	Quality policies and procedures incorporate DFSS into the processes
Workshops provided for teams at all points along the product development process, to drive learning and immediate application of learning	Team leaders and members held accountable by leadership to follow the DFSS process and use the tools properly

planning (ERP) software was thought to be the savior? You then heard the horror stories of how much ERP really wound up costing organizations. Those organizations thought that ERP by itself would fix their problems for them, but ERP proved to be only as good as the business processes it enabled. Some organizations were quick to see this and embarked on redesigns of their core and supporting business processes. For example, many of the early DFSS service applications occurred when GE Capital used DMADVI to redesign business processes that were then enabled by software such as Oracle or SAP. Other organizations didn't get this message and continued to throw money at the ERP effort, only to curse ERP after millions of dollars were spent with little to show for the effort.

While ERP is the most memorable example of software being thought of as a solution rather than an enabler, there are many more, smaller examples we could share with you. For example, recently one organization put into place a software tool for requirements management. Within two years, the rumbling across the organization was that this software was the worst thing that they'd ever used and the biggest waste of time. A thorough inspection by the team chartered to fix the problem found that teams were struggling with requirements management itself, not with the software. So the team made a focused effort to improve the engineers' abilities to cascade the requirements, develop transfer functions, and manage the requirements. Once the effort was complete, the teams knew how to manage requirements and used the software once again to enable them to manage those requirements.

Other software tools that enable Monte Carlo simulation of tolerances and other transfer functions, design of experiments, and finite element analysis can make it easier for teams to truly design for Six Sigma. Be careful not to deploy a software package that teams are forced to use. Software should be something that makes people's jobs easier. Few of us would go back to a typewriter given the availability of word-processing software. Even we prefer to use statistical software like Minitab or JMP rather than the hand calculations we did 20 years ago. If software makes someone's job easier, they will want to use it. If the software is forced upon someone, they may learn to use the software, not necessarily the process. Have you ever seen people use Excel to manage their budgets, when they really didn't know how to categorize debits and credits in the first place?

Training Aids

Another enabler that is helpful in most process changes is up-to-date and easy-to-follow training material. Classroom training is one factor in changing behavior, but associates also need reference material that they can use when the time comes to actually apply what they have learned. The material should be easy to access and easy to follow. One best practice is to have a website dedicated to DFSS support. The website, if put together well, will allow users to navigate through training material, tools and templates they can download, and contact names of subject matter experts who can help them through any given tool (designing the website could be a DFSS project!). Within the training material, there should be concise, easy-to-follow quick guides for any given tool or element of the roadmap. If the website is easy to use, people will make it their first stop to get help. Putting a website together usually takes a dedicated effort, and is best when organized by a group of people who can think through a typical navigator's thought process. Think of the websites you like to use the most. The navigation is intuitive and you don't have to click through many pages to get to what you want. If you're given a tool like this, you'll be more than happy to abandon your previous research method (like the online yellow pages).

Subject Matter Experts

The subject matter experts (SMEs) listed on your website should know and agree that they are indeed experts on the subject listed. They should also be held accountable to keep up-to-date on that subject, or you should have a process to rotate and reestablish experts on a timely basis. These SMEs should be given an estimated expectation of time spent helping others, and they should be held accountable to make that time available whenever they can. An SME can be held accountable by adding this expectation into his or her performance plan.

One model for sustaining DFSS is the Green Belt, Black Belt, and Master Black Belt certification model (discussed in Chapter 6). The subject matter experts can keep their skills fresh by delivering their given subject in the training course. Advanced training should be made available to the SMEs, so that they can maintain and improve their status as experts. The Black Belts and Master Black Belts can be identified by their specialized area of knowledge. For instance, one Black Belt may be known as the go-to person for design of experiments, while another may be the Monte Carlo simulation expert. These experts should be identified in a publicized format, not just by word of mouth.

Just-in-Time Workshops

Making an internal or external expert (or several, as needed) available to facilitate just-in-time workshops will help teams learn the roadmap and tools by allowing team members opportunity to immediately apply each tool or process. While this is more costly than organizing traditional classroom-style training, the organizations we have worked with have been successful when they use the just-in-time workshop approach. We have found the organizations that have just used traditional training have really struggled to sustain any process improvements once the training was done. We could speculate whether the companies that insisted on this type of training really didn't take the time either to understand their culture before blindly deploying the DFSS training or to understand whether the poor training plan was to blame for their lack of sustainability. In either case, we hope you learn from their mistakes and take the time to understand the cultural needs of your organization before you consider the DFSS deployment completed.

These top enablers have been compiled from dozens of organizations we have worked with. Organizations that use a combination of enablers and enforcers have shown the most complete cultural change in their implementation of Design for Six Sigma. In fact, the most successful organizations we have worked with have been those organizations that combine all of these enablers as well as most of the enforcers listed.

ENFORCERS

Performance Management

How many times have you heard the phrase "what gets measured gets attention"? This holds true when it comes to individuals' performance plans. Associates at all levels know that their performance is the key metric for annual raises and/or bonus distributions. The more an organization values performance and individual contribution, the more the individuals will work toward their performance plans. Depending upon the culture of your organization, this value placed on individual performance can help drive DFSS forward through your organization. For instance, if there is a strong emphasis placed on individual performance plans within your organization, you can enforce the DFSS culture by including DFSS metrics in each person's performance plan. For project leaders, performance plans may include metrics based on driving the DFSS culture through their teams and using the DFSS process throughout their project. For team members, metrics may include using the DFSS process and tools in their areas on the team. A design engineer may be responsible to drive design-for-manufacturability as well as optimizing customer requirements. A manufacturing engineer may be responsible for design-for-manufacturability and design-for-assembly, as well as low-cost design. As noted, the goal of being certified as a Green or Black Belt may be included in annual goals.

There is one tricky thing to watch out for when it comes to individual metrics and DFSS. DFSS is not a serial process. The product development does *not* get tossed over wall after wall from marketing to design to manufacturing. DFSS demands that team members be engaged at some level from start to finish of the project. Manufacturing engineers need to know what the customers really want. Marketing members need to know the trade-offs in the design and cost implications of features. Design engineers need to optimize their designs for the customers and the manufacturers. All disciplines need to help optimize the product from start to finish, to cascade from the customer needs down to the nuts and bolts and assembly process and back up again to the customer. So be careful when you implement metrics into performance plans; be sure that the responsibility of each discipline does not contribute to the *silo,* or over-the-wall, mentality. Team members should be encouraged to think outside their silos or disciplines, using the DFSS process and tools to ensure that nothing gets thrown over the wall to the next discipline. An enforcer like performance management should take that into account.

Project Reviews

If there is one thing we have been able to take away from every organization we have worked with, it is the need for management to actively engage in the DFSS cultural change. Without management's engagement, a grass-roots effort to drive DFSS culture has a small chance at working in the short term. With the engagement of leaders, DFSS has a great chance of working long-term. We have been lucky enough to work with many leaders who were committed to improving their processes. These leaders believed in the benefits and advocated DFSS' benefits to the rest of the organization as we worked to change processes, coach teams, and build DFSS infrastructure.

One organization enforced the DFSS culture by expecting its leadership to be trained before anyone else. This show of commitment resonated throughout the organization, through each level into the teams and sponsors, and the result was a culture that knew they were being supported all the way from the top. The teams knew that they were going to be asked some very specific questions by leadership at each phase review. They understood that the leadership really knew what they were looking for and would continue to ask questions until they felt comfortable the teams were doing the right thing. Teams knew that they would be held accountable for following the process, to "walk the walk" and not just "talk the talk." The knowledgeable and engaged leadership would accept no less than full commitment from any team.

Policies and Procedures

We have worked with some highly regulated industries. The FDA regulates the medical device, pharmaceutical, and food industries; the Nuclear Regulatory Commission regulates nuclear power plants; and the organizations we have worked with have committed substantial resources to be the best ambassadors of quality and compliance. In other organizations, commitment to quality has been shown by companies' ISO or QS certification and compliance. In all of these cases, the level of commitment is evident from the individual contributor at every level to the highest-ranking leader in the organization. In our experience, the commitment to DFSS is just one more step in any organization's commitment to quality. Organizations that commit to DFSS do their employees the biggest favor when they integrate the DFSS processes into their quality systems.

As an example, we worked with one organization for almost three years, teaching the tools and processes. But teams were still complaining about the extra work they needed to do to satisfy all of the company requirements. It seemed to them that they had to follow the DFSS processes and use the tools to satisfy their immediate management, then they had to fill out piles and piles of forms to satisfy their stakeholders in quality systems, and finally they felt they had to make some fancy presentations to satisfy their business stakeholders at the gate reviews. After digging into the problem, we found that members of this organization took all of their quality policies so literally that they really shouldn't have been called quality systems but "forms to fill out" systems. Some members of this organization were so driven to follow policies that they almost forgot they still had to produce a product. They looked through every policy, procedure, and work instruction, searching for the list of forms to complete as if those forms were the maps to lost treasures. They went straight to those forms, as if completing them was the company's primary purpose for existence. We should note that this was a company whose products and processes were regulated by the Food and Drug Administration (FDA) and the "complete-the-form" culture seemed to have been ingrained during the initial deployment of quality systems many years back. It seems that the original drive for quality systems took an overzealous approach to forms, and the organization had made the inference that all of those years of audits without findings must have been caused by rigorous forms.

It took a cross-functional team a month of focused effort to dig into the culture and policies before they came out with one integrated procedure that told teams how to develop products the best way. That new procedure integrated the management requirements at each gate, the DFSS process to follow, and the compliance to FDA guidelines to ensure they produced the best product for the customer while satisfying all their stakeholders. It was a long and painful lesson, so if we can help one organization see these signs and fix the problem early, we will have achieved our goal.

Accountability

Quality policies are one way to enforce the DFSS process, but without a deeper level of accountability teams may revert back to the more compliance aspects of the quality system, filling forms as required but not really following the process behind the forms. It takes leadership commitment to drive the process through the teams by holding them accountable at all steps along the product development process. In one organization we have worked with, the leadership was first trained on the benefits of DFSS and then trained in more detail in small snippets (about 40 minutes per month) in the processes along the DFSS path. The product development teams were trained in just-in-time workshops. After a year of training for teams and management, both were ready to come together in project reviews where they spoke the same language. We trained the leaders to conduct thorough assessments at each stage in the new product development process and then set up assessments for each team. The fact that leadership was willing to commit the amount of time necessary to assess every team at the end of every stage spoke volumes to the organization. Two years later, we are happy to say that teams and management still come together at each stage and review their progress. It is that level of commitment that helped DFSS sustain in that organization.

The key to these effective assessments is to provide the leaders understanding of the process so they can ask the right questions. You also want to set the teams up for success. In one organization where we implemented assessments, we made sure that teams were assessed only on the areas they had been trained on. Because we trained just-in-time, some teams were half-way through their product development when we started DFSS deployment. We couldn't ask teams to go backward and spend another year on phases they had already passed, so we showed them the benefits of DFSS from that point forward and trained them as they went through the next phases. Management was made aware of each team's level of training, so teams were held accountable for only the training they had to date. Because teams knew their sponsors and top management expected them to follow the DFSS roadmap, they were even more driven to follow the roadmap and use the tools correctly. It was definitely a win-win-win situation in that organization, as teams used the right tools at the right time, their projects benefited from it, and the leadership saw the benefits of each project along the way. In the end, everyone won, including the customers, who received the products they wanted sooner and with higher quality.

Each organization's culture may look at enforcement differently. While some organizations may be able to deliver an edict for change, others may be expected only to softly suggest the change is needed. It is important for your implementation team to assess where your organization lies within this spectrum and establish the appropriate enforcers to fit your culture. There is one thing we want to stress: If you really expect a sustainable DFSS improvement, there have to be *some* enablers and *some* enforcers to provide the foundation the change needs to stand on.

OWNERSHIP FOR THE NEW PROCESS

The chances are pretty high that the DFSS implementation will not be perfect in your organization at the time your team considers the deployment complete. As the implementation team plans their hand-off to the long-term owner, you should also be setting up the proper transition of each critical element. Any enablers or enforcers you have put into place need to be transitioned to a long-term owner. You may have a full-time Master Black Belt responsible for all of these elements for sustaining and continuous improvement. Or, for example, the owner of the enabling software tools might be your information technologies liaison. The training and subject matter expert list might be transferred to an owner in your training or Six Sigma program office or similar group.

Each element that you have put into place needs to have a designated owner to sustain the DFSS gains achieved. Remember, the DFSS system is likely to take several years before it is considered "perfect," if it ever will be considered perfect. Your job as the implementation team is to get it as good as you can get it, considering the culture you have today, and to turn a sustainable process over to owners who are just as passionate about the DFSS process and its continuous improvement.

KEY POINTS

Your job as the implementation team is to assess your culture and identify the forces required to sustain the positive changes you have been seeing. You can identify and implement the right combination of enablers and enforcers in your organization, whether they are software tools, training material and guides, or quality procedures and work instructions.

Your last responsibility as the DFSS implementation team is to transition each of these sustaining elements to an appropriate owner who is motivated and expected to maintain these processes or structures. Help these new owners identify the reasons you put each enabler or enforcer into place, and give them a sustainable process to follow to maintain them. In the product development world, you'll recognize this as ensuring that transfer of design intent has occurred.

10

Where Do You Go from Here?

INTRODUCTION

Improving the new product development process is a challenge that never ends. Implementing DFSS may just be one part of your new product development *improvement* strategy. This chapter will provide you with ideas for how to capitalize on the improved development processes.

For example, now that your organization can reliably develop a Six Sigma product, you may decide to improve the development cycle time by identifying and eliminating non-value-added design activities. Your growth/improvement plans may involve developing your suppliers' design capabilities (potential small-scale DFSS implementations).

Table 10.1 contains some suggested improvement themes and their potential impact on your development process.

ADVANCED VERSUS NEW PRODUCT DEVELOPMENT

You have probably noticed that we emphasized the application of *mature technology* within DFSS. We have seen too many development projects where the need to invent something has caused significant project delays. You may see these science projects in your own organization. On the other hand, your development process may just be churning out line extensions of existing products using existing technology. You may find that you frequently have to buy or license technologies to come up with truly new products.

Table 10.1 Suggested improvement themes and their potential impact.

Improvement theme	Potential improvement in:			
	Quality	Cost	Speed	Safety
Advanced development vs. new product development	X		X	
Axiomatic design	X			
Customer "listening" and ethnography	X		X	
Design infrastructure	X	X	X	X
Holistic development	X			
Leaning the NPD process		X	X	
Organizational change management	X	X	X	X
Schedule performance improvement		X	X	
Supplier development	X	X	X	X
Systematic innovation technique	X		X	
Taguchi robust design	X	X	X	
Theory of inventive problem solving	X		X	

Let's address the science project issue first. If this is prevalent in your organization, you should consider decoupling advanced development from new product development. Conceptually this is easy, but there are several practical difficulties.

First, you'll have to develop an advanced technology process. For example, in *Design for Six Sigma,* C. M. "Skip" Creveling describes a generic technology development model—I^{2}DOV (Invention and innovation, develop technology concept, optimize robustness, and verify technologies). We helped one of our telecommunications clients design an innovation process with the following steps:

Idea entry—The company gathers filters and prioritizes product/technology ideas. If the idea has merit and high enough priority, a decision is made to proceed with placing the idea into one of their innovation centers. Otherwise, the idea may be shelved, postponed, or killed.

Defining the innovation—A team of company staff, suppliers, and customers is chartered and inducted into the innovation center to work on the idea. The core team drafts a charter for the project, defining goals, metrics, and scope. Based on the innovation framework, they identify some key project milestones to work toward.

As they scope the project, they begin to identify additional skill sets to help them design the innovation (including company staff and vendors).

Design the innovation—The team gathers voice of customer information (using a goal-directed design approach) and develops/obtains technologies to fill the customer needs. The output of this step is the ability to *make it for one customer.*

Optimize the innovation—The team further develops the technology so that it is robust and capable of scalability. This phase is known as *make it for many.*

Transfer to business unit—The developed technology is transferred to the company's product development process. Team members are rewarded, recognized, and repatriated to their business units. A core of the team continues to work the idea through the normal development/commercialization processes and launch.

So, this sounds easy; where's the hard part? Well, first, you are going to battle the tyranny of the present. Most reward systems are set up with a short-term (one year or less) view. You will be deploying valuable development resources into a process that has an uncertain return on investment. Second, you have to make sure that the advanced development stays focused on the long term. It's easy to drag them back into short-term projects. A consumer products company decided to deploy resources to platform teams—whose charters were to look for the next big ideas in their market. Within about six months, these teams were all focused on short-term, incremental gains.

You will also have to consider how to transition the output of the advanced development effort into DMADVI. Will some of the same team members continue on the project (providing continuity), or do they go back and start the next advanced development project? What will have to change in DMADVI to accommodate the learnings of the advanced development process? For example, much of the voice of customer work may already be done; hence the Measure step of DMADVI may be shortened. Finally, we've seen a lack of trust between the advanced development group and the new product development staff. The new product development staff often feels that they have to reinvent what the advanced development folks have accomplished. This is a difficult trust to establish.

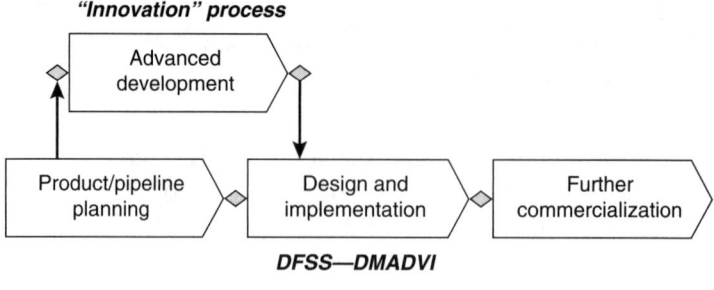

Figure 10.1 Relationship—advanced development to DMADVI.

Use your multigenerational plans as a communication/prioritization vehicle between new product and advanced development. If the product team has developed a vision of future product generations, they may already know what technology is needed to develop these generations. These technology needs should be a key input to your advanced technology group's work plan. Figure 10.1 shows how pipeline planning, advanced technology, and product development should work together.

AXIOMATIC DESIGN

Dr. Nam Pyo Suh notes that although product developers are generally good at design *analysis,* they exhibit significant weaknesses in design *synthesis.* He has postulated a series of design axioms that govern the development of the product or system.

For example, in his view, four "domains" govern the design of any product: (1) customer, (2) functional, (3) physical, and (4) process. Further, mapping these domains will establish a clear line of sight from customer to the product to the process. Mapping the customer's needs (or attributes) to the functional domain results in the definition of the product's functional requirements (FRs). Similarly, the functional requirements can be mapped to the physical—identifying design parameters (DPs) and then the design parameters mapped to the process parameters.

As these domains are mapped, the design team should apply Suh's design axioms. Suh's first axiom, *Maintain the independence of the functional requirements,* is followed by axiom 2, *Minimize the information content of the design.* Practically, this means that the design team should select a physical design (defining the design parameters, or DPs) so that each functional requirement can be met without affecting the others.

The benefit of such a design is that it will be inherently robust—design parameters can be adjusted to achieve target values for each functional requirement without affecting other functional requirements. Axiomatic design provides some of the underlying theory for Taguchi's design approach and may be enabled by Genrich Altshuller's theory of inventive problem solving (TRIZ) (see discussions on these improvement opportunities later in this chapter).

CUSTOMER LISTENING

Quality function deployment (QFD) is a powerful tool to help you gather and translate customer needs into product requirements and further deploy them to process Xs. However, it is not the only way to bring the customers' voice into your product development efforts. Some teams find the matrix analysis painful (recently, we spoke with one woman who pleaded, "Please don't make me do another house of quality!"). There are also a few weaknesses of QFD that other methods overcome. A brief survey of alternatives to QFD follows:

> *Kano analysis*—Dr. Noriaki Kano developed his theory of customer needs in the 1970s. While many are familiar with his theory of *must-be, one-dimensional,* and *delighter* needs, few actually practice the surveying and analysis method he developed to systematically distinguish the different types of needs.
>
> Kano's approach involves asking customers a two-part question. First, the customer is asked, "How would you feel if this [insert requirement here!] was present?" Next, the customer is asked, "How would you feel if this [insert requirement here] wasn't present?" Analysis of these responses can then differentiate what your customer finds essential (the must-be needs) to the product, requirements where you can dial in the degree of satisfaction your customer will experience (the one-dimensional needs) and finally, which requirements, if met, will excite or delight them.
>
> *Market-driven product definition (MDPD)*—In her book, *Customer-Centric Product Definition,* Sheila Mello

advocates a four-phase approach to listening to the customers, analyzing their voices, developing product requirements, and then developing design concepts that meet these requirements. Her approach starts with planning and conducting customer interviews, in which the entire development team (not just marketing) is involved in the listening process.

One of the unique aspects of Mello's approach is the creation of *image* and *requirements* diagrams to process the customers' voices. Whereas QFD can tend to result in product requirements that are basically features, MDPD emphasizes the definition of *solution-free* product requirements—those that define the desired product function and the degree of performance desired for that function. With image diagrams, Mello reminds us that customers experience products with both their left (logical) and right (emotional) brains. These provide a picture of what life is like for the customer using the product—their feelings, fears, excitement, and so forth.

One of our clients has adapted and woven the MDPD approach into its DMADVI development method. Although that company is still on a learning curve, we are seeing fewer features masquerading as requirements.

Interaction Design—Alan Cooper's *The Inmates Are Running the Asylum* describes the horrors of most software development processes. A few quotes[1] from a *10 Worst Products* list lend support to his hypothesis:

- For a GPS system: "Marred by an awful interface and a poor data-entry keypad, it failed our tests."

- For an MP3 player: "With ergonomics straight from a Klingon warship, balky software, and a poor display, this one deserves a place in the remainder rack."

- For a media player: "The screen is terrible, the interface abysmal, and the physical buttons erratic."

- For a DVD projector: "Marred by a minuscule remote, nasty interface, and terrible video quality, it'll be quickly relegated to the garage or eBay."

---

[1] Jim Louderback, "Ten to Avoid—The Worst Products of 2005," *PC Magazine*, November 22, 2005.

- For a monitor touch screen: "Alas, it works more slowly than the midnight shift at an all-night diner, and often gets your order wrong, too."

One of Cooper's contentions is that some software developers design for themselves—the advanced or expert group. Further, they are always trying to fend off the pleas of their marketing people who want them to design for the first-time users. The resulting software products will then usually ignore the bulk of users—the perpetual intermediates (such as you and me).

Cooper admits that *Inmates* gave him a chance to rant and rave about poor development practices. His follow-on, *About Face 2.0—The Essentials of Interaction Design,* provides a framework and methods to help you help your customers better achieve their goals. He describes designing the product before coding starts, better understanding the customer through ethnographic research, defining user goals, recognizing the difference between a user's mental model and the product's implementation model, designing to a persona, and translating user goals into the design.

So, why *do* we click the Start button to shut down our PCs?

Human factors/industrial design—One of the many characters in our nuclear engineering department was a strange guy named Bill Klein. Although no one could really figure out what Klein did, we were supposed to take our designs to him so he could check them out for *human factors*. After the Three Mile Island event in 1979, the Nuclear Regulatory Commission forced nuclear utilities to consider human factors in the design of control rooms. Despite this, a lot of us just didn't *get* human factors!

Fast forward a decade or so, and we're sitting with one of our client's human factors/ industrial design staff. His description of how the human factors staff is helping the organization get closer to the customer and design better products is knocking our socks off.

He shows us process maps of how the customer uses the company's products in a team environment and how he can incorporate many layers of information—for example, what emotional state and stress levels they experience at different moments during use of the product. He shows us rapid prototyping methods that can get the product's *form* into the customers' hands and quickly gather feedback about the product. He shows us an example of how this prototyping helped shape a new product concept—significantly away from traditional concepts (and much better in the customers' eyes).

He shows us how usability testing can confirm the perceptions of the customer around the product and measure their ability to perform their functions better with the new product.

In short, if you have a human-factors/industrial design staff in your organization, go talk to them, learn what they can do, and challenge them to help you develop better products.

DESIGN INFRASTRUCTURE IMPROVEMENTS

If you consider the fishbone diagram of factors that lead to good design, DFSS is the main factor on the method bone. What other bones need work to improve your design and development process? A few suggestions follow:

> *Capability data*—DMADVI asks our development staff to predict the capability of the design's Ys as a function of part and process variation. This requires that they know something about the mean, standard deviation, and shape (for example, probability distribution) of the X variation. How easy is it to identify such information in your organization?

In a DFSS demonstration project a few years back, it took us about 20 minutes to clarify a design requirement, about 1 hour to build the transfer function between the requirement and its associated Xs, but *two weeks* before the engineer could obtain information about part and process variation.

One of our clients has invested in a database of process capability data. The developers can enter the database, determine the kind of process that will produce their design, and then obtain typical variation data for that process. Could something like this help your new product development teams?

> *Material properties*—Likewise, how easy is it to identify properties of materials you are using in your products? One company found that this was one of the bigger frustrations for its developers trying to practice the DFSS discipline. Similar to the capability database, they developed and populated a materials database. The relief on the engineers' faces when they realized they could simply call up a material in the database and pull all of the properties in a minute was worth every minute of effort building the database.
>
> *Simulation capabilities*—How well can you predict the performance of your designs? Are you forced to make expensive (and time-consuming) prototypes to test the

design? Modern simulation software is powerful, but somebody needs to know how to use it, what its strengths and weaknesses are, and how to interpret the results.

We've mentioned Monte Carlo simulation several times in this book. This is an essential DFSS simulation tool. With Monte Carlo (and understanding the product's CTQ transfer functions), you can predict how part and process variation will impact the variation your customers will see. We've introduced the Crystal Ball Monte Carlo package to many engineers. With this particular package, the engineer can build a simulation model in Excel (or use an existing engineering calculation spreadsheet) and define the expected variation in the product/process parameters that affect the CTQ. Running the simulation provides the engineer with a prediction of how much the CTQ will vary, what percentage of product will fall outside the specification limits, and what the sensitivity of the design will be to the sources of variation in the model (for identifying improvement opportunities). During a recent open house at one of our clients, an engineer walked up to one of us. He said, "You probably don't remember me, but I was in your Monte Carlo class a few years back. I just wanted you to know that I use that Crystal Ball program almost every day!" He was right, we didn't quite remember him, but we were sure glad to see that Monte Carlo had become part of his development process.

One of our clients has a two-person group whose sole function is to perform finite element analysis (FEA) in support of development projects. This group has developed very impressive capabilities in finite element modeling and analysis. They have brought in and validated FEA computer codes, are building a supercomputer to support the calculation loads, and have developed sophisticated models that allow them to predict product performance in its intended environment. This group has demonstrated their value over and over in their ability to provide x-ray vision into the designs, identify weak points, optimize the designs, and minimize the need for prototypes, with savings in development team burn rate (cost/hour of development resources) and design cycle time. It's definitely a worthwhile investment.

Monte Carlo and finite element analysis are just two of the simulation capabilities you may need, and they don't answer all the engineering questions you may have. Simulation packages are available to help you model fluid dynamics, heat transfer, plastic injection mold flow, product and process reliability, process dynamics, and on and on.

HOLISTIC DEVELOPMENT

John was sitting with his teenage daughter one night watching TV. A commercial came on for a skin-cleansing product; it just happened to have been developed by one of our clients. Even before the commercial was over, she exploded, "This commercial is crap! Here they show this beautiful model, with perfect skin and she gets a zit that nobody can even see! If this product is any good, show me how it will fix my skin, not someone who doesn't have a blemish on her body!" So, even if our client's product is great at performing its intended functions, the advertising campaign blew it for my daughter (and, we wonder, how many others?).

In *Innovation and Entrepreneurship,* Peter Drucker discusses cases in which a good product was presented to the public through poor distribution channels. Contrary to some early pundits, pure Internet distribution companies are being challenged by the websites of the bricks and mortar businesses. For some products, such as higher-end electronics, it seems that customers want to be able to touch and see the product before they purchase. The ability to pick up the ordered product at the customers' convenience may also have something to do with their purchase patterns.

The message here—look beyond DFSS—refers to what's between the produced product and your customers. Are you getting the *right* message out through the *right* communication channels and through the *right* distribution channels?

LEANING THE NEW PRODUCT DEVELOPMENT PROCESS

One of our clients has three pillars that support their business improvements—Six Sigma, DFSS, and lean. Their DFSS strategy included a full-scale implementation of most of DFSS' methods and tools (even here, they focused their DFSS implementation on better voice of customer/requirements definition and flow-down of requirements/flow-up of design capabilities). Once they started getting good at DFSS, they took a hard look at the value-added/non-value-added activities in their development process. They identified several *value streams* in the development process—for example, *from customer to requirements* is one value stream. They mapped in detail all of the activities and interfaces that occur in these streams.

One of this leaning effort's outcomes was the development of *tailoring* decision support tools. Instead of performing a full voice of customer effort every time, each team now tailors its VOC efforts to the specific design challenge. For example, if the product is the next generation of an existing platform, the VOC effort is focused on the gaps between what is already known and what the new product is intended to deliver.

Another area they are exploring tentatively is the opportunity to reduce the number and scope of design verification/validation activities. One development leader noted, "With all the design analysis we now do, when we walk into the Verify/Validate step, it seems like we throw all that knowledge away." He's convinced that there is an opportunity to perform risk-based verification/validation activities. If the team is confident that the design analyses provide them with the verification knowledge they need, then either no or minimal verification efforts will be planned for that requirement. For those requirements with higher uncertainty or risk, more verification will be performed. They are moving toward the design, analyze, and confirm philosophy of DFSS.

Here's another lean element you may consider for further development process improvement. In *Managing the Design Factory,* Donald Reinertsen focuses on the capacity of the development process and treats development as a factory that has constraints just like any production process. For example, a consumer products company has its R&D staff working on anywhere from 5 to 15 development projects at one time. On average, that's 4–5 hours per week devoted to any one project. And they wonder why they aren't getting innovative products out the door.

In our nuclear engineering department, at one time we had 400 designs in progress for an *operating* nuclear plant. Our Monday afternoon scope and schedule discussions were hilarious. We were so overloaded that we developed a form to give the plant the scope and schedule for when we would actually provide the scope and schedule for the project, let alone actually getting the work done.

ORGANIZATIONAL CHANGE MANAGEMENT

One day, we were sitting in a client's conference room waiting for the next development team to show up for DFSS coaching. One of our acquaintances wandered in and started talking about the work he was doing looking at the portfolio of their projects. He had analyzed the portfolio of projects in terms of their risks and rewards (the teams' charters were helpful here). The picture wasn't pretty. Most of their projects were in the low-risk, low-reward quartile. They were

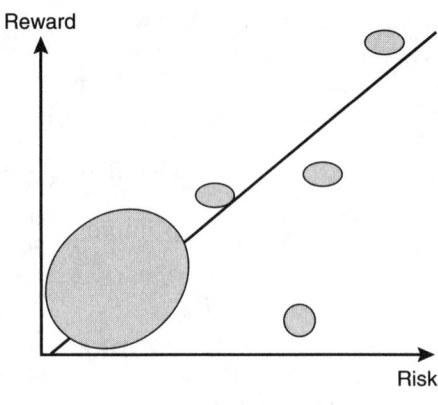

Figure 10.2 Product portfolio risk/reward profile.

only working on a few potentially innovative projects and one high-risk, low-reward project (see Figure 10.2).

When he started to ask why, some of the real, organizational impediments to innovation surfaced. The organization had a low tolerance for risk; product development schedules were always tight; marketing staff were assigned to their positions for only 18 months—they had to launch something to meet their goals (and get their bonuses); and capital for new production equipment (to produce something other than what they'd always done) was generally hard to obtain. He'd stumbled on to some of the behaviors that DFSS by itself can't fix. General Electric uses a change management equation: $Q \times A = E$ where Q = quality (of a decision or action), A = acceptance, and E = effectiveness. DFSS definitely helps you improve the Q side, but this company needed some A-side work.

SCHEDULE PERFORMANCE IMPROVEMENT

There's a bit of an overlap of this topic with leaning the NPD process. The Define–Measure–Analyze steps of DMADVI are tough to pin down on a schedule—these being the VOC gathering, concept development, and feasibility steps. Moving forward into Design, Verify/Validate, and Implement, the work should be predictable enough to wrap into a schedule. One of our clients found, though, that the traditional critical-path approach to project management resulted in predictable schedule overruns; they just weren't launching when the schedule said they should!

Diagnosis of the root causes led them to take a closer look at the just-off-critical path activities. They discovered that, because of variation in the time it takes to perform development activities, frequently a non-critical-path activity would make its way to the critical path. They are now exploring how to incorporate variation into their estimates of development cycle time (e.g., through Monte Carlo simulation of the schedule) and trying to improve their schedule risk management.

SUPPLIER DEVELOPMENT

How much of your product is produced by suppliers? Do you rely heavily on the quality of their parts/assemblies for your products to work well? Are you a virtual development organization, with perhaps market research and concepting/feasibility done in-house, detailed design done by a contract development/engineering firm, and production by a contract manufacturer?

Your DFSS strategy, then, will be shaped by these realities. For example, the business strategy of one of our clients is to delegate some of their production and design activities to China. They've developed a careful, measured plan to build capability at their key Chinese suppliers. They focused first on ensuring that the suppliers can produce parts and assemblies at the required Sigma levels. Next, they began to work with their suppliers' design group to introduce some basic DFSS methods (e.g., design scorecards, failure modes and effects analysis, and design for manufacturability/assembly).

A more difficult challenge is faced by the virtual development organization. While they can improve their voice of customer and concepting/feasibility processes themselves, convincing the contract development and manufacturing organizations to adopt DFSS/Six Sigma may be a challenge. One of our clients is having a difficult time with their contract manufacturer; even adoption of some basic quality assurance methods such as statistical process control is being resisted.

SYSTEMATIC INNOVATION TECHNIQUE

DFSS is all about the customer. By now, you've realized that the Measure step is focused on obtaining solid voice of customer information, which in turn is translated into product requirements that guide the design. Two Israeli professors, Jacob Goldenberg and David Mazursky, ask a slightly different question: "What if we start with the voice of the product?"

Their systematic innovation technique (SIT) guides you to think about how your product could evolve—by applying creativity templates based on predictable patterns of product evolution. These ideas must be validated by your customers; for example, do they have needs this new product may satisfy.

Systematic innovation may help you in the fuzzy front-end of DFSS. For example, one product team was stuck; they felt their product was mature and, other than incremental improvements, didn't have much place to go. They decided to try systematic innovation and were led through a two-day session by experienced facilitators. Applying SIT and the creativity templates helped them identify more than 100 new directions for their product, about 30 of which seem to have commercial potential.

TAGUCHI'S ROBUST DESIGN

We would argue that Genichi Taguchi's robust design approach is an integral part of DFSS. His core ideas of ensuring that the design is made robust to sources of noise (manufacturing, environmental, deterioration) is consistent with DFSS' message of ensuring that the design minimizes the variation seen by the customer (e.g., at the CTQ or product level). However, there are two ways to make this happen: the brute force or the more elegant Taguchi approach.

In the brute force approach, the requirements are defined and the design is developed. Variation predictions then identify and prioritize the design or process Xs that significantly affect the CTQ variation. Achieving the allowable CTQ variation is then accomplished by setting tight enough specifications at the X level. Quality is then achieved, but the cost may be high.

Taguchi argues that an effort called *parameter design* should follow the concepting phase. Here, the design is tested by expected noises (manufacturing, environmental, deterioration) through an experimental approach. Changing some design parameters will affect not only the average response of the CTQ, but also the *variation response*. In Figure 10.3, if we set the X at X_2 the CTQ will be higher on average than if we set the X at X_1. However, if we consider manufacturing noise in this X, setting the X at X_1 results in less variation in the CTQ (and this is what the customer sees).

Taguchi would recommend setting this parameter at X_1 (to minimize CTQ variation *for free*). He would then try to find another parameter which can be used to adjust the average value of the CTQ,

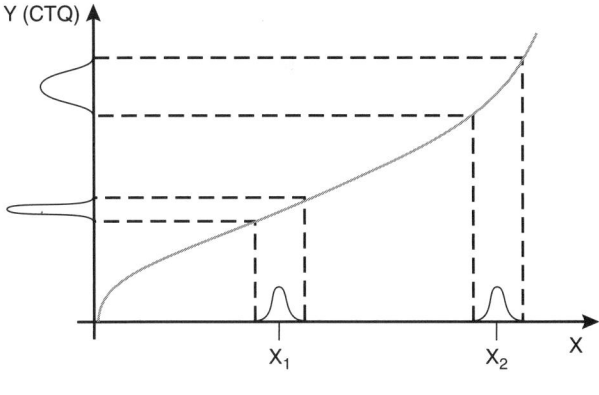

Figure 10.3 Variable noise transmission from X to CTQ.

but whose variation doesn't cause a change in the CTQ variation (see Figure 10.4).

Whatever quality that cannot be achieved through *parameter design* is then addressed by Taguchi's tolerance design phase, where the required CTQ variation is achieved by balancing design cost with the "quality loss" to society.

Taguchi's parameter design activities fit nicely into the Analyze step of DMADVI—part of establishing design feasibility.

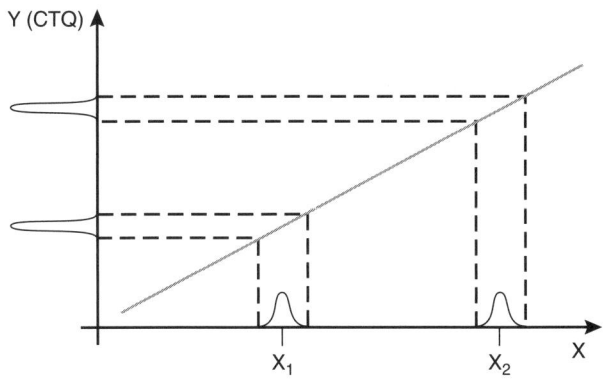

Figure 10.4 Constant noise transmission from X to CTQ.

THEORY OF INVENTIVE PROBLEM SOLVING (TRIZ)

The Russian engineer Genrich Altshuller noted that 90% of problems that engineers face have already been solved. Perhaps these problems weren't solved by your company or industry, but they were solved somewhere before.

His insight led to the development of the theory of inventive problem-solving (Russian acronym, TRIZ). TRIZ has a wide variety of applications in product development—initial idea generation (the systematic innovation technique has its basis in TRIZ), design concepts (unique solutions to design problems, especially "busting" technical or physical design conflicts), and in-process development (again, breaking through process design conflicts).

In our view, TRIZ thinking will significantly benefit almost any product development process. However, TRIZ is not the easiest method to learn. The methodology is captured in the algorithm for inventive problem solving (ARIZ), and the last time we looked it was in its 71st version! One practitioner told us that it took a year for him to rewire his brain in the TRIZ thinking patterns.

Recognizing this, Kalevi Rantanen and Ellen Domb published *Simplified TRIZ*. This book is a very readable, *applicable* treatment of TRIZ.

KEY POINTS

You should walk away from reading this chapter with some thoughts about where to go next after you have implemented DFSS, including these possibilities:

- Leaning your process
- Improving your customer listening/VOC collection and translation
- Improving your suppliers' capabilities
- Innovative thinking

11
DFSS Case Study

INTRODUCTION

Although this is a book about implementing DFSS, one of the strong needs that we identified during our research was "give me a DFSS example." Unfortunately, this is difficult for two reasons. First, the real DFSS examples that we've participated in are proprietary and the details are hide to disguise. Second, even if the design information isn't proprietary, a full description of a typical product design effort would be a book in itself.

So here's how we're going close this book and try to meet your need for an end-to-end DFSS example. You might remember Jethro Tull as a rock band from the 1970s. Well, it turns out there was a *real* Jethro Tull, who lived from 1674 until 1741. Tull is credited with several inventions that revolutionized the world of agriculture. We've chosen one of his simpler designs: the wheat seed drill.

Before Tull's invention, farmers would plant their fields by simply scattering seed around on the ground. His idea was to develop a device that placed seeds in the ground, in rows, and at regular intervals (yes, you can already *smell* the CTQs).

Let's take a historical trip and see how Mr. Tull could have used DFSS' DMADV to develop his seed drill. We'll focus on some key DFSS issues that he would have faced.

DEFINE PHASE: THE OPPORTUNITY

Mr. Tull has been interested in improving farm productivity for a number of years. He owns and manages the Prosperous Farm near Basildon, Berkshire, in England and is known in his town for promoting innovations in farming methods. Recently, he has been investigating the process of planting wheat. The current method employed by farmers in his area is to scatter seeds by hand across the field, in hopes that some of them will germinate. Mr. Tull tried to have his workers plant seeds manually at regular intervals in rows, but they didn't seem capable of this work.

He decides to embark on developing a device that will do this work automatically. Mr. Tull starts the project by developing a charter—this helps him clarify the scope, goals, and resources required for the project. When he finishes the charter, Figure 11.1, Mrs. Tull will review and approve it as his sponsor.

Next, he thinks strategically about how his new product could expand and records these thoughts in a multigenerational product plan (MGPP). This MGPP provides him with two major benefits:

- Managing the scope of the current project (getting a product to market quickly).

- Identifying potential design features to be included in the current generation that will help him develop future generations.

- Identifying technology that might be needed for future generations that he doesn't currently possess. In his spare time he can work on these advanced technology projects.

Jethro Tull considers his MGPP, shown in Figure 11.2, to be a draft for now. He may learn things in the Measure or Analyze steps that will cause him to revise the MGPP.

Before his Define phase gate, Mr. Tull also develops a more detailed project plan than the milestones shown in his charter. He wants to begin his voice of customer activities as soon as he passes his Define gate.

Define Phase Gate

As his sponsor, Mrs. Tull has a few questions about the charter and MGPP. She's concerned about the two red risk items: technology and adoption. She suggests that Mr. Tull investigate the adoption issue as he is gathering the voice of customer in the Measure phase. As for the technology issue, even though he's not sure how to solve the problem, he's had success inventing other farm improvement devices and is confident he will figure it out. Mrs. Tull is satisfied with these responses and agrees with his recommendation: Move to the Measure phase.

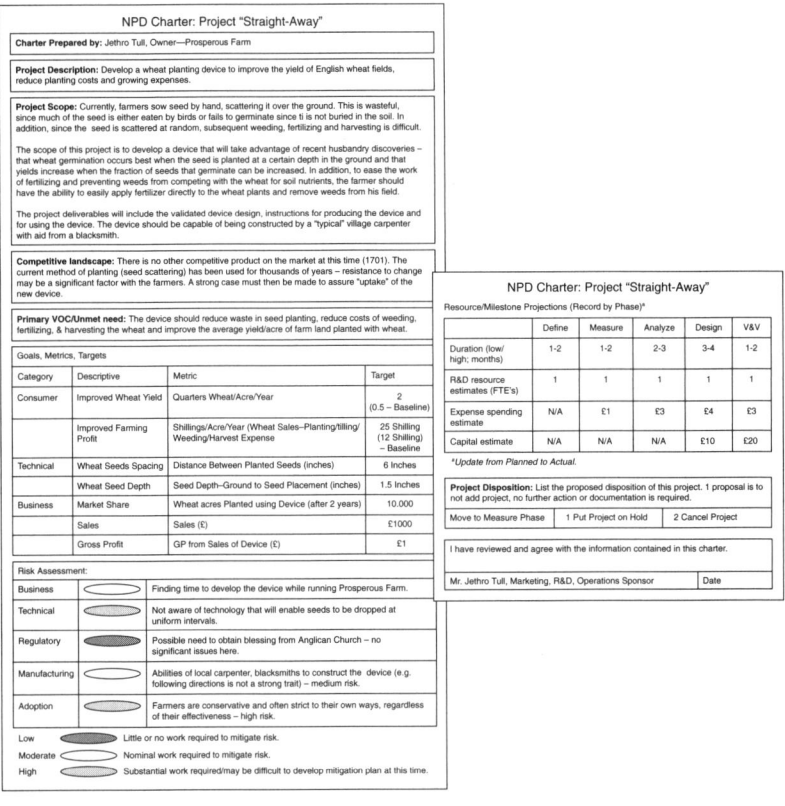

Figure 11.1 Tull's wheat planting device charter.

MEASURE PHASE: DEFINING CUSTOMER REQUIREMENTS AND CTQs

As a typical engineer, Mr. Tull thinks he knows what the device should do. However, he's humble enough to gather customer input (especially because of the adoption risk issue). His voice of customer plan includes the following:

- Write down what he would want in such a device (as a farmer, he knows quite a bit already).
- Segment the market and identify unique customer groups/segments.

MULTIGENERATIONAL PRODUCT PLAN

Project: "Straight-Away"
Date: 2 Jan 1701
Revision: 1

	GENERATION		
	I - Step	II - Stretch	III - Leap
Vision	Improve Wheat Yields & Reduce Farm Expenses	Improve Yields & Reduce Expenses of Other English Crops	Improve Productivity of Seeding – Reduce Time to Plant an Acre
Product/Process Generations	A seeding device that can plant wheat at regular intervals & at uniform depth in the soil.	A seeding device that can plant any field crop planted in England at regular iintervals & at uniform depth in the soil.	A seeding device that can plant any field crop across multiple rows of a typical English farm field.
Platforms & Techology	Wood cutting & shaping Possible iron/steel working Horse harness	Wood cutting & shaping Possible iron/steel working Horse harness	Wood cutting & shaping Possible iron/steel working Horse harness

Figure 11.2 Tull's multigenerational plan.

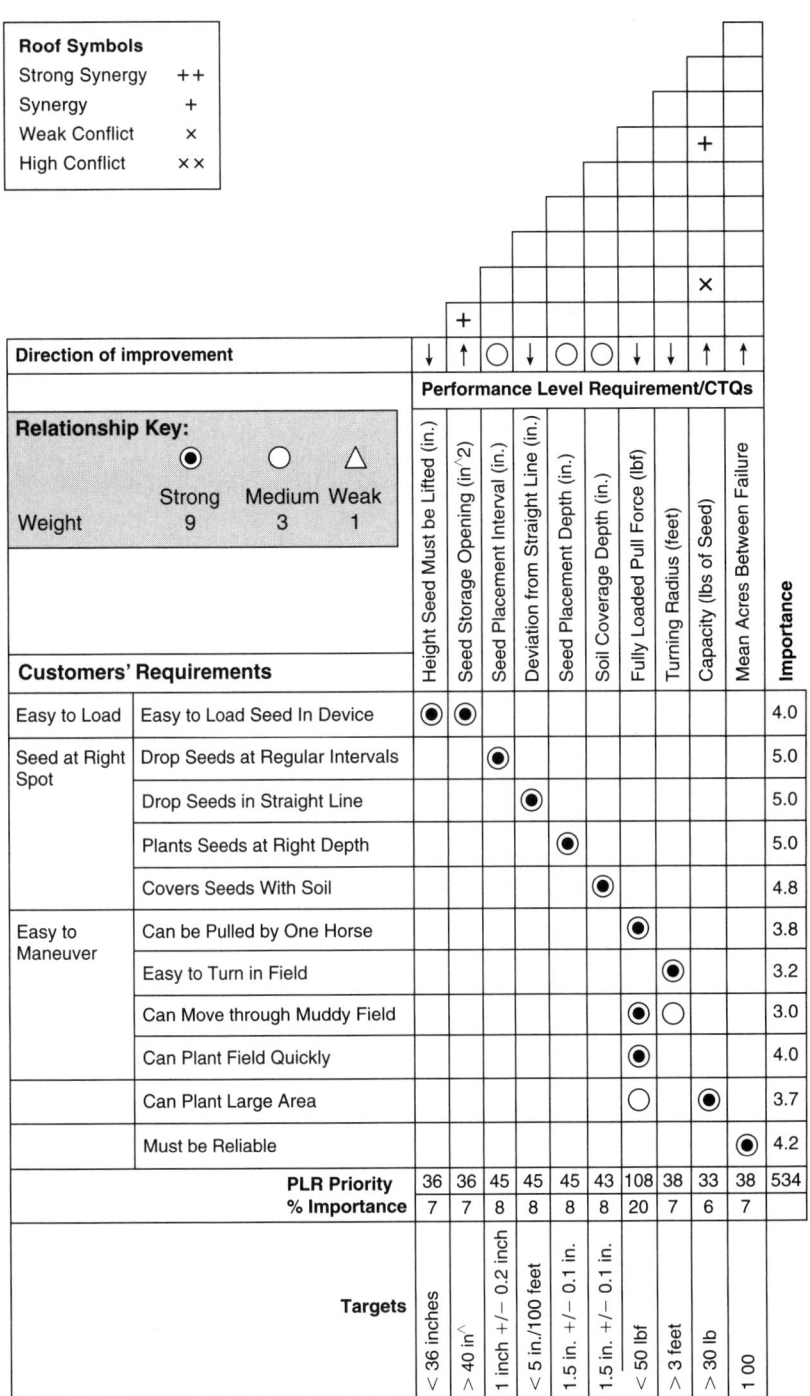

Figure 11.3 Planting device house of quality.

- Plan and conduct interviews of 8–10 customers in each segment. He thinks this should give him enough information to understand a large percentage of the needs.
- Organize this qualitative research through affinitizing the needs.
- Conduct a survey of the customers, using the organized needs to identify their priorities and confirm their requirements.
- Translate the customer needs into product-level requirements and select the critical-to-quality (CTQ) requirements.

Fortunately, it's winter in Basildon so the farmers can spend some time discussing their needs with him. (He remembers this for future product development efforts—conduct VOC in the winter to get best access to his customers.)

He enjoys using matrices to organize his thinking and so develops a house of quality (see Figure 11.3) to define and prioritize the requirements.

Sitting in front of his fireplace, he realizes that the VOC work has helped. He was very focused on developing a device that spaces the seeds equally and at a constant depth. The farmers' voices have also said that the device must be easy to move through the fields, especially the muddy conditions that are found around planting time in England.

The other good news is while there are a few synergies among requirements, there is only one conflict—that of the pulling force and the seed capacity.

After some thought, Mr. Tull selects the three most important product-level requirements and records these on his design scorecard (see Figure 11.4). The first two were selected because they are new and unique capabilities, the third because it may be difficult to achieve.

Measure Phase Gate

Mr. Tull reviews the results of his Measure phase work with Mrs. Tull. She concurs that the requirements he's identified make sense and that he should focus on the three CTQs, as confirmed by a representative sample of his potential customers. She questions the target of 2 inches for seed placement interval, especially because the charter lists 6 inches. Mr. Tull explains that he was thinking of corn plant

	B	C	D	E	F	G	H	I
1	**CTQ Scorecard**							
3	Product/System:	Seed Planting Device						
4	Project Leader	Jethro Tull						
5	CTQ	Measure	Target/ Nominal	Upper Spec Limit	Lower Spec Limit	Sigma Target (ST)	Mean	Std. Dev.
6								
7	Seed Placement Interval	Inches	2.0	2.2	1.8	4		
8								
9	Seed Placement Depth	Inches	1.5	1.6	1.4	4		
10								
11	Fully Loaded Pull Force	Pounds-force		50.0		3		
12								
13								
14								

Figure 11.4 CTQ design scorecard.

placement in the Define phase—discussions with the wheat farmers (and his own practice) resulted in the revision to the target to reflect the higher density of wheat plants in the fields. He tells her that he will update the charter with the new information.

ANALYZE PHASE: IDENTIFYING CONCEPTS AND ASSESSING FEASIBILITY

Mr. Tull is systematic in his thinking. He first identifies the functions that the product will have to perform:

- Load seed
- Store seed
- Disburse seed
- Bury seed
- Cover seed
- Turn at row end

He begins to research ways of accomplishing these functions. The most difficult function is disbursing seeds; this function will be responsible for ensuring that the seeds are placed at regular intervals. After consideration of many ideas, he identifies a design concept that includes a rotating, grooved spindle, with a tongue to control the disbursement of the seed. Here are his words:

> When I was young, My Diversion was Musick: I had also the Curiosity to acquaint my self thoroughly with the Fabrick of every Part of an Organ; but as little thinking that I should take from thence, the first Rudiments of a Drill. . . . that I could contrive an Engine to plant St. Foin more faithfully than such Hands [i.e., his labourers] would do. To that Purpose I examin'd and compar'd all the mechanical Ideas that ever had enter'd my Imagination, and at last, repitch'd upon a *Groove, Tongue and Spring* in the Sound-Board of the Organ: with these, a little alter'd, and some Parts of 2 other Instruments as foreign to the Field as the Organ is, added to them, I compos'd my Machine: 'Twas nam'd a Drill. . . .

In his first design concept, the spindle will be rotated by two small wheels, connected to the main wheels (we'll call this the *seed disbursement subsystem*). A hopper above the spindle will store the seed during planting (the *seed storage subsystem*). Steel tubes will deposit the seed at the correct depth (the *seed delivery subsystem*), and two steel harrows will spread soil over the seed (the *seed coverage subsystem*). These subsystems will be mounted on a base with two large wheels. The entire device will be pulled by a horse and led by a worker through the field (the *propulsion/guidance subsystem*). He develops a sketch of his overall concept as shown in Figure 11.5.

From here, we will focus on the design of the seed disbursement subsystem and how Mr. Tull applies DFSS to achieve the *seed placement interval* CTQ. First, how can Mr. Tull apply his musical organ insight to the seed disbursement subsystem? He knows that an organ works by a tongue that admits air to the pipe, with the tongue being controlled by the organ keys. For his seeding device, though, he wants to admit a controlled flow of seeds, not air. His concept for the disbursement subsystem involves a rotating spindle with grooves for the seeds. The flow of seeds is controlled by a tongue, which is held against the spindle. Seeds enter the grooves in the spindle from the seed storage subsystem, and are then disbursed to the seed delivery subsystem by rotation of the spindle. A cover fitted over the top of the spindle prevents seeds from falling out of the front of the device. The sketch of this subsystem appears in Figure 11.6.

The spindle's rotation is controlled by the spindle wheels, which are, in turn, rotated by their friction with the axle of the main wheels (see Figure 11.7).

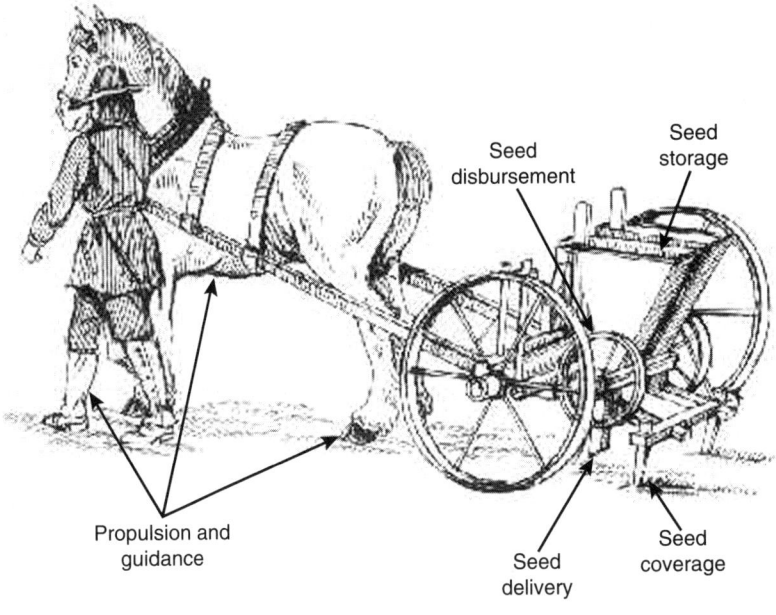

Figure 11.5 Seeding device—conceptual sketch.

At this point, let's illustrate the idea of cascade. The CTQ of interest is *seed disbursement interval*. The target for this CTQ is 2 inches. For this Y, we'll invoke geometry to identify the important design parameters. In Mr. Tull's concept, for every 360° rotation of the main wheel, the spindle rotates $r_{axle}/r_{spindle\ wheel} \times 360°$.

Therefore, the disbursement interval depends on the main wheel radius (which determines the distance the device travels forward each rotation), the ratio of the axle radius to spindle wheel radius, and the number of grooves in the spindle. This qualitative cascade is depicted in Figure 11.8.

If Mr. Tull equally spaces the spindle grooves, the transfer function expressing the CTQ as a function of the design parameters is easily determined:

$$Interval = \frac{2\pi \times r_{Wheel}}{\dfrac{r_{Axle}}{r_{Spindle\ Wheel}} \times \#Grooves}$$

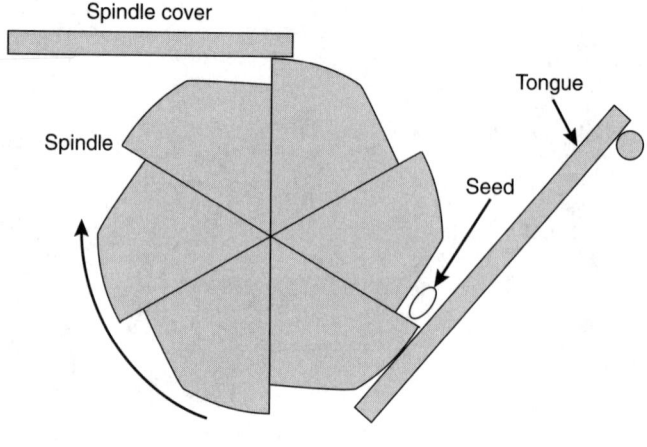

Figure 11.6 Seeding device—seed disbursement subsystem concept.

For example, if the main wheel radius is set at 12 inches, the axle radius at 2 inches, and the spindle wheel at 6 inches and 12 grooves are cut into the spindle, the disbursement interval is:

$$Interval = \frac{2\pi \times 12}{\frac{2}{6} \times 12} = 18.85 \; inches$$

So with this early concept, he's pretty far off the mark. Time to go back to the drawing board.

Mr. Tull rethinks his first concept. He decides to decouple the spindle wheels from the main wheels and let them contact the ground. Now, the spindle rotates at the same rate as the spindle wheels. The new transfer function is:

$$Interval = \frac{2\pi \times r_{Spindle \; Wheel}}{\# Grooves}$$

For a 9.5-inch-diameter spindle wheel (4.75-inch radius) and 15 equally spaced grooves, he will achieve a seed interval of 1.99 inches—pretty close to his target on the scorecard.

He's now comfortable that his design is feasible, at least for the CTQ we've examined. He'll work on the rest of the subsystem

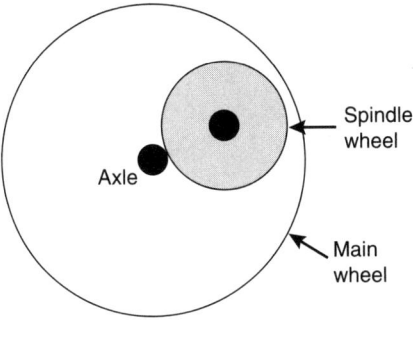

Figure 11.7 Seed disbursement subsystem—propulsion concept.

design and try to achieve the other product requirements identified in the Measure phase.

As part of his feasibility work, he'll also identify the technologies needed to produce his device. For example, he'll consider the capabilities of the local craftsmen to build his device. He shows Mr. Ferguson, the carpenter, his spindle concept and says that it will need 15 equally spaced grooves cut into a wooden cylinder.

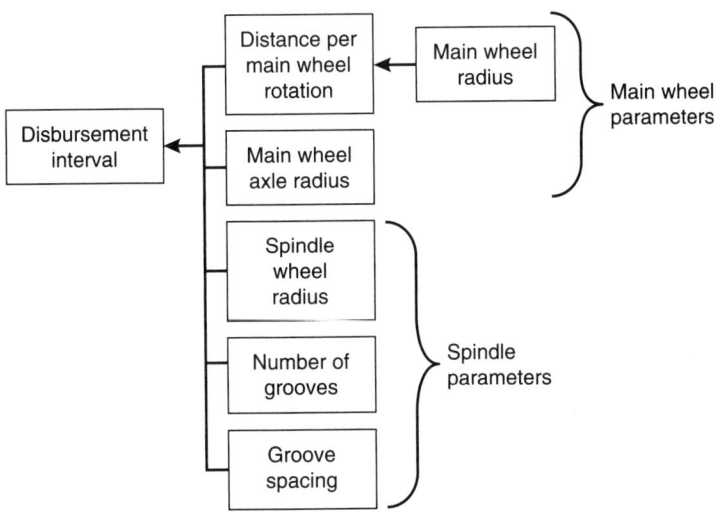

Figure 11.8 Disbursement interval cascade to design parameters.

Mr. Ferguson assures Mr. Tull that this is easily done with his tools and measurement methods.

Because reliability is important, Mr. Tull sits in front of the fire one night with his sketches and identifies the failure modes that could occur and their effects. He recognizes that not all of these are equally important and so tries to rank them by their frequency and severity (he multiplies these two factors together and calls the result a *risk priority number,* or RPN). So that he can easily refer to these potential problems in the future, he records them on a matrix that he calls a failure modes and effects analysis (FMEA).

He makes several design changes to reduce the high RPN and high severity failure modes. He also identifies several investigations that he needs to perform in the Design phase (seed arching, which we'll address).

Before his gate review with Mrs. Tull, Mr. Tull calls together a group of his neighbors (a few pints of ale and a roast beef provided the motivation to attend). He explains his conceptual design to them and asks for their input. They give him a number of suggestions to improve the design, most of which he incorporates (one or two were good, but not in the scope of the first-generation design; he'll save those for later).

Analyze Phase Gate

Mr. Tull reviews the results of his Analyze phase work with Mrs. Tull. He starts with his Design Scorecard (Figure 11.9) and shows her the facts—how close he is to the targets (and how far away from the spec limits he is for the one-sided CTQs).

She reviews the results of the neighbors' review and concurs with how Mr. Tull dispositioned the comments. She questions the financial aspect of the design: how much will it cost to build and what profit they may expect from the sales. Mr. Tull provides her with preliminary figures, and she's satisfied.

DESIGN PHASE: DETAILED PRODUCT AND PRODUCTION PROCESS DESIGN

Mr. Tull based his Analyze phase feasibility work on calculations. A prototype wasn't needed to demonstrate that, at least theoretically, the product requirements could be met. He commences to develop the production version of the device. Here, we'll focus on the seed

	B	C	D	E	F	G	H	I
1	CTQ Scorecard							
3	Product/System:	Seed Planting Device						
4	Project Leader	Jethro Tull						
5	CTQ	Measure	Target/ Nominal	Upper Spec Limit	Lower Spec Limit	Sigma Target (ST)	Mean	Std. Dev.
6								
7	Seed Placement Interval	Inches	2.0	2.2	1.8	4	1.99	
8								
9	Seed Placement Depth	Inches	1.5	1.6	1.4	4	1.5	
10								
11	Fully Loaded Pull Force	Pounds-force		50.0		3	34	
12								
13								
14								

Figure 11.9 Analyze phase design scorecard.

storage and seed disbursement subsystems. The drawings in Figures 11.10 and 11.11 show his detailed design of these subsystems.

We'll describe four key DFSS activities here:

- Design optimization through designed experiments
- Variation prediction through Monte Carlo simulation
- Reliability assurance through testing
- Production process controls—critical control points to achieve CTQs

Design Optimization—Bevel to Prevent Seed Arching

Mr. Tull builds a working prototype of the two subsystems to test their functions. The interior walls of the seed storage system were, at first, parallel (easy to construct). Testing, though, revealed that sometimes the seed would *arch,* which interrupted seed flow through the spindle (see Figure 11.12).

He decides to perform an experiment to ensure that his design will not have this problem. Although he has performed experiments on his device (now called a *seed drill*) by changing one factor at a time, he suspects that some of the design parameters may interact with one another.

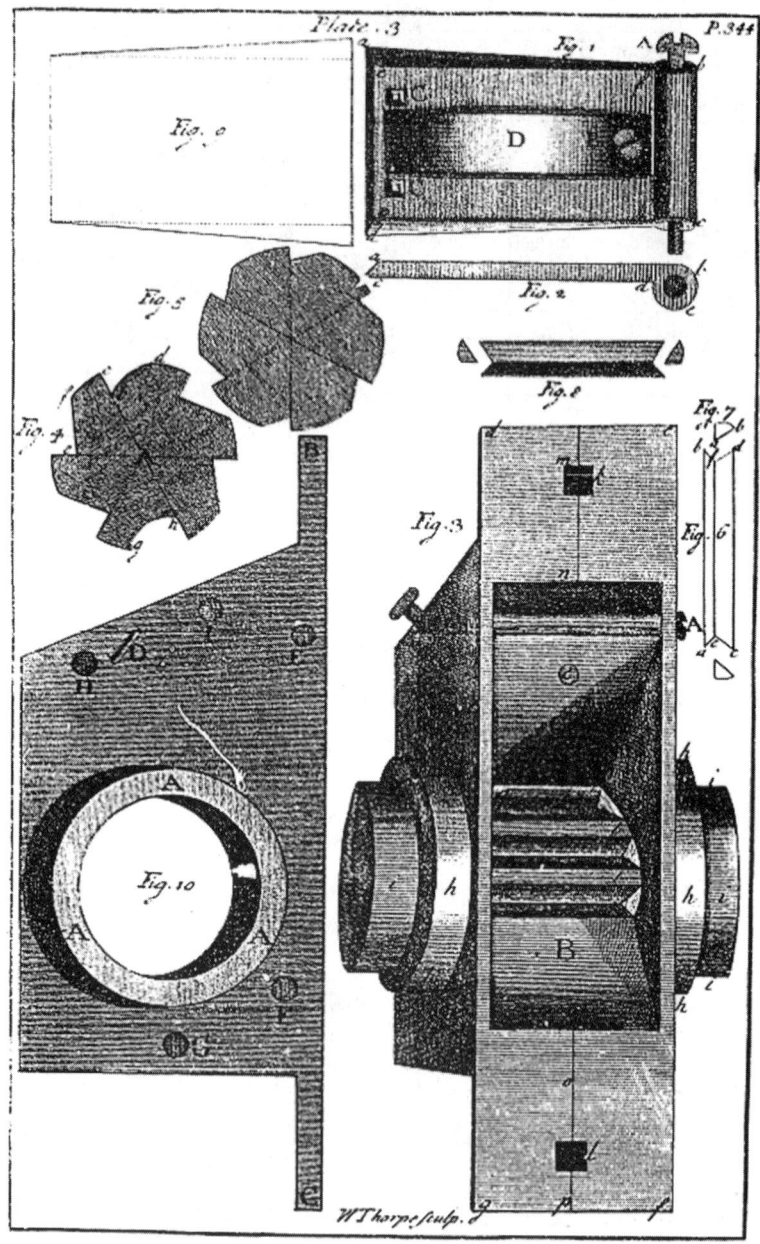

Figure 11.10 Components for seed storage and disbursement subsystems.

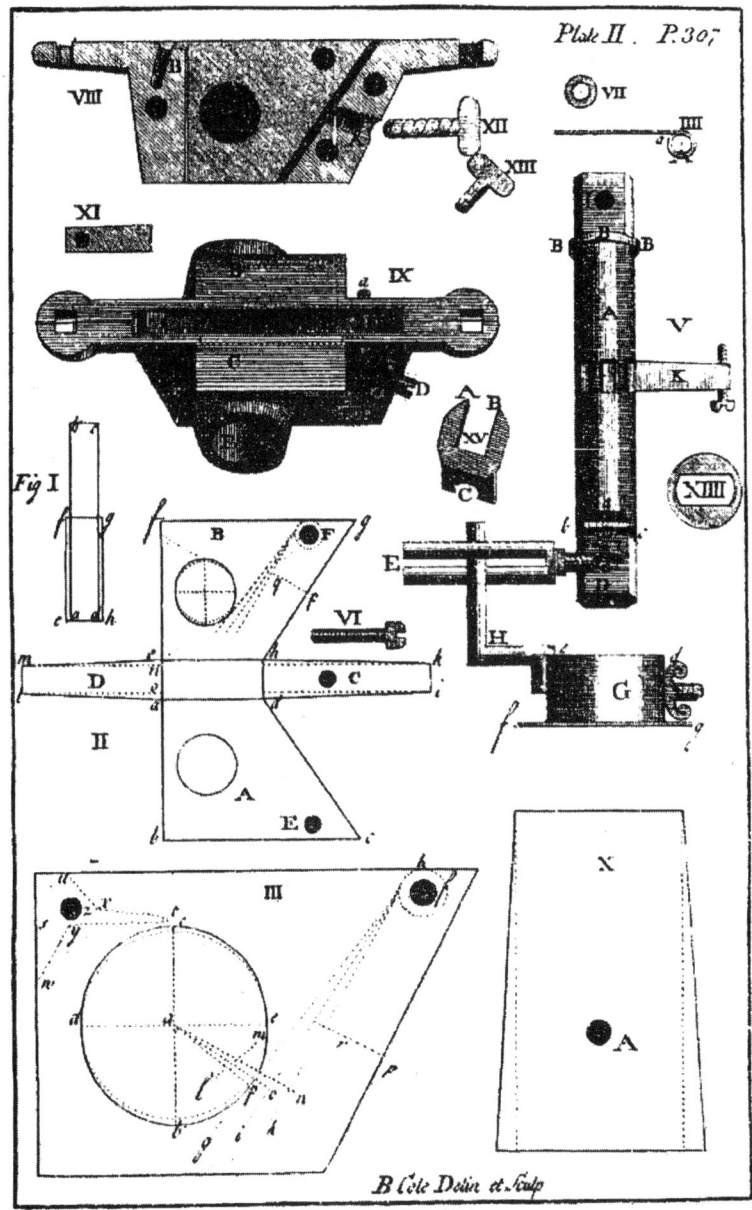

Figure 11.11 Components for seed storage and disbursement subsystems.

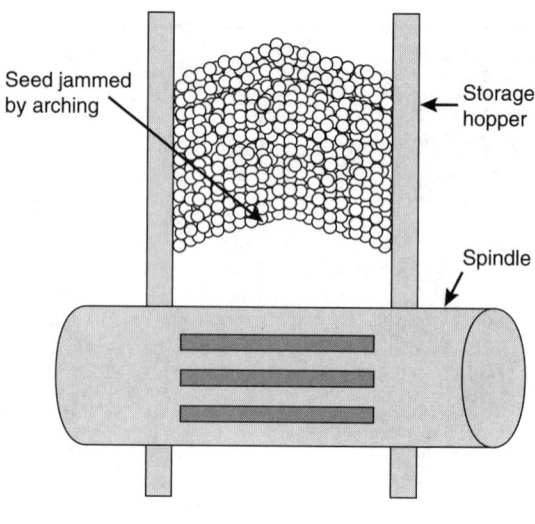

Figure 11.12 Seed arching in seed storage/disbursement subsystems.

He asks a friend from London, Mr. Isaac Newton, to help him design an experiment that will allow him to efficiently optimize his design. They choose three parameters: storage hopper wall smoothness (rough, smooth), side-to-side bevel (parallel, angled), and front-to-back bevel (parallel, angled). Figure 11.13 illustrates the latter two factors.

Mr. Newton shows him a way of performing and analyzing these experiments so that they will be able to detect the main effects and

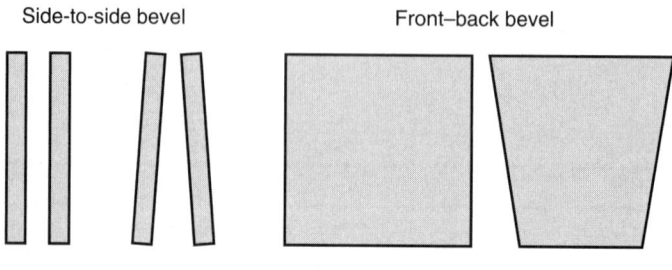

Figure 11.13 Seed storage system—DOE bevel factors.

	C1	C2	C3	C4	C5	C6	C7
	Std Order	Run Order	Center Pt	Blocks	Wall Surface	Side-Side Bevel	Front-Back Bevel
1	1	1	1	1	Rough	0	0
2	2	2	1	1	Smooth	0	0
3	3	3	1	1	Rough	10	0
4	4	4	1	1	Smooth	10	0
5	5	5	1	1	Rough	0	30
6	6	6	1	1	Smooth	0	30
7	7	7	1	1	Rough	10	30
8	8	8	1	1	Smooth	10	30

Figure 11.14 Full-factorial design of experiments—seed storage subsystem.

two-way interactions of these parameters that he calls a full-factorial experiment. The experimental layout is shown in Figure 11.14.

Mr. Newton recommends that Mr. Tull *randomize* the order of these experiments to prevent other factors from influencing his results. Mr. Tull performs the experiments, and Mr. Newton helps him analyze the results. The significant factors are shown in the Pareto chart of Figure 11.15.

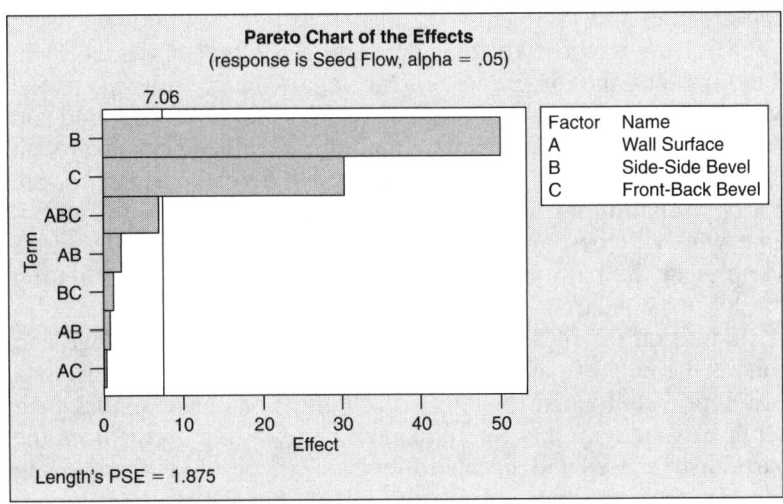

Figure 11.15 Pareto chart of effects—seed storage subsystem DOE.

He finds that Factor B, side-to-side bevel, is the most important factor affecting seed flow, followed by the front-to-back bevel (Factor C). The smoothness of the wall surface (Factor A) isn't important. Mr. Tull also records the transfer function obtained from the experiment; this will be useful to him in setting the final design parameter values:

$$\text{Seed Flow} = 99 + 5 \times \text{Bevel}_{\text{Side-to-Side}} + 1 \times \text{Bevel}_{\text{Front-to-Back}}$$

Interestingly, these two factors explained 98% of the variation in seed flow. With this problem solved, he turns his attention to the force applied by the tongue to the spindle.

Variation Prediction—Tongue/Spring to Spindle Force

The tongue/spring assembly controls the number of seeds entering each groove on the spindle. If the force applied by the tongue is too small, there will be too much *play* (Mr. Tull's term) and the seed will pass out too quickly. If the force is too large, the tongue will either slow the seed flow or prevent the seed from passing through the grooves. From his previous cascade and design work, Mr. Tull has developed a subsystem tongue/spring to spindle force requirement of 1 pound-force +/− 0.2 pound-force. He records this on a subsystem design scorecard shown on Figure 11.16.

Mr. Tull has worked out the parts for this subsystem, which appears in Figure 11.17.

Mr. Tull would like to understand the effect of variation in these parts on the tongue force. Once again, he consults his friend Mr. Newton. Mr. Newton examines the physics of the situation and decides that he can approximate the force that the spring exerts on the tongue as a beam being deflected. He derives an appropriate transfer function for Mr. Tull. Next, Mr. Tull talks with the craftsmen who will be building his device. He asks them to produce samples of the parts and measures their dimensions—calculating means and standard deviations.

Based on the measured variation, he visits a local college and solicits the help of the mathematics department. They take his data and fit probability distributions to each of the parameters. They then set up an assembly line where random numbers are drawn from the parts' distributions and repeatedly calculate the resulting force (using Mr. Newton's equation). Since the actual calculations were lost to history, we'll re-create this analysis using Crystal Ball, a modern Monte Carlo Simulator.

	B	C	D	E	F	G	H	I	J	K	L	M	N	O
1	**CTQ Scorecard**													
3	Product/System:	Seed Planting Device – Seed Disbursement Subsystem								Date				
4	Project Leader	Jethro Tull								Revision:				
5	CTQ	Measure	Target/ Nominal	Upper Spec Limit	Lower Spec Limit	Sigma Target (ST)	Mean	Std. Dev.	Data-Short or Long?	Shift (1.5 - Default)	DPU	No. Opps	DPMO (LT)	Predicted Sigma (ST)
6														
7	Tongue/spring Force	lbf	1.0	1.2	0.8	4								
8														
9														
10														
11														

Figure 11.16 Seed disbursement subsystem—design scorecard.

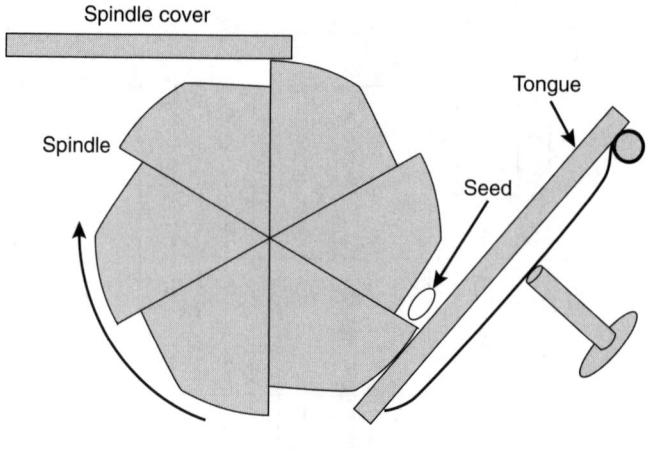

Figure 11.17 Seed disbursement subsystem—parts design.

First, we'll set up an Excel spreadsheet with the design parameters and Mr. Newton's transfer function shown on Figure 11.18.

Next, we'll assign probability distributions to each of the design parameters (Xs). An example appears in Figure 11.19.

Then, we'll run the Monte Carlo simulation (10,000 trials) and examine the results as shown on Figure 11.20.

Based on Mr. Tull's specifications for the force, over 99% of the tongue/spring assemblies will fall within the spec limits. The parameters that most influence the variation are shown on Figure 11.21, the sensitivity chart.

	A	B	C	D
1	Cantilevered Beam			
2				
3	Design Parameter	Nominal	Standard Dev.	Distribution
4	Modulus E (lbf/inch^2)	29000000	480000	Normal
5	Width at base wb (inch)	0.500	0.02	Normal
6	Width at end we (inch)	0.500	0.02	Normal
7	Thickness at end te (inch)	0.090	0.001	Normal
8	Thickness at base tb (inch)	0.100	0.001	Normal
9	Length L (inch)	8.000	0.02	Normal
11	Thickness at end te (inch)	0.160	0.001	Normal
12				
13	Force F (lbf)	1.047		
14				

Figure 11.18 Cantilevered beam spreadsheet.

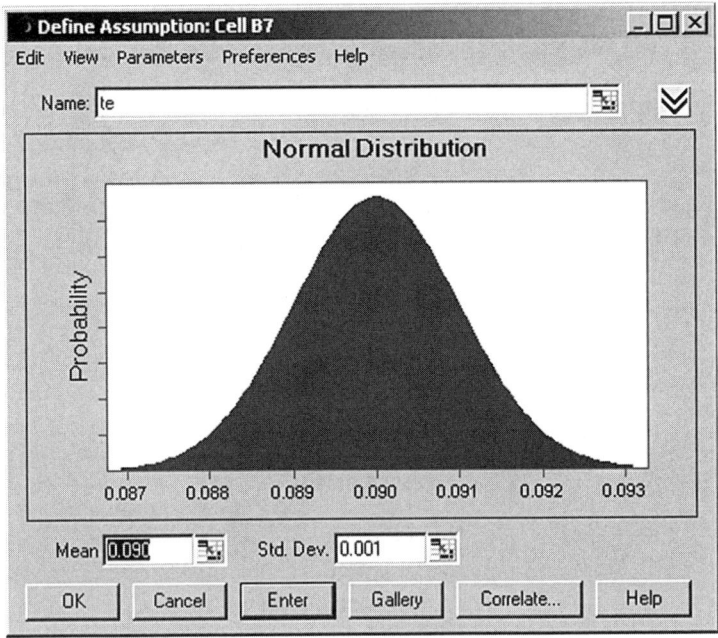

Figure 11.19 Normal probability distribution—assigned to end thickness design parameter.

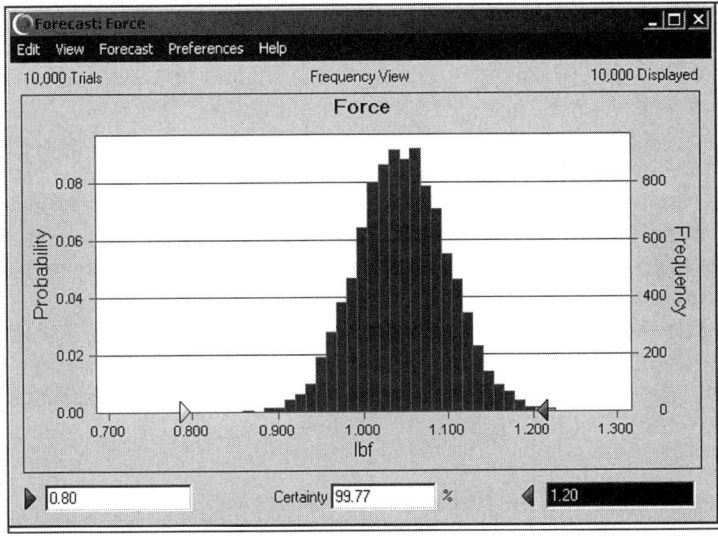

Figure 11.20 Deflection force simulation—initial run.

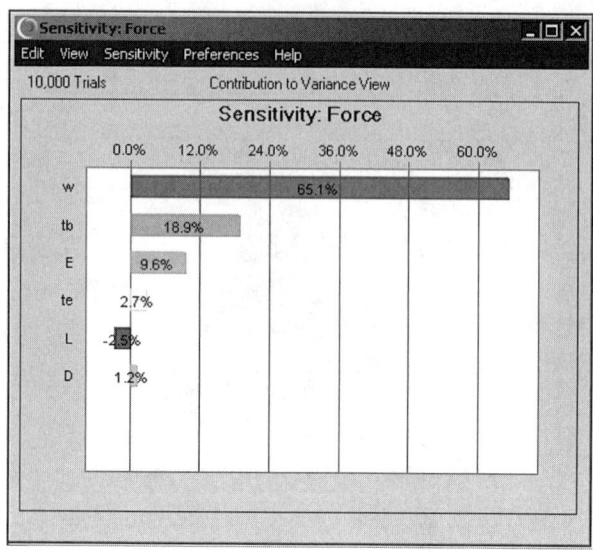

Figure 11.21 Deflection force—sensitivity chart—initial run.

The variation in the width of the spring (w) is the largest contributor (65%). Mr. Tull could investigate the benefit of trying to reduce this variation. For example, if he could cut the spring width variation in half through an improved fabrication process, the assembly variation would also be reduced as shown on Figure 11.22.

The design's sensitivity to the width has been reduced as shown by the new sensitivity chart (Figure 11.23).

Base thickness (tb) has replaced the width (w) as the most important source of variation. Mr. Tull records the results of his work on his subsystem design scorecard (see Figure 11.24, assuming he made the improvement to the width variation).

The design is predicted to meet its Sigma level target. Mr. Tull files the results of this analysis; he will confirm the results when he verifies the design later. By the end of the Design phase, Mr. Tull will roll up these predictions to the CTQ level.

Reliability Testing—Spring Cycle Test

Over a typical day's seeding, Mr. Tull has calculated, the spring will flex over 100,000 times. Because it would be very inconvenient to

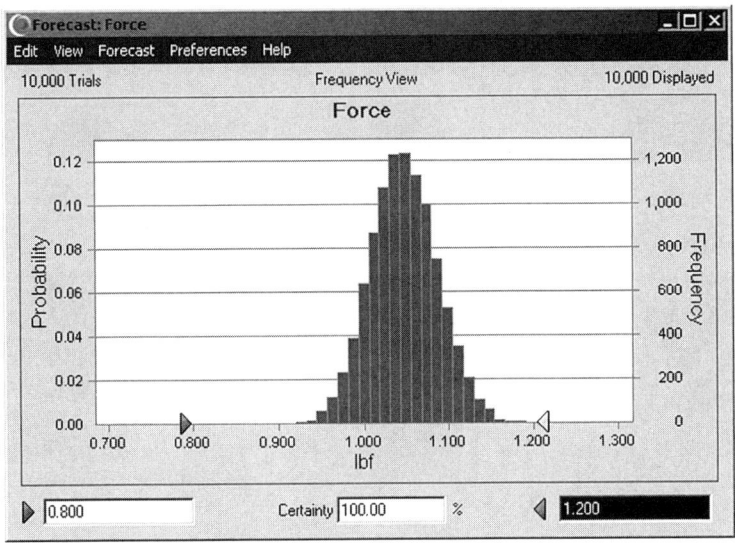

Figure 11.22 Deflection force simulation—second run.

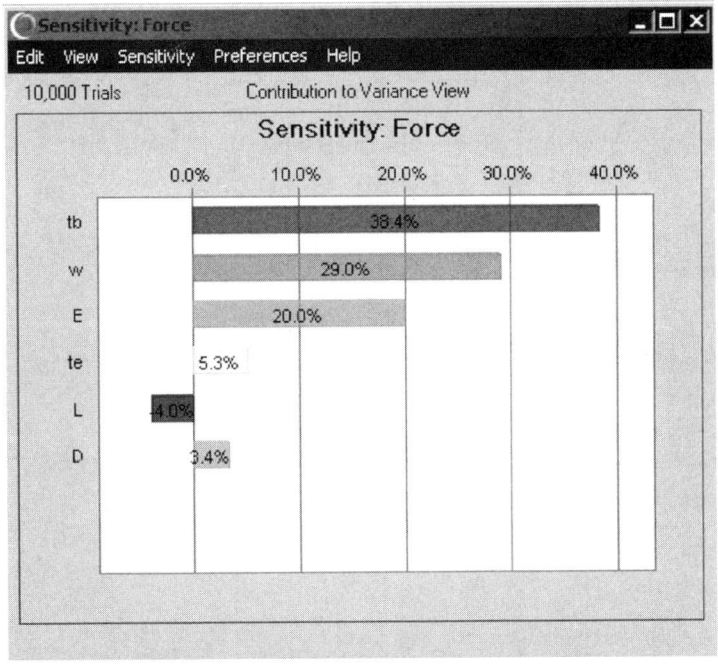

Figure 11.23 Deflection force—sensitivity chart—second run.

	B	C	D	E	F	G	H	I	J	K	L	M	N	O
1	**CTQ Scorecard**													
3	Product/System:	Seed Planting Device – Seed Disbursement Subsystem									Date				
4	Project Leader	Jethro Tull									Revision:				
5	CTQ	Measure	Target/ Nominal	Upper Spec Limit	Lower Spec Limit	Sigma Target (ST)	Mean	Std. Dev.	Data- Short or Long?	Shift (1.5 - Default)	DPU	No. Opps	DPMO (LT)	Predicted Sigma (ST)
7	Tongue/spring Force	lbf	1.0	1.2	0.8	4	1.047	0.039	1				4.37E+01	5.42

Figure 11.24 Updated subsystem design scorecard—seed disbursement subsystem.

Table 11.1 Spindle spring reliability test—cycles to failure.

Spring	Cycle to Failure
1	1,229,890
2	2,135,667
3	1,478,277
4	1,945,319
5	1,933,260
6	2,293,196
7	1,565,735
8	1,939,551
9	1,722,570
10	1,825,213

have to replace the spring during planting, he decides to test its reliability. His blacksmith fabricates 10 springs, which are flexed under simulated operating conditions. The cycles to failure are recorded in Table 11.1.

Planting a typical English farm will take about five days or 500,000 cycles. Because, on average, the spring lasts over 1,800,000 cycles, Mr. Tull is happy with the results of his test. We, however, will take his data and perform a Weibull analysis (see Figure 11.25).

We learn that his springs fail through a *wearout* mechanism (the shape or *beta* is 6.07—greater than 1 indicates wearout). We also learn that there is a 99% probability that the springs will last at least 900,000 cycles before failure (where the straight line intersects the 1% point. We're 95% confident that they will last at least 600,000 cycles at 99% reliability (where the lower bound—curved line intersects the 1% point). Based on this information, Mr. Tull could offer a warranty with his seed drill, and/or recommend a replacement schedule for the springs (6 acres or 600,000 seeds).

Production Design and Control Points

As he was developing the product design, Mr. Tull was also working out the details of the production process. His book *Horse-Hoeing Husbandry* (a catchy title for the 1700s) provides detailed instructions for building the seed drill. Here, for example, is a part of his instructions on shaping the side-to-side bevel of the seed storage subsystem:

> Take care that these opposite Sides be sure to be *true Planes*, especially all that Part of their Areas, that is before

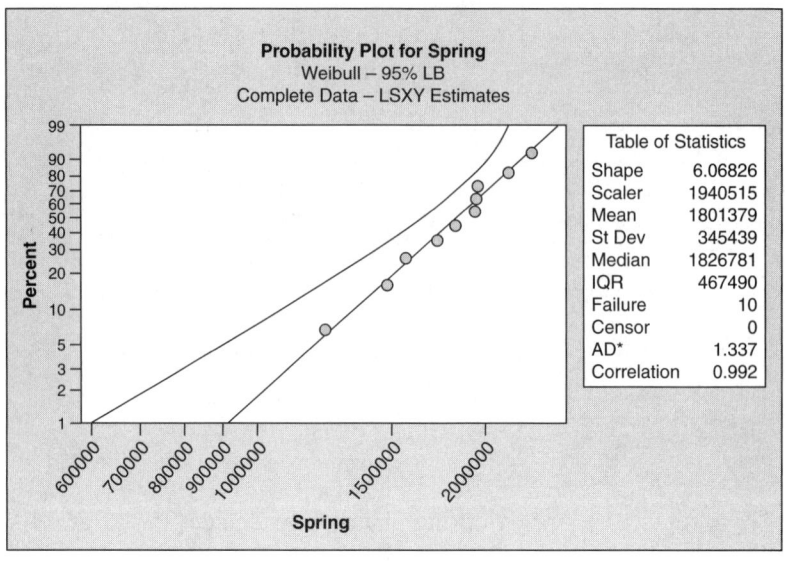

Figure 11.25 Weibull analysis—spindle spring cycles to failure.

the transverse Axes of their Ellipses herein after described; for should they be otherwise, the Bevel of the Mortise would be spoiled, and so would the Ellipses, and the acute Triangles, on the Sides of the Tongue; which how necessary they are to be true, is shewn in the proper Place. Workmen are very apt to fail in this when they file by Hand, and make these Sides of the Mortise convex instead of plane. Therefore this might be done with less Difficulty, and more Exactness, with a File placed in a Frame, whereby it might move upon a true Level without rising or sinking of either End.

These critical control points (a *control point* is any process operation where a product or lower level requirement can be controlled within specifications; critical control points are those operations where a CTQ can be controlled within specifications and/or high-risk failure's risk minimized) are included on the process control plan for the device. Today, Mr. Tull's instructions would be translated into a control plan for manufacturing as shown on Figure 11.26.

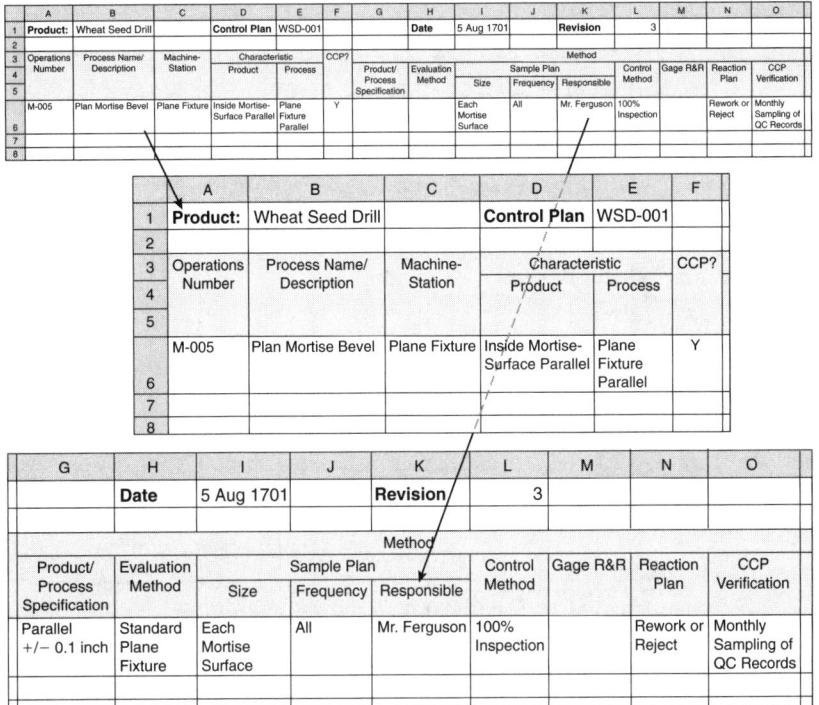

Figure 11.26 Process control plan example.

Design Phase Gate

Mr. Tull reviews the results of his Design Phase work with Mrs. Tull. He starts with his Design Scorecard (Figure 11.27) and shows her the facts—how close he is to the targets and, now, how much variation he predicts in the CTQs.

After some discussion, Mrs. Tull agrees that they should invest the capital required to produce the seed drills. As part of her approval, though, she asks Mr. Tull to visit Portsmouth where the British navy has been applying the new concept of *lean thinking* to the construction of ships. She thinks some of these principles will be useful in laying out the production process and associated supply chain for the seed drill. Mr. Tull agrees.

	B	C	D	E	F	G	H	I	J	K	L	M	N	O
1	**CTQ Scorecard**													
3	Product/System:	Seed Planting Device								Date				
4	Project Leader	Jethro Tull								Revision:				
5	CTQ	Measure	Target/ Nominal	Upper Spec Limit	Lower Spec Limit	Sigma Target (ST)	Mean	Std. Dev.	Data- Short or Long?	Shift (1.5 - Default)	DPU	No. Opps	DPMO (LT)	Predicted Sigma (ST)
6														
7	Seed Placement Interval	Inches	2.0	2.2	1.8	4	1.99	0.04	s				6.07E+02	4.74
8														
9	Seed Placement Depth	Inches	1.5	1.8	1.2	4	1.54	0.05	s				1.08E+02	5.20
10														
11	Fully Loaded Pull Force	Pounds-Force		50.0		3	32	4	s				1.35E+03	4.50
12														
13														

Figure 11.27 Final CTQ scorecard with design predictions.

VERIFY/VALIDATE PHASE: VERIFY AGAINST REQUIREMENTS; VALIDATE AGAINST CUSTOMER NEEDS

After building all the tools and laying out the production process, Mr. Tull and his craftsmen qualify the process. They assure themselves that each manufacturing station is *operationally qualified* to fabricate or assemble the parts within specifications. They then build a number of the devices as part of the *performance qualification* of the process. Measurements from these devices are made, the statistics calculated, and the design scorecard updated with this verification data as shown on Figure 11.28.

Although they see a small Sigma level dip from their design predictions to the verification data, the process is still performing satisfactorily. After another review with Mrs. Tull, the product is approved for release.

To validate the product, Mr. Tull uses several of the production models to plant his winter wheat for 1702. Some of his neighbors (those who helped him with the design review) also use the devices. Favorable results are reported, both on the use of the device and the effect it has on improved yields and lower farming costs (confirming Mr. Tull's goals in the Define phase charter).

IMPLEMENT PHASE: PRODUCTION AND QUALITY/BUSINESS RESULTS

Production and sales begin. From his visit to Portsmouth, Mr. Tull has implemented a lean production process. When a farmer orders a seed drill, that triggers the production process through a kan-ban system. Mr. Tull manages to keep his costs low by maintaining a very low inventory of parts and finished goods and, because he has used DFSS to design and implement the production process, there is very little in the way of scrap and waste.

Six months pass. . . .

Postlaunch Gate

Mr. Tull reviews the quality, sales, and financial figures with Mrs. Tull. While overall sales are good, the breakdown by segment is interesting. Unfortunately, the wider market of English farmers is slow to change and domestic sales of Mr. Tull's seed drill are low.

CTQ Scorecard

Product/System:	Seed Planting Device												
Project Leader	Jethro Tull												
						Design Prediction				Design Verification			
CTQ	Measure	Target/ Nominal	Upper Spec Limit	Lower Spec Limit	Sigma Target (ST)	Mean	Std. Dev.	Data-Short or Long?	DPM (LT)	Predicted Sigma (ST)	Mean	Std. Dev.	DPMO	Verified Sigma Level
Seed Placement Interval	Inches	2.0	2.2	1.8	4	1.99	0.04	S	6.07E+02	4.74	2.01	0.05	3516.28	4.20
Seed Placement Depth	Inches	1.5	1.8	1.2	4	1.54	0.05	S	1.08E+02	5.20	1.50	0.06	383.18	4.86
Fully Loaded Pull Force	Pounds-Force		50.0		3	32	4	S	1.35E+03	4.50	33.0	4.00	29879.72	4.25

Figure 11.28 Updated design scorecard—design verification results.

However, the British colonies across the Atlantic learned of the new seed planting device and are eagerly adopting it on their farms. Mr. Tull now enjoys a brisk export trade, so much so that he is planning to set up a factory in New England to manufacture and sell the devices in the colonies.

Glossary

analysis of variance (ANOVA)—An analytical process that identifies the contribution of each individual input factor to the overall output response. (Chapter 2)

axiomatic design—A theory by Dr. Nam Pyo Suh that stresses that each functional requirement be designed to achieve robustness without affecting other functional requirements. (Chapter 10)

benchmarking—The act of seeking out relative processes to compare your methods against. The goal of benchmarking is to find a new standard to live up to, whether it is inside your industry or not. For example, a laundry detergent manufacturer might benchmark other consumer products for advertising best practices or other chemical companies to benchmark manufacturing and quality-control processes. (Chapter 5)

best practice—The "new standard" to live up to. The best current set of processes or products you have found to compare to, measure against, and learn from. For example, Motorola is known as a best practice in Six Sigma deployment. And Toyota is known to have best practices in automotive manufacturing. (Chapter 5)

Black Belt—Typically a person assigned full-time to lead Six Sigma (DMAIC, lean, or DFSS) projects that reach out past his or her field of expertise. Black Belts are also typically assigned to mentor Green Belts. (Chapter 2)

build-and-test—A traditional method of designing products that results in multiple iterations, low levels of actual learning from each iteration, and wasted design time. Build-and-test methods can be replaced with predictive design and software-based simulation in best-practice design organizations. (Chapter 4)

cascade—A flow-down of requirements from the product level down through the subsystem level and component level to the process level. The cascade allows us to link requirements from the top down, as well as from the bottom up.

Typical cascade: Performance requirement → subsystem requirement → parts requirement → process requirement → process variable. (Chapter 2)

cause-and-effect analysis—The process of identifying the likely causes of any outcome. Some cause-and-effect analyses produce an output like a fishbone diagram. Others produce a cause-and-effect tree, with multiple sub-branches. (Chapter 4)

concept feasibility—Predicted ability to fulfill performance level requirements with considerations of variations of customer use, balancing of performance-level requirements, and manufacturability. (Chapter 4)

concept selection—The selection of the concept that best fulfills the performance-level requirements. Clamping concepts could include mechanical (spring-force, linkage), electrical (electromagnetic), and biologic (finger compression). (Chapter 4)

control charts—Charts that track a process input (or output) over time, showing the trends and tracking the tendency to produce a failure. Control charts use statistical methods to predict the trend to failure in time to fix the process, minimizing the traditional desire to tweak the process. (Chapter 4)

control plans—Principle: If you keep the critical X-parameters under control, the outputs (Ys) will also be under control. Follow-up of Ys outcomes: Identify the difference between signal and noise. Define actions: When to take action and what actions you should take in case of parameters moving out of control. (Chapter 4)

cost-benefit analysis—An analysis of any change to identify whether the costs outweigh the benefits. All costs, both financial and intangible, and all benefits are weighted in a cost-benefit analysis. (Chapter 4)

Cpk (short-term capability index)—A measure of short-term process capability that takes into account both the process center as well as the variation. It is the minimum of {CPU,CPL}. (Chapter 2)

critical parts factors (CPD)—Dimensions, material, or surface properties of parts responsible for achieving the target and/or allowable variation associated with critical-to-quality product requirements. (Chapter 4)

critical process variable (CPV)—A variable associated with the manufacture or assembly of the product that is responsible for achieving the target and/or allowable variation associated with critical-to-quality product requirements. (Chapter 4)

critical to quality (CTQ)—The select few requirements that your team can focus on to deliver a differentiated and superior product for your customers. Must be measurable, with targets and ranges. The recommended method of determining CTQs is to identify performance-level requirements that are linked to VOC and are new, unique, or difficult to fulfill (NUD). For example, a vehicle must provide 30 miles per gallon of regular gasoline or better. Target 35 miles per gallon, no upper limit. Or a drill must provide 50 inch-pounds of torque or higher. Target 60 inch-pounds, upper limit 80 inch-pounds. Drill requires less than 40 pounds of force to actuate. Target 30 pounds, upper spec 40 pounds, lower spec 15 pounds. (Chapter 2)

defect—Any event that does not meet a customer specification (must be measurable). (Chapter 2)

defect opportunity—A measurable chance for a defect to occur. For example, an assembly with three components and two connections might have five opportunities for defect (one for each component, and one for each connection/assembly step). (Chapter 2)

design of experiments (DOE)—A structured approach to experimenting, effectively and efficiently exploring the cause-and-effect relationship between numerous process variables (Xs) and the output or process performance variables (Ys). Designed experiments can produce a useful transfer function to identify the relationship between inputs and outputs. (Chapter 4)

design freeze—A situation that is declared when:
- Engineering analysis is complete.
- Tolerance analysis budgeting is complete.
- Product testing specifications are identified and testing methods are defined.
- Design cascade on CTQs is complete with transfer functions.
- Tunable features are identified.
- Risk analysis is complete. (Chapter 4)

design for manufacturability and assembly (DFM/A)—A collection of principles and design analysis techniques aimed at ensuring the product can be produced at a minimum of cost, complexity, and defects. (Chapter 4)

DMADV—Phases of DFSS used by GE and many other companies. Phases are: Define, Measure, Analyze, Design, and Verify. Variations of DMADV include DMADVI, DMADI, and I2DOV. (Chapters 4 and 11)

failure modes and effects analysis (FMEA)—A process used to identify the potential failures of a design, process, or equipment. By identifying all the ways something can go wrong, the team can create a robust design with all misuses and other failure modes accounted for. (Chapter 4)

fault tree analysis (FTA)—Systematic logic diagram used to explore causes of failure or to identify factors (CPF and/or CPV) responsible for achieving critical-to-quality product requirements. (Chapter 4)

finite element analysis (FEA)—A design tool to model stresses, heat flow, or other physical phenomena in a design. (Chapter 10)

flow-down—The design act of allocating targets and specifications associated with product requirements/CTQs to lower-level (such as subsystem or parts) requirements. (Chapter 4)

flow-up—The design act of predicting the capability of a design to achieve product requirement targets and specifications as a function of parts/process variation. (Chapter 4)

gage R&R (repeatability and reproducibility)—A method to assess the repeatability and reproducibility of a measurement system. Measurement methods can contribute a large percent of the observed variation on quality characteristics. Gage R&R allows us to measure the extent of this variation and alerts us if we need to take action to reduce variation caused by measurement methods. Typical gage repeatability and reproducibility < 10% of process variation. Gage R&R < 10% of process tolerance. (Chapter 4)

gemba visit—"Place of work." A gemba visit is a method of obtaining voice of customer information that requires the design team to watch customers use the product in their environment. (Chapter 4)

Green Belt—Typically a person assigned part-time to lead Six Sigma (DMAIC, lean, or DFSS) projects that are fairly narrowly scoped to match the Green Belt's field of expertise. (Chapter 2)

histogram—A graphical display of the frequency distribution. The height of each bar represents the number of respondents in each category. The histogram shows whether the distribution is approximately bell-shaped, U-shaped, or skewed. (Chapter 2)

house of quality—The name given to any of several matrix-based analyses performed to translate customer requirements into product requirements or to lower-level requirements. (Chapter 2)

hypothesis testing—A statistical test that quantifies the validity of a statement. A statistical method to test a hypothesis by comparing the data to values predicted by the hypothesis. It may be used to detect differences between groups. For example, a hypothesis test may be used in consumer testing to determine whether there is a significant difference in consumer preference between two or more products. (Chapter 4)

independence day—The day (or week or month) on which you can verify that your deployment team has succeeded in implementing DFSS into your organization and you can transfer to a sustaining mode. (Chapter 8)

Kano survey—A voice of customer method used to distinguish which customer needs are must-be, one-dimensional (or "more is better"), or delights. (Chapter 4)

Master Black Belt—Typically a person assigned full-time to train and mentor Black Belts as well as lead the strategy to ensure the projects chartered are the right strategic projects for the organization. Master Black Belts are usually the authorizing body that certifies Green and Black Belts. (Chapter 2)

mean—The average value of a sample of data. (Chapter 2)

measurement system analysis—An analysis that determines the dependability of your measurement system, revealing how much variation exists in the measurement system, either from the measurement device itself, from the humans operating the device, or from a random effect. This ensures that the conclusions drawn from the data are valid. A typical measurement system analysis is the Gage R&R. (Chapter 4)

Monte Carlo simulation—The predictive simulation of an outcome created by identifying the variation and distribution of each of its inputs. A Monte Carlo simulation predicts the variation you would expect to see in your output. (Chapter 4)

multigenerational plan (MGP)—A planning tool to determine a series of product releases and associated technology requirements based on a market- and business-driven vision of the product's "direction." (Chapter 4)

new product development (NPD) process—The process of developing products or processes: Defining the opportunity; Collecting and Measuring the voice of the customer; Creating, Analyzing, and Selecting the best concept; Designing; and Verifying that all requirements and CTQs have been met. (Chapter 3)

NPD project charter—A charter that clearly defines what the new product development (NPD) team will be charged to accomplish, which customers will be satisfied by the new product, and what those customers are missing from today's options. (Chapter 4)

optimization of product and process—Adjusting the inputs to where the performance requirement targets are met and are least sensitive to variation. (Chapter 4)

parameter estimation—The process of estimating the variation of each factor in a design. (Chapter 4)

Pareto analysis—A process used to identify the factors that are most responsible for the outcome. A Pareto analysis will show the largest contributors so you can focus on those factors. (Chapter 4)

phase—A period in new product development that specifies certain activities. In the process we describe in this book, the phases are Define, Measure, Analyze, Design, and Verify. (Chapter 2)

prediction—The design act of calculating the capability of a design to meet the targets and specification limits as a function of parts and process characteristics. (Chapter 2)

probability distributions—The histograms showing the distributions of a population or sample and the probability of delivering outside of the upper or lower specification limit. (Chapter 2)

process capability—The ability of a process to deliver according to the requirements. Often measured in terms of Ppk or Cpk, process capability can also be measured in terms of Sigma level. In a normal process, the process capability can easily be converted from Cpk to Sigma level (Z).

$$Z = 3 \, Cpk$$

Example: A process running at a Cpk of 2 can be said to be producing at Six Sigma. (Chapter 4)

product-level requirement (or simply product requirement)— A characteristic that can be directly traced to customer and procedural requirements; it also includes requirements necessary for developing and delivering the product. (Includes performance measures, appearance, packaging requirements, human factors, and so forth.) Examples include vehicle mileage, torque delivered through a tool, and force to actuate a tool. (Chapter 2)

production process design—Preparing the product for commercialization. This includes DFM/A analysis, capacity analysis, and tooling plan. (Chapter 4)

Pugh matrix—A qualitative decision-making tool used to assess the strengths and weaknesses of design concept relative to customer and business criteria. A Pugh concept selection matrix can help a team select the best ideas from among many alternatives, using objective criteria. (Chapter 4)

quality function deployment (QFD)—A method used to translate voice of customer information into product requirements/CTQs and to continue deployment (for instance, cascading) of requirements to parts and process requirements. (Chapter 4)

radar charts (spider diagrams)—Graphical outputs typically used to represent the gaps between importance and satisfaction of any requirement. (Chapter 4)

reliability testing/accelerated testing—A set of tests designed to understand and predict the failure rate of a system or component. There are many ways to perform reliability testing, including accelerated testing and worse-conditions testing. (Chapter 4)

response surface methods (RSM)—A collection of statistical techniques used to optimize a dependent variable (for instance, a product requirement/CTQ) as a function of one or more independent variables. (Chapter 4)

sampling—When collecting data, it is a good idea to have a sampling plan. A good sampling plan includes a properly estimated sample size and steps to ensure that the sample is representative. There are several approaches to sampling, including random sampling, stratified random sampling, systematic sampling, and subgroup sampling. (Chapter 4)

scorecard—A summary of the predicted and measured capability/reliability of critical requirements at all levels defined within the cascade. Examples include CTQ: Force to actuate < 40 lb (USL) @ 4 Sigma; capability: Mean force = 30 lb; standard deviation = 2 lb; predicted Sigma level = 5. (Chapter 4)

sigma(s)—Standard deviation. The English letter s is the standard deviation of a sample. The Greek character sigma (σ) is reserved for the standard deviation of the entire population. (Chapter 4)

Sigma level (Z)—A measure of the capability of a design. Specifically, the Sigma level is the number of standard deviations that fit between the sample mean and the specification limit. *Six Sigma* is the term used in a centered normal process when 6 standard deviations fit between the process mean and the specification limit. (Chapter 4)

Defects per million opportunities	Sigma level
66,807	3
6,210	4
233	5
3.4	6

Six Sigma—A term used when a normal process is performing centered at 6 standard deviations from the specification limit. A Six Sigma process can be predicted to produce 3.4 defects per million opportunities. (Chapter 2)

standard deviation—A statistical measure of the spread of the data. It is the square root of the variance. Symbols to represent the standard deviation are *s* for the sample standard deviation and *s* for the population standard deviation. (Chapter 4)

$$S^2 = \sum_{i=1}^{n} \frac{(x_i - \bar{x})^2}{n-1}$$

supplier-input-process-output-customer (SIPOC)—A high-level process map that depicts the suppliers that provide the input, the input they are providing, how the process operates, the output from the process, and the customer of the output. It is used as a communication/visualization tool so that everyone has the same understanding of the process and a key analysis tool that is a starting point for risk analysis, identifying sources of variation, simulation, and process improvement. (Chapter 4)

stakeholder analysis—Understanding the key stakeholders in your organization and identifying what information they need and "what is in it for them" if you implement a change. Making an action plan to bring each stakeholder up to the level of support needed for a successful change. (Chapter 5)

systematic innovation technique (SIT)—A technique that helps teams solve design problems or create ideas by using a systematic process designed to build the maximum amount of useful ideas. (Chapter 1)

Taguchi robust design—Setting appropriate parameters in the design in order to optimize not only the output, but also the variation. (Chapter 10)

tolerance design—Setting appropriate tolerances on process parameters and critical characteristics of raw materials to achieve a good process capability on the quality characteristics. (Chapter 4)

transfer function—A quantifiable relationship between inputs and outputs. There are three methods of developing transfer functions: (a) explicit mathematical equation, (b) computer simulation modeling, and (c) experimentation, or combinations of (a), (b), and (c). A transfer function is also used to predict the variability of the outputs. (Chapter 4)

For example:

Sleeve Bend Strength

$$M = Ultimate\ Stress \times \frac{I}{C}$$

$$I = \frac{\pi}{4}(OD^4 - ID^4),\ C = 1/2 \times OD$$

TRIZ—Russian acronym for theory of inventive problem solving, a systematic means of inventing and solving design conflicts. (Chapter 4)

voice of the customer process—A broadly defined process for collecting the customers' needs and reactions. For detailed process to collect and confirm the VOC, see *Voices into Choices* by Christina Hepner Brodie or *Customer-Centric Product Definition* by Sheila Mello. (Chapter 2)

voices of the customer—Things you hear directly from the customers about their needs or actual measurable requirements. For instance, "I don't want to go broke driving the car!" or "I want the tool to do the tough jobs for me." (Chapter 4)

References

Bertels, Thomas (Ed.). (2003). *Rath & Strong's Six Sigma Leadership Handbook*. New York: Wiley & Sons.

Breyfogle, Forrest W., III. (1999). *Implementing Design for Six Sigma*. New York: John Wiley & Sons.

Brodie, Christina Hepner, and Gary Burchill. (1997). *Voices into Choices*. Madison, WI: Joiner.

Clausing, Don. (1994). *Total Quality Development—A Step-by-Step Guide to World-Class Concurrent Engineering*. New York: ASME Press.

Cohen, Lou. (1995). *Quality Function Deployment—How to Make QFD Work for You*. New York: Addison-Wesley.

Cooper, Alan. (2004). *The Inmates Are Running the Asylum—Why High-Tech Products Drive Us Crazy and How to Restore the Sanity*. Indianapolis, IN: SAMS Publishing.

Cooper, Alan, and Robert Reimann. (2003). *About Face 2.0—The Essentials of Interaction Design*. New York: John Wiley & Sons.

Cooper, Robert G. (2001). *Winning at New Products*. New York: Perseus.

Creveling, C. M., J. L. Slutsky, and D. Antis Jr. (2003). *Design for Six Sigma*. Upper Saddle River, NJ: *Pearson*.

Drucker, Peter F. (1985). *Innovation and Entrepreneurship—Practice and Principles*. New York: Harper & Row.

Goldenberg, Jacob, and David Mazursky. (2002). *Creativity in Product Innovation*. Cambridge, UK: Cambridge University Press.

Goldratt, Eliyahu M., and Jeff Cox. (2004). *The Goal—A Process of Ongoing Improvement.* Croton-on-Hudson, NY: North River Press.

Huthwaite, Bart. (2004). *The Lean Design Solution.* Macinac Island, MI: Institute for Lean Design.

Mello, Sheila. (2003). *Customer-Centric Product Definition.* New York: AMACOM, American Management Association.

Rantanen, Kalevi, and Ellen Domb. (2002). *Simplified TRIZ—New Problem-Solving Applications for Engineers and Manufacturing Professionals.* Boca Raton, FL: St. Lucie Press.

Reinertsen, Donald G. (1997). *Managing the Design Factory—A Product Developer's Toolkit.* New York: Free Press.

Tull, Jethro. (1731). *The New Horse-Houghing Husbandry, or, an Essay on the Principles of Tillage and Vegetation.* Dublin: Cyber Library, College of Bioresource Science, Nihun University.

Yang, Kai, and Basem El-Haik. (2003). *Design for Six Sigma.* New York: McGraw-Hill.

Index

A

About Face 2.0—The Essentials of Interaction Design (Cooper), 179
accountability, 125, 170–171
additivity of variances, 28–29
adult learning principles, 115
advanced development, 174–176
affinity sort, 60
algorithm for inventive problem solving (ARIZ), 188
aligning organization, 112–113
Altshuller, Genrich, 177, 188
analysis. *See also* gap analysis
  change-management, 103–104
  competitive, 58
  conjoint, 60
  fault tree, 64, 68
  intellectual property, 63, 68
  Kano, 60, 177
  process, 15–16
  reliability, 64
  root cause, 71, 72, 73, 74
  stakeholder, 96–98, 112, 133
  Weibull, 213, 214
  worst-case, 88
analyze phase (DMADVI), 51–53, 61–65, 83, 187, 195–201
ARIZ (algorithm for inventive problem solving), 188
Asaka, Tetsuichi, 78–79
assessment
  business case, 79–81, 158–161
  concept development, 86–87
  customer requirements, 85–86, 89
  decision-making process, 91
  define phase, 84–85
  development processes/resources, 84–91
  DFSS process, 158–161
  organizational gap analysis, 90
  past change, 102–104
  product requirements, 86
  project management process, 91–92
  readiness for DFSS, 77–82
  requirements cascade, 87–89
  team, 147–148
  technology, 58
  training, 156–157
  verification phase, 89
  voice of customer collection, 85–86
axiomatic design, 176–177

B

benchmarking, 9, 58, 63, 68, 158
Black Belts, 22, 115–116, 118, 119, 167
books as DFSS tools, 139–140
budget, DFSS and, 24, 125, 128
business case assessment tool, 79–81, 158–161
business reviews, 40

C

capability evaluation, 66–67, 180
cascade, requirements
  analyze phase, 62, 64
  assessing, 87–89
  benefits, 38, 40, 62
  design phase, 66, 68

233

cascade, requirements, *continued*
  difficulties defining, 130
  example, 27
  overview, 30
  purpose, 8
  qualitative, 62
  timing, 114
case study
  analyze phase, 195–200, 201
  background, 189
  chartering, 190–191
  define phase, 189–191
  design phase, 200–216
  design scorecards, 201, 206–207, 216–218
  implement phase, 217, 219
  measure phase, 191, 192–195
  verify/validate phase, 217
  voice of customer, 191, 194
catch-ball, 110
certification, 118, 119
Champions, 22, 110
change
  assessing past, 102–104
  distribution of, 112
  fear of, 101
  leaders/managers and, 74, 77–78, 99–100
  organizational, 183–184
  planning for, 103–104
  prioritizing, 93, 126
  during product development, 40
  requirements for, 9–10
  resistance to, 112, 134
  tolerance/motivation for, 91, 101–103, 143
change-management analysis, 103–104
chartering, 37–38, 58, 84–85, 109–111, 190–191
coaching reports, 147
commitment, organizational, 101–103, 145
competitive analysis, 58
concept development, assessing, 86–87
concept selection/identification, 9, 63

configuration control/management, 64, 68, 74
conjoint analysis, 60
consultants, 109, 115–116, 126, 128
control planning, 69, 214–215
control points, 214
controls, project, 56
Cooper, Alan, 178–179
cooperation, departmental, 101
copyrights, 63, 68
corrections, course, 129
correlation thinking, 145
cost reduction, Six Sigma and, 24
Cpk (operational process capabilities), 18
creativity techniques, 63, 67
critical control points, 214
critical mass for acceptance, 163
critical process parameters, identifying, 66
critical-to-quality (CTQ) requirements
  characteristics, 16–17
  controlling, 27
  defining, 30
  described, 8
  identifying, 9, 59
  manufacturing variation and, 114–115
  prioritizing, 86
  tools for, 181
  variation predictions, 70
Crystal Ball Monte Carlo software, 181
CTQ requirements. *See* critical-to-quality requirements
culture, organizational
  DFSS implementation and, 132–135, 167, 169–170, 171, 184
  risk tolerance, 6
  throw-it-over-the-wall approach, 2, 5, 40, 168
  tolerance for labeling, 92
Customer-Centric Product Definition (Mello), 177–178

customers. *See also* voice of customer
  communication with, 182
  feedback from, 64, 69
  identifying, 58
  listening to, 177–178
  requirements of, 59, 85–86, 89
customization, 117–118

D

dashboard tool, 153–154
decision-making, 91, 182–183
defect rates, Six Sigma, 16
Define, Measure, Analyze, Design, Verify (DMADV), 50–51
Define, Measure, Analyze, Design, Verify/Validate, Implement (DMADVI). *See* DMADVI
Define, Measure, Analyze, Identify, Execute, Control (DMAIEC), 23
Define, Measure, Analyze, Improve, Control (DMAIC), 20
Define, Measure, Analyze, Improve, Control, Replicate (DMAIC-R), 20–21
define phase (DMADVI), 51–52, 54–58, 83, 84–85, 189–191
deliverables
  advantages, 40–41
  analyze phase, 65
  design phase, 56–57, 69–70
  implement phase, 74
  measure phase, 60–61
  verify/validate phase, 72
departmental cooperation, 101
deployment, product, 155–156, 161, 172
design. *See also* product design
  axiomatic, 176–177
  concepts, developing, 86–87
  concepts, selecting/identifying, 9, 63
  evaluation of, 31
  industrial, 64, 68, 179–180
  parameter, 63, 186–187
  poor, costs of, 36–37
  prediction, 9, 31, 38, 39
  process, feedback on, 73–74
  process of, 25–26
  reviews of, 40, 64, 69, 72
  tolerance, 187
  tooling, 66
design control, 64, 68
Design for Six Sigma (Creveling), 174
Design for X, 63, 64, 68, 87
design of experiments (DOE), 64, 68
design phase (DMADVI), 52, 53, 66–70, 83, 200–216
design scorecards, 8, 67, 70, 201, 206–207, 216–218
development processes
  assessing, 84–91
  capacity, 183
  current vs. best practice, 82–83
  DFSS strategy and, 84
  integrating into existing process, 123, 125
  software for, 178–179
  terminating, 89
DFSS
  assessing readiness for, 77–82
  engineering benefits, 35, 41–42
  evolution, 15
  financial benefits, 35–39
  increasing use of, 6
  limitations, 7
  methods for, 49. *See also* DMADVI
  organizational benefits, 35, 39–41
  process, 8, 30–31
  scope, 8–9
  successes, 7–8
  tools for, 9
DMADV (Define-Measure-Analyze-Design-Verify), 50–51
DMADVI (Define-Measure-Analyze-Design-Verify/Validate-Implement)
  advanced development and, 175–176
  analyze phase, 51–53, 61–65, 83, 187, 195–201
  define phase, 51–52, 54–58, 83, 84–85, 189–191
  ending, 54
  history, 50–51

DMADVI (Define-Measure-
    Analyze-Design-Verify/
    Validate-Implement), *continued*
  implement phase, 52–54, 73–75, 84,
    217, 219
  incorporating, 54
  measure phase, 51, 52, 57–61, 83,
    191–195
  nonlinear nature, 54
  phases, overview, 51–54, 83–84,
    184
  verify/validate phase, 52, 53, 70–72,
    84, 217
DMAIC (Define, Measure, Analyze,
    Improve, Control), 20
DMAIC-R (Define, Measure,
    Analyze, Improve, Control,
    Replicate), 20–21
DMAIEC (Define, Measure, Analyze,
    Identify, Execute, Control), 23
DOE (design of experiments), 64, 68

E

early adopters, 112
early measures, 125, 146–149,
    150–151, 152
80% rule, 158
Einstein, Albert, 43
enablers, 164–167, 172
enforcers, 164, 165, 167, 168–171,
    172
enterprise resource planning (ERP)
    software, 164–165
Entrepreneurship and Innovation
    (Drucker), 182
examples. *See also* case study
  consumer products, 37–38
  global positioning company, 42–47
  LightSpeed Computed Tomography
    Scanner, 7–8
  medical device company, 38–39
  nutrition products company, 39–40
  wheel and axle, 26–29
excess cost of production, 28, 36–37

F

failure, DFSS, 36–37, 107, 135–140,
    148–149

failure mode and effects analysis
    (FMEA), 9, 64, 68, 87, 200
fault tree analysis (FTA), 64, 68
FEA (finite element analysis), 64, 181
fear, organizational, 101
feasibility studies, 87
features, product, 85, 130
feedback, customer, 64, 69
feedback, organizational, 93
Finance role, Six Sigma, 22
finite element analysis (FEA), 64, 181
flexibility, 117–118
Florida Power & Light (FPL), 78–79,
    96, 98–99
flow-down. *See* cascade, requirements
flow-up, 63
FMEA (failure mode and effects
    analysis), 9, 64, 68, 87, 200
forms, overuse of, 170
FPL (Florida Power & Light), 78–79,
    96, 98–99
FTA (fault tree analysis), 64, 68
full-factorial experiments, 204–205
functional analysis, 62, 63, 67

G

gap analysis
  acceptance-side, 91, 93, 96–104,
    143, 145
  assessing organizational, 90
  process, 71, 73
  quality-side, 82–89, 90–95
  reasons for, 82
  results of, 111–112
gap, defined, 82
gargle and spit approach, 3–4
gate process, 91, 107
GE Capital, 165
GE (General Electric)
  adoption of Six Sigma, 15, 20
  change management approach, 82
  consultants, use of, 126, 128
  CT scanner example, 7–8
  leadership knowledge, 128
  process development at, 50
  reward behavior, 90
goals
  implementation and, 109

individual performance, 168
misalignment of, 5
prioritizing, 9
for product requirements, 59
project, 56
strategic, 24
Goldenberg, Jacob, 185–186
grandfathering, 123
grass-roots approach, 138–139
Green Belts, 22, 115, 118–119, 120–122, 167

H

heroes, view of implementation team as, 137–138
Honda, Soichiro, 35
house of quality, 177, 193. *See also* QFD
human factors, 64, 68, 179–180

I

I²DOV (Invention and innovation, develop technology concept, optimize robustness, and verify technologies), 174
image diagrams, 60, 178
implement phase (DMADVI), 52–54, 73–75, 84, 144, 217, 219
implementation. *See also* chartering
approaches to, 155
failure, causes of, 107, 135–140
overview, 108
phased process, 134
planning for, 71
Six Sigma, 22
success, keys to, 131–135
support needed for, 108
time requirement, 108, 110
transfer to post-deployment, 155, 161, 172
variation in, 107–108
implementation teams, 56, 90, 92–95, 110, 133–134, 137–138
Independence Day, 155, 161, 172
independence phase, metrics in DFSS, 144, 149–150, 152
industrial design, 64, 68, 179–180
infrastructure projects, 114–115

initial idea generation technique, 188
The Inmates Are Running the Asylum (Cooper), 178
innovators, 112
in-process indicators, 125, 146–149, 150–151, 152
installation qualification, 71, 72, 217
intangibles, measuring, 145–146
integration plans, 113–115
intellectual property, 63, 68
introduction phase, DFSS, 144
Invention and innovation, develop technology concept, optimize robustness, and verify technologies (I²DOV), 174
Iversen, Elizabeth, 50

J

Johnson & Johnson, process development at, 50–51
Juran, Joseph, 35, 101
just-in-time production, 69
just-in-time training, 123, 167

K

Kano analysis, 60, 177
Kano, Noriaki, 177
Kansai Electric Power Company (KEPCO), 78

L

labeling, tolerance for, 92
lagging indicators, 144, 149–150, 152
late adopters, 112
launch, project, 55
leaders
commitment of, 96–101, 145
defined, 96
opposition from, 98
personal involvement of, 99
prioritization by, 5–6, 93, 126
risk tolerance, 6
role of, 128–129
support from, 108, 117, 138–139, 169, 170–171
training, 128–129, 170–171
understanding, 98–99
working with, 112

238 Index

lean production, 69
legal liability, 36
LightSpeed Computed Tomography Scanner example, 7–8
little y's, 125, 126

M

MAIC (Measure, Analyze, Improve, Control), 20
maintenance plans, 68
managers, 96. *See also* leaders
Managing the Design Factory (Reinertsen), 183
manufacturing. *See* production
Manufacturing Processes Reference Guide (Todd, Allen, & Alting), 115
market research, 9, 58, 60
market-driven product definition (MDPD), 177–178
Master Black Belts, 22, 115–116, 118–119, 167, 172
materials, properties of, 180
Mattenson, Eric, 50
Mazursky, David, 185–186
MDPD (market-driven product definition), 177–178
mean, 16
Measure, Analyze, Improve, Control (MAIC), 20
measure phase (DMADVI), 51, 52, 57–61, 83, 191–195
measurement, 66, 143, 151–152, 153–154. *See also* metrics
mentorship, 115–116, 129
metric system, acceptance of, 93, 96
metrics. *See also* measurement
  choosing, 109, 125, 151–152
  communicating, 159–161
  early, 144–146, 150–151, 152
  example, 111
  independence phase, 144, 149–150, 152
  in-process, 125, 146–149, 150–151, 152
  post-independence, 150
  responsibility for, 152–153

  timing, 144
  training-related, 135–136, 156–157
MGPP (multigenerational product plan), 58, 190, 192
milestones, 109–110, 111
mistrust within organizations, 5
Money Belts, 22
monitoring process, 129–130
Monte Carlo simulation, 8, 29–30, 114, 181
motivation, team, 90
Motorola, 15
multigenerational product development, 38, 176
multigenerational product plan (MGPP), 58, 190, 192

N

new product development (NPD), 31–33

O

operational process capabilities (Cpk), 18
operational qualification, 71, 217. *See also* qualification, product/process
opportunity statements, 109
optimization, 87, 201, 204–206
outcomes, project, 56
outputs, DMADVI. *See* deliverables

P

parameter design, 63, 186–187
Pareto charts, 205
Pareto principle, 86
patents, 63, 68
performance management, 168
performance qualification, 71, 217. *See also* qualification, product/process
phase-gate process, 91, 107
pilot projects, 130
pilot teams, 118, 128, 134–135
pilot testing, 70, 71, 72, 118–119
planning, as Six Sigma project, 131–132

policies, organizational, 169–170
post-design phase reviews, 57
prediction
    affect of variation on, 114–115
    design, 9, 31, 38, 39
    of variation, 67, 70, 88, 123, 125, 206–212
preventive maintenance plans, 67
prioritization, 5–6, 93, 126
problem statements, 109, 111
procedures, organizational, 169–170
process analysis methods, 15–16
process capability studies, 58
process control, 67, 74
process variables, critical, 9
product design
    axiomatic view, 176–177
    conceptual, 62
    development of, 66
    reviews of, 40, 64, 69, 72
product development. *See also* new product development
    changes during, 40
    characteristics, 3
    improvement methods, 173–174, 182–183
    infrastructure, 180–181
    model, 173–176
    multigenerational, 38, 176
    problems with, 1–2, 3–7
    requirements, identifying, 38
    role, organizational, 7
    turnover to operations, 73
product failure, 36–37
product planning, 58, 72, 74, 91–92
product requirements, 38, 59, 60, 86
production
    excess cost of, 28, 36–37
    instructions for, 74
    problems with, 39–40
    process design, 9, 66, 213–215
    processes, 62, 69, 71, 73, 87
    variation in, 88, 114–115, 123, 125
project approach, 56
project chartering. *See* chartering
projects
    managing, 58, 72, 74, 91–92

planning, 56, 58, 109–110, 111
reviewing, 169
scope, 55–56, 109, 111
terminating, 73–74
prototypes, 32, 88–89, 179
Pugh concept convergence, 62, 64, 68

Q

QFD (quality function deployment)
    analyze phase, 63
    benefits, 4–5, 59
    design phase, 67
    measure phase, 60
    opting not to use, 133
    shortcomings, 178
    usage scenario, 4
    uses, 177
qualification, product/process, 71, 72, 217
qualitative cascade, 62
quality function deployment (QFD). *See* QFD
quality loss, 36–37
quality policies, 170
quality systems, 130

R

radar charts, 60
randomization of experiments, 205
Rath & Strong's Six Sigma Leadership Handbook (Rath & Strong), 158
recalls, 36
recognition, 5, 90, 130
regulatory requirements, 58, 130, 169, 170
reliability analysis, 64, 68, 210, 213
requirements
    critical. *See* critical-to-quality requirements
    customer, 85–86, 89
    defining, 129–130
    lower-level, 30
    product, 38, 59, 60, 86
    regulatory, 58, 130, 169, 170
requirements cascade. *See* cascade, requirements

requirements diagrams, 60
requirements management software, 165
resistance to change, 112, 134
resistors, 112
resources, assessing/distributing, 90, 99
reviews
  analyze phase, 65
  business, 40
  design, 40, 64, 69, 72
  design phase, 57, 67, 70
  implement phase, 73–74, 75
  measure phase, 61
  project, 169
  verify/validate phase, 72
reward, 5, 90, 130, 175
rework, 40
risk, organizational tolerance for, 6
risk priority number (RPN), 200
risk/opportunity management, 58
risks, identifying product, 63
robust design approach, 186–187
robustness, 31
root cause analysis, 71, 72, 73, 74
RPN (risk priority number), 200

S

safety factors, 88
scale-up potential, 71
scheduling, 184–185
science projects, 87, 173–175
scorecard tool, 153–154
seed drill example. *See* case study
Sigma, 18
Sigma level, 16, 18, 27–28
Sigma targets, 59
silo mentality, 5, 168
Simplified TRIZ (Rantanen & Domb), 188
simulation
  Monte Carlo, 8, 29–30, 114, 181
  product, 63, 64, 68, 87
  tools for, 114, 180–181
SIPOC (Supplier-Input-Process-Output-Customer) mapping, 58
SIT (systematic innovation technique), 185–186

6Ms, 3
Six Sigma, 15–16, 18, 21–22, 24
"The Six Sigma Zone" (Wheeler), 18
skill development. *See* training
SMEs (subject matter experts), 116–117, 166–167
Society for Plastics Engineers, 114–115
software development processes, 178–179
software tools, 164–166
sort, affinity, 60
spare-parts planning, 67, 68
spider diagrams, 60
Sponsors, 22, 110
staff, training/working with, 73, 112–113
stakeholder analysis, 96–98, 112, 133
stakeholders, 56, 96–99
standard deviation, 16, 18
start-up testing, 73
statistical methods, Six Sigma, 15–16
steering committee, 112
stock value, company, 36
structure tree, 60
subject matter experts (SMEs), 116–117, 166–167
success
  communicating, 125, 145, 158
  comparing to others', 158
  DFSS examples, 7–8
  identifying, 156–161
  in implementation, 131–135
  limiting factors, 13
  measuring, 125
  requirements for, 13
success drivers, 125, 126
success measures, planning, 125
Suh, Nam Pyo, 176–177
supplier development, 185
Supplier-Input-Process-Output-Customer (SIPOC) mapping, 58
sustaining phase, 163, 172. *See also* enablers; enforcers
systematic innovation technique (SIT), 185–186

T

Taguchi, Genichi, 63, 186–187
targets, 59
teams
  assessment of, 147–148
  development, 56, 90, 92–95, 110, 133–134, 137–138
  gap analysis, 92–95
  management of, 58
  motivation of, 90
  pilot, 118, 128, 134–135
  training, 171
teamwork, 4–5
technologies, 9, 39, 58, 63
test plans, 67
testing
  pilot, 70, 71, 72, 118–119
  production processes, 71
  start-up, 73
  usability, 179
theory of inventive problem solving (TRIZ), 177, 188
throw-it-over-the-wall culture, 2, 5, 40, 168. *See also* culture, organizational
tolerance, allocating, 30
tolerance design, 187
tolerance limits, 59
tolerance stack-ups, 67
tooling design, 66
tools
  define phase, 58
  design phase, 67–69
  implement phase, 74
  learning, 139–140
  measure phase, 60
  overemphasis on, 136–137
  simulation, 114, 180–181
  verify/validate phase, 72
trade secrets, 63, 68
trademarks, 63, 68
training
  aids for, 166
  assessment of, 156–157
  failure of, 148–149
  feedback from, 129
  Green Belt, 115
  just-in-time, 123, 167
  leader/manager, 128–129, 170–171
  limitations, 137
  method for, 135–136
  metrics and, 135–136, 156–157
  plans for, 115, 117–123
  scheduling, 118–119, 123, 124
  by SMEs, 117
  staff, 73
  team, 171
  tracking, 145
training spreadsheets, 118–119, 123, 124
transfer functions
  analyze phase, 64
  building, 114, 130
  defined, 27
  design phase, 68
  purpose, 8
transition plans, 71
tree diagrams, 63, 67
TRIZ (theory of inventive problem solving), 177, 188
Tull, Jethro, 189
2X safety factor, 88

U

usability testing, 179

V

validation, defined, 53, 70. *See also* verify/validate phase
value proposition, 58
variables, critical process, 9
variances, additivity of, 28–29
variation
  affect on product, 67
  in implementation, 107–108
  manufacturing/assembly, 88, 114–115, 123, 125
  measuring, 16
  predicting, 67, 70, 88, 123, 125, 206–212
verification, 53, 70, 89, 183. *See also* verify/validate phase
verification/validation plans, 67
verify/validate phase (DMADVI), 52, 53, 70–72, 84, 217

voice of customer (VOC). *See also* requirements, customer
assessing collection of, 85–86
case study, 191, 194
described, 59, 60
example, 38

W

warning signs, recognizing, 1–2, 145
websites, DFSS support, 166

Weibull analysis, 213, 214
worst-case analysis, 88

X

X-factors, 68. *See also* Design for X
X-Y charts, 125, 126

Y

Ys. *See* critical-to-quality requirements